Books By Dorothy Clarke Wilson

NOVELS

The Brother
A Story of James the Brother of Jesus

The Herdsman
A Story of the Prophet Amos

Prince of Egypt
A Story of Moses

House of Earth
A Novel of India

Jezebel

The Gifts
A Story of the Boyhood of Jesus

BIOGRAPHIES

Dr. Ida
The Story of Dr. Ida Scudder of Vellore

Take My Hands
The Remarkable Story of Dr. Mary Verghese

Ten Fingers for God
The Story of Dr. Paul Brand

Handicap Race
The Story of Roger Arnett

Palace of Healing
*The Story of Dr. Clara Swain, First Woman
Missionary Doctor, and the Hospital She Founded*

Lone Woman
*The Story of Elizabeth Blackwell,
the First Woman Doctor*

The Big-Little World of Doc Pritham
The Story of a Maine Doctor

Hilary
Story of Hilary Pole

Bright Eyes
The Story of Susette La Flesche, an Omaha Indian

PLAYS

Twelve Months of Drama for the Average Church
A Collection of Religious Plays

FOR YOUNG PEOPLE

The Journey
Stories of the Boyhood of Jesus

The Three Gifts
Stories of the Boyhood of Jesus

Stranger and Traveler

Dorothea Lynde Dix

Stranger and Traveler

The Story of Dorothea Dix,
American Reformer

by

Dorothy Clarke Wilson

Little, Brown and Company—Boston—Toronto

FIRST EDITION

T 10/75

LIBRARY OF CONGRESS CATALOGING IN PUBLICATION DATA

Wilson, Dorothy Clarke.
    Stranger and Traveler.

    Bibliography: p.
    Includes index.
    1.   Dix, Dorothea Lynde, 1802-1887.   2.   Reformers—
Biography.   I.   Title.
HV28.D6W54   361'.92'4[B]   75-15711
ISBN 0-316-544963

Designed by D. Christine Benders

Published simultaneously in Canada
by Little, Brown & Company (Canada) Limited

PRINTED IN THE UNITED STATES OF AMERICA

Stranger and traveler!
Drink freely and bestow
A kindly thought on her
  Who bade this fountain flow;
Yet hath for it no claim
  Save as the minister
Of blessing in God's name.
                    —John Greenleaf Whittier

(Written for Dorothea Dix to describe
the fountain she donated for thirsty
animals in Custom House Square,
Boston)

Contents

Illustrations

Acknowledgments

THOUGH SHE LIVED in our state for only her first ten years, we Maine natives feel that Dorothea Dix belongs to us. Riding along Route 1A at the southern end of the lovely old town of Hampden, one passes a stately stone archway bearing the words DOROTHEA DIX PARK, on one side of which is a plaque, reading:

In Memory of
DOROTHEA LYNDE DIX
who by devoted care to sick and wounded
soldiers during the Civil War earned the
gratitude of the Nation, and by her labors
in the cause of prison reform and of humane
treatment of the insane won the admiration
and reverence of the civilized world
1802–1887
HER BIRTHPLACE

So of course when I decided to write her story, the first place I went for information was Hampden. Refreshing, after travels to India, Palestine, Egypt, England, researching for previous books, to find material less than twenty miles from home! Members of the Hampden Historical Society, especially Mrs. Ralph Millner and Miss Miriam Hall, were eager to share facts relating to the town's early history and the Dorothea Dix Memorial Association, founded in 1899 and responsible for the creation of the Park. Records of its festive dedication on July 4, 1899, of Dorothea's birth, of the purchase of a Dix pew in the town Meeting House, were all available. Mrs. Newton A. Robbins took me for an interesting tour of the park, the site of Dorothea's birthplace, the steep rocky river bank where she played as a child, and other historical spots in the town, including Mrs. Robbins's own family home, built in 1783, close to the farm where Dorothea was born and lived in her early years.

Persons in the nearby town of Dixmont, founded by and named for Dr. Elijah Dix, Dorothea's grandfather, were equally helpful. Miss Eleanor Toothaker took me on a tour of historical sites which included Dr. Dix's grave, old houses, locations of lots owned by Dix heirs; and she shared her father's manuscript history of the town. Mrs. Doris Gray was also a help. Mr. Amos Kimball, the area's acknowledged historian and collector of archives, produced invaluable old documents, letters, and other material relating to the Dix and Harris families. (If you are ever in the neighborhood, don't fail to visit his old Country Store. It's a museum of Americana.)

Helpful in supplying information regarding Maine coastal navigation in the year 1809 were Mr. Robert B. Applebee of Stockton Springs, Maine, and Mr. Frank P. Adams of Salem, Massachusetts.

Professor Charles M. Snyder of State University College, Oswego, New York, provided useful information concerning the letters of Dorothea Dix to President Millard Fillmore.

Information concerning the family of Reverend John G. T. Nichols, responsible for Dorothea's first interest in work for the insane, was given by Mr. William B. Jordan of Portland, Maine.

Superintendents of several state hospitals founded by Dorothea Dix were most cooperative in furnishing historical data, pictures, and other materials relating to their several institutions. Special recognition is due Mr. Edwin P. Kwiatanowski, chairman of the Historical Committee of the Dixmont State Hospital, Sewickley, Pennsylvania; Dr. John P. Logan, Superintendent of the Harrisburg State Hospital, Harrisburg, Pennsylvania; and Dr. Martin H. Weinberg, Medical Director of the Trenton Psychiatric Hospital, Trenton, New Jersey.

I am in great debt to many librarians and curators. Miss Carolyn E. Jakeman, Assistant Librarian for Reference of the Houghton Library at Harvard, gave invaluable assistance during long weeks of study of the Dorothea Dix papers. Mrs. Vincent A. Hartgen of the University of Maine Library, Special Collections department, gave constant help in securing source materials, besides permitting me to keep valuable books out for months on end. Helpful also were assistants in the Bangor Public Library, Bangor, Maine; the Boston Athenaeum; the Massachusetts Historical Society; and the Boston Public Library.

And of course this, as well as all my other books, could

not have been written without the cooperation of my husband, Reverend Elwin L. Wilson, who has cheerfully endured through the years my absences for research of days, weeks, and sometimes months, given valuable criticism, helped prepare indexes, and patiently suffered the exigencies of life with a temperamental author.

My thanks to all of these.

D. C. W.
Orono, Maine
January, 1975

Prologue

IT WAS A DAY in the mid–1800s. In a small town in
Michigan a carriage of doubtful vintage drawn by a
husky farm horse clattered up to the entrance of the town's
only hotel. Its driver, a lad in his late teens, wound the
reins about the whipstock, jumped down from his high
perch over the front axle, and fastened the halter to a hitching post. All four — horse, driver, carriage, hotel — were
eloquent examples of the raw frontier, rough, obviously
intended for work, not beauty, devoid of all luxuries and
niceties.

The boy swaggered into the hotel, glanced about the
deserted lobby, then, heavy boots pounding on the bare
pine floor, approached the desk.

"Okay, I'm here. Where is he?"

The clerk looked up indifferently from his whittling.
"Where's who?"

"My passenger. This crazy bloke I'm supposed to cart
off into the wilderness. I'm from the livery stable."

A droll gleam livened the clerk's dull eyes. "Oh, yeah,
your passenger." He tapped a bell, and a small boy ap-

peared. "Look, sonny. Tell the — the person up in Room Three that the carriage is ready. Be sure to knock first," he called after the retreating figure.

The driver leaned against the counter. "I hope this fool knows what he's likely to get into. That's just about the god-forsakenest road north o' *De*-troit — if you can call it a road. They say there's been holdups there lately. But I'll be ready for 'em." He patted a bulge on either hip. "I say, what in tarnation does this city feller want in that backwoods town, anyways? Nothin' there."

"There's a jail and a poorhouse, most likely," said the clerk. "This — person seems to be interested in such."

"You mean he's one o' them lousy guvment —"

"Not exactly." The clerk was obviously highly amused.

"Well, then, what —"

The small boy reappeared, toting a heavy carpetbag. "I found 'er. She's comin' right down."

The driver's jaw dropped. "D-did he say — *she*?"

"He sure did." The clerk was grinning broadly.

"Y-you mean some *woman* — travelin' alone — on *that* road — to *that* godforsaken town —"

"Not just *some* woman. Wait till you see her."

"I don't need to." The driver winked knowingly. "There's only one kind of woman travels alone into frontier towns on funny business. I've seen *them* women."

"You haven't seen this one. And she's not that kind of woman. This is Miss Dorothea Dix."

"Who's she?"

"Heck, she's just about the most important woman you'll ever set eyes on! She hobnobs with judges and guv'nors and maybe even presidents. She goes around the country huntin' up poor loonies in jails and poorhouses, and then gets people to build 'em better places to live in."

The driver's eyes narrowed suspiciously. "Huh! Sounds like a loony herself. If you think I'm goin' to travel on a lonely road —"

A woman came down the stairs and crossed the room. She was tall, very straight of shoulders. She was dressed simply, a black shawl covering most of a plain gray dress with the barest touch of white at the throat. A dark bonnet did not quite hide two wings of waving red-brown hair framing a face with strong, yet delicately patrician features. The young driver's jaw dropped again. Instinctively he removed his cap and held it awkwardly in both hands. This was no "loony"; neither was she one of "*them* women." This was a *lady*.

"So you are to be my driver. I hope you don't mind taking a single passenger."

The boy stood twirling his cap, momentarily speechless. The woman's voice, low yet peculiarly vibrant, held him spellbound. It sounded a little like the fiddle the caller played at Saturday night dances, yet somehow he knew that this person would never use the word "fiddle." What would she call it? Vi — viol — The clerk brought him sharply back to reality. "Hey! What's the matter, Bub? The lady asked you a question."

"Y-yes, sir — I mean ma'am." He blushed furiously. "I mean, no, ma'am."

The woman smiled. "Then let us go, shall we?"

He picked up the carpetbag, finding it unexpectedly heavy. "It contains a lot of books," explained the woman. "I take them with me to give to the people I visit, in jails and poorhouses."

"Oh, it ain't really heavy, ma'am. That is, I'm real strong."

"Yes, I can see you are. I always feel safer with a strong driver."

Leading the way jauntily to his conveyance, the boy regarded it with sudden dismay. Certainly it was no proper carriage for a *lady*. A discard from the fashionable East, it had obviously seen better days. Built in the style known as a "brougham," it might once have contained features of comfort, even elegance, but no longer. Paint was faded and scraped, body dented. The iron-bound wheels, with their dozen slender wooden spokes, were noticeably dished. The glass was gone from the openings over the doors. There were better carriages in the stable, but the owner had begrudged them to a single passenger and a road which was little more than two wagon tracks and a forest trail.

"You shouldn't ought to ride in a trap like this," the boy blurted. "It's not for the likes of you."

She smiled again. "It's quite all right. Beside some of the conveyances I have ridden in, it is like a chariot."

He opened the creaking door. Before he could reach a hand to help, her daintily booted foot was on the iron step, and she hoisted herself easily into the small compartment. He had turned toward the hitching post when she called him back.

"Young man!" The melodious voice held a sharpened note, as if the fiddler had drawn hard on his bow.

"Yes, sir — I mean ma'am."

"Are those pistols I see protruding from your rear pockets?"

"Yes, ma'am. You see, there might be bandits on this road we're goin'. I've heard tell as how robbers have stopped carriages and taken money from passengers — not long ago, neither." He squared his shoulders. "But don't you worry none, ma'am. I'll protect you. That's why I've got these here pistols."

"Please — give them to me."

His mouth fell open. "Wh-what?"

"I said, give them to me. I will take care of them for you. You may have them back at the end of the journey."

"B-but — I tell you, ma'am, it ain't safe —"

"Safer than to run the risk of someone's being hurt or even killed. There will be no shooting from any conveyance which I have hired. Give them to me."

The boy hesitated. Had he made a mistake? Maybe the woman was a "loony," after all! But the voice still cast its spell, and it held authority now as well as gentleness. Reluctantly he handed over the two pistols. She took them, and he saw her place them on the floor under the seat.

The road was even worse than he had feared. Farm wagons lumbering through spring mud had worn deep ruts. For ease of riding the once-luxurious carriage might have been an ox cart. It swayed, tipped crazily, sank into the soft muck that felt like quicksand, rattled over rock outcroppings and through beds of stones that almost made one's teeth chatter. More than once the driver was almost jolted from his high seat. To his surprise there came no protests from behind.

But these hazards were nothing beside what lay ahead. Farmhouses grew less and less frequent. After several hours they entered a dark and lonely wood. For some miles the road tunneled through thick growths of pine, spruce, and cedar, so dense that one could see no further than a few yards on either side. The boy sat tense and watchful, eyes darting like ferrets from side to side. Once, startled by the sound of an animal's scuttling, he stiffened. His hand flew to his hip pocket, and he swore softly. He felt naked, bereft of his pistols. He should never have let her take 'em. These woods were known to be a hideout for ruffians, maybe even escaped criminals.

Then suddenly it happened. A man rushed into the road, seized the horse by the bridle, and stood brandishing a pistol.

"All right, you there. Stop! Don't reach for your gun, or I'll shoot!"

"I — I ain't got no gun."

"Says you!"

"Honest to God I ain't! I had two, but she took 'em."

"Who?"

"The woman. In there, in the carriage. My passenger."

"Woman!" The man burst into raucous laughter. "You're lying."

"I ain't." The boy's voice was shrill with desperation, for the pistol was pointed directly at him. "Go look! See for yourself!"

Warily, gun still poised, the man approached the window, peered inside.

"By God, it *is* a woman — and alone! Okay, ma'am, hand it over — your purse."

The young driver waited, trembling. This would show 'er. Maybe now she wished she'd left him his guns! Or would she use 'em? Maybe she wasn't so dumb as he'd thought. But, no. She was just talkin' to him, in that same voice, quiet like.

"Are you not ashamed, my good man, to rob a woman? I have but little money, and I need it to defray my expenses in visiting prisons and poorhouses, and occasionally in giving to objects of charity. But if you have been unfortunate, are in distress and in want of money, I will gladly give you some."

Noting that the gun was no longer pointed in his direction, the driver peered around the corner of the carriage. He could not believe his eyes. Under his stubble of beard the robber had turned strangely pale. He was staring at the woman, wide-eyed, his pistol, forgotten, dangling at his side.

"My God," he exclaimed, "that voice!"

The boy stared, eyes bugging and mouth agape, listening to the conversation that ensued. While an inmate in the Philadelphia penitentiary, explained the bandit, he had heard the woman talking to some of the prisoners in an adjoining cell, speaking to them kindly, giving them good advice. Now he recognized her voice. He would have known it anywhere.

"You may go on," he said with deep emotion. "Please forgive me for this outrage I have committed."

But the woman was not ready to go on. "I want to give you something," she said, "some money to support you until you can get honest employment."

"Oh, no — no, I couldn't —!"

The woman insisted. "You might be tempted to rob someone else," she told him, "before you found something honest to do." The boy heard the clink of coins. "Good-bye, my good man, and God bless you."

Not until they had left the man far behind did the young driver draw a long breath, as much of bewilderment as of relief. He still could scarcely believe his eyes and ears. They went on to the town, and he deposited the woman at its one makeshift inn. When she paid him, she insisted on adding a few coins so he could sleep in a good bed that night before returning home in the morning. That evening he told the story at least a dozen times to as many groups of incredulous listeners.

"But I tell you it's true! If you don't believe it, go ask the woman yourselves. She's right over there in the inn!"

It was by no means the last time he would tell it. As long as he lived, he knew, even if he grew to be a hundred, nothing any more strange or memorable would ever happen to him.

Stranger and Traveler

Runaway

I never had a childhood

1

ONCE MORE THE GATES of Paradise were closing. The child clutched the iron rail of the schooner's deck until her thin fingers whitened. Unshed tears blurred the

retreating shoreline of Boston so that hills and housetops, church spires and ship masts blended in hopeless confu-

3

sion. Adam and Eve must have felt like this, being expelled from the Garden of Eden. In fact, the sunlight blazing across the harbor waters was like an angel's flaming sword.

But, she thought, she had one advantage over Adam and Eve, for she was taking Jehovah with her! . . . then gasped in horror, half expecting the sword to smite her. Sacrilege! Father would exclaim harshly. But not Grandfather. She looked up at the tall figure beside her with a devotion akin to worship. Some people might call Dr. Elijah Dix stern, stubborn, dictatorial, and could quote words and incidents to prove it. Yet in all her seven years he had never frowned at her or chided. When she pictured God, it was as a strong sturdy man in his early sixties, with thick graying hair and beard, a square chin with a hidden dimple, lips that smiled at a child's prattle, and piercing eyes that could snap with impatience but for her always held a twinkle.

"Have a tart, Dolly," he said now, understanding her need for a tangible reminder that the joys of Paradise were not all left behind. "Here's one cram full of your Grandmother's prize pear preserves."

Made with his own prize pears, his proud tone implied. In the garden behind his great red brick house in Orange Court he had grafted and crossed trees until they produced some of the biggest and most famous pears in the country. The child's mouth watered just to think of them. Eve's apple could not have been more tempting. In fact, whoever said it was an apple? Much more likely it was a pear like Grandfather's.

"Careful, Dorothea, don't spill! You might know that mother of yours would never teach you proper manners!"

It did not take Grandmother's stern admonitions, still fresh in her ears, to prompt caution as she bit into the juicy tart. The new gray poplin dress with its tight bodice, full ankle-length skirt, and crisp ruffles, made by Aunt Mary's dressmaker in the latest fashion of this year, 1809, must do for best until her next visit to Boston, and only heaven knew when that would be! Not that there was any need of "best" for the Joseph Dixes in the little Maine village of Hampden, except for the few hours in meeting house on Sunday. But the spell of the big brick house with its polished furniture, its snowy linens, its gleaming glass and silver, its fragrance of flowers and old gentility, was still all-powerful, and she ate daintily, careful not to let fall a single luscious morsel.

There had been other visits to Boston, but this one eclipsed them all. She relived it now, savoring some of its moments with each delectable bite. It was springtime, and gardens were bursting into bloom. Grandfather took her walking along the Mall by the Common, full of budding trees and sweeping gulls and grazing cows. He showed her Old North Church where the lanterns were hung and the graves of John Hancock and "Mother Goose" in the Granary burial ground and the place where the despised British tea had been flung into the bay. He took her riding in his fine carriage while he called on his patients, gravely related their various ailments as if she were old enough to understand all the big words. They visited his drugstore on the south side of Faneuil Hall, and he showed her some of the medical books and surgical instruments he had brought back from Europe, becoming a dealer in physicians' supplies.

Once they drove across the long wooden bridge just four years old to South Boston where he had a big chemical shop for refining sulphur and purifying camphor, stopping on the way back to revel in the breathtaking view from the bridge. One could even see the dome of Bulfinch's State House high on the hill above the Common, and all along the waterfront was a forest of masts and spars, some with snowy sails flying like huge gulls. The bridge seemed to be a popular place, for many people were gathered along the wooden railing, some of them young men and women more interested in each other than in the view.

"A real lovers' lane," commented Grandfather dryly.

5

"Already they're beginning to call it 'The Bridge of Sighs'." His eyes twinkled down at her. "Sometime, Pet, you may be walking here with the man you're going to marry."

"Oh, no!" she retorted. "Never!"

"No? And why not?"

"Because — " Her voice trailed off. How explain, even to Grandfather, the way she felt seeing wings soaring or sails billowing, like this, how she wanted to be bound by nothing and nobody on earth — man, child, house — not like the married women she knew, Grandmother and Aunt Mary and the housewives in Hampden? Certainly not like Mother!

Grandfather nodded. He never probed, like Grandmother. "What are you thinking, child?" . . . "Why do you stare out of the window like that?" . . . "You mean you are seven and have never made a sampler?"

But even Grandmother's rigid code of discipline could not mar the perfection of Paradise. Now it was over. Memories faded into the shoreline along with spires and masts, and once outside the harbor there was nothing but sky and sea, a windy sky and a tumultuous sea.

"Good!" exulted Grandfather, lifting eager eyes to the bellying topsail. "With this down-easter we should make the Penobscot in fewer days than you can count on five fingers!"

Already he had left Boston, patients, drugstore, chemical works far behind and was sniffing the heady air of the vast wooded tracts he had purchased years before as an investment in the District of Maine, over 20,000 acres bought from the Bowdoin College allotment at a little more than a dollar an acre. The same indomitable energy and enterprise which had made him doctor's office boy at seventeen, physician and surgeon at twenty-three, salesman and manufacturer of drugs, promoter of a commercial fleet between Boston and the West Indies, had made this venture in land speculation prosper. In the first years he had charted his wilderness acres on foot, blazing trees to mark paths; then had begun slowly to survey it into farm sections. To promote settlement of his lands he had installed his son Joseph on a rented farm in Wheelersborough, later renamed Hampden, the town nearest the larger of his two tracts. The first settlers had arrived about 1795. By 1800 Collegetown, as it was called, had fifty-nine inhabitants, and now, nearly ten years later, it had over three hundred.

The route between Cape Cod and Penobscot Bay was exposed to the full force of the Atlantic, with wild weather possible. Though late in the spring, near the middle of May, the seas were rough. The small topsail schooner, known as a "Bay-coaster", rode the waves gallantly but with torturing discomfort for the uninitiated. While Grandfather paced the decks with mounting excitement, already savoring the heady ozone of his northern hills, Dorothea lay huddled on her bunk, head whirling, stomach churning. The trip up to Boston with Grandfather had been so different, just enough breeze for slow but steady progress, sky and sea blue-gold with anticipation. Even the change in smells was symbolic, instead of the sweet pungency of fresh lumber, bound for southern cities, the reek of pitch, tar, and turpentine for the northern shipbuilders. But, like the sojourn in Paradise, the days of agony came to an end.

"Come, Pet, we've entered the bay. No more rock and roll and not much wind, worse luck. Get up on those sea legs and come out."

The next days were a reprieve from exile. She skipped along the deck beside Grandfather, taking at least three steps to his one. In defiance of Grandmother's lingering authority she removed her new bonnet and let her fine rich brown hair blow in the breeze. The bay with its hundreds of islands hugged the wooded shore like a robe of blue watered silk sewn with emeralds. It was so beautiful she was glad when the sails hung limp. She wished the journey would never end.

Grandfather was as much at home among the islands

and inlets of Penobscot Bay as in the streets and alleys around Faneuil Hall and Old North Church.

"See, Dolly? Those houses on the beautiful little harbor under the high hills? Camden. Named after Lord Camden, one of our British friends during the Revolution, strongly opposed to taxation. . . ."

"Castine over there to the right. Oldest trading post in these parts. Named after a French baron who settled there in the sixteen hundreds. The British had a garrison there in the Revolution. Sometime I'll take you over to see the fort."

Sometime! She snatched at the crumb of promise like a starving bird.

He pointed toward a cluster of buildings deep in a wooded cove. "No wonder that colony of Irish Presbyterians wanted to change their settlement from over in New Hampshire! Belfast! A little bit of Ireland, yes, and a little bit of heaven."

The child looked and listened, enchanted. It was Grandfather, she decided, who made any place Paradise — except the ugly little house in Hampden. Already her muscles were tightening at the prospect of impending tensions.

Winds and tides were favorable on their arrival at the Bucksport Narrows, famed for their depth of waters and swirling eddies, and they passed between the high wooded banks without difficulty. After rounding Fort Point with its little lighthouse late in the afternoon, they dropped anchor in Fort Point Cove before attempting the hazardous trip up the river. Other vessels, several of them seagoing ships, were there before them. The embargo, Grandfather explained, had been lifted just two months before, a few days before Jefferson went out of office, and the New England merchants, their trade with Europe long stifled, were hastening to get shiploads of lumber, furs, dried and pickled fish off to foreign ports. Dorothea woke the next morning to the crackle of halyards being pulled and the sharp click of windlasses. Grandfather was jubilant. A south wind was blowing, strong and steady, and it was also flood tide, the best of combinations for travel up the treacherous Penobscot.

But progress was too slow to suit him. The crooked river with its mud flats, shoals, outstretching points ending in huge boulders, some close to the channels, must be ascended cautiously, and the high banks played havoc with the winds. Grandfather was no longer the genial and communicative companion. He paced the decks with such impatience that the child had to run to keep up with him. To her embarrassment he kept berating the skipper and mate for the craft's slowness. It was her first experience with the quick temper and dictatorial manner which had made the honest and public spirited doctor a bit less than popular in both Worcester and Boston. The ship's officers, who knew him well, hid their annoyance behind friendly grins.

"Let's hope that father of yours is at the wharf to meet us and that he has the horses and provisions ready for our trek into the wilderness! There's no time to lose."

Dorothea began to worry. Old far beyond her years, she was fully aware of the tensions between the Boston and the Hampden Dixes and knew the reasons for them. On this same visit she had overheard a conversation between Grandmother and Aunt Mary.

"My poor Joseph! Of course it's that wife of his who has been his ruination. How could he have been so stupid! He knew of course that Harvard would permit no married man to remain as a student. Leaving his theological training to marry a woman almost twenty years his senior and not even from a respectable Boston or Worcester family, one of those Bigelows from Sudbury! Poor, ignorant, uncouth, and quite unfit to become a member of the Dix household!"

"Unfit also, Mother, for life on the frontier farm where Father placed them. You or I might not have managed much better."

9

"Pah! You think we would have sent that child to Boston looking like that? Not a decent stitch to her back, and such manners! And it isn't as if they were poor. Your father pays Joseph good money for managing his lands, what little managing he does when he's not running around the country preaching!"

"I would be a poor one, Mother, to blame Joseph for that, after marrying a minister myself."

"Stuff and nonsense! You mean to compare your husband, the Reverend Thaddeus Mason Harris, pastor of a respectable Congregational church, with a fly-by-night circuit-rider who neglects his work and family to go around spouting Methodist heresies? How Elijah Dix came to father such a weak son I will never understand."

Dorothea had shrunk deeper into the heavily curtained window seat where she had curled with a book, and it had seemed an eternity before she could make her escape unnoticed. The words still burned in her ears.

Her father, she knew, was not the only one of Dr. Dix's six sons who had brought disappointment to his parents. Uncle William, the oldest, had died in Dominique, the West Indies, ten years ago. Just a few months before Uncle Alexander had been killed in Canada. She had heard whispers of their extravagance and dissipation. Joseph, her father, was the third son. As a fresh breeze whipped the sails and the vessel moved briskly upriver, she gripped the railing and prayed, "Please, don't let Father do anything to make Grandfather angry!"

The schooner reached Hampden in the late afternoon, anchoring in the strong current of mid-channel, and, since it was the turn of tide, swinging directly across it. News of her approach had been bruited by some of the small boys playing along the shore, and already half the town was assembling on or about General Crosby's long wharf at the mouth of Sowadabscook Stream. Though any arrival was of interest, this vessel was one of John Crosby's merchant fleet, built there at Hampden and manned by local sailors, and it was greeted with wild waving and loud cheers. Anxiously Dorothea scanned the faces. Surely Father must be there, even though she couldn't see him. He was so slight of figure he never stood out in a crowd.

The small boats were let down, and she was lowered into the arms of a sailor. Grandfather and his luggage were conveyed in the first boat as a matter of course. He was as important a man in these parts as General Crosby himself, who was the most prosperous importer on the river and had married the daughter of Benjamin Wheeler, the first settler for whom the town had originally been named, and builder of the thriving grist- and saw-mills near the long wharf. Townsmen pressed forward to greet the distinguished visitor.

"Dr. Dix — welcome to town! Heard you was comin'."

"Surveyin' some more farmland this spring, be ye?"

"Heard they're fixin' to name that settlement after you and the big mountain over there. Dixmont! Much more sensible than Collegetown."

Dr. Dix made dutiful responses while his keen eyes roamed the surrounding faces. The child saw his lips tighten, and her heart sank. Father had not come. Please — just let him be late, not gone away somewhere!

A man approached, respectfully doffing his cap. "I've got a horse and wagon, sir. General Crosby sent me, knowin' you was comin' and how your son was out of town."

Grandfather brusquely accepted the offer. The dirt road up from the wharf was rough, still deeply rutted from the spring mud. Perched on the high wooden seat between the driver and Grandfather, Dorothea clenched her teeth hard to keep them from chattering, partly from the joggle of the wagon but more from fright. She had never seen Grandfather look like that, face hard like stone and unnaturally white above his dark beard, eyes knife-sharp with anger. And all the time he said never a word.

They climbed the hill from the wharf; passed John Crosby's elegant big house still in process of building and his new brick store three stories tall, where he sold his lumber and grain and the cloth manufactured in Wheeler's mills and the sugar and molasses he imported from the West Indies; passed the Meeting House, used for all public gatherings as well as church, where Grandfather had bought a pew for the family. Dorothea felt a stirring of pride at sight of the Academy on the left, its bricks still bright-red from the kiln, and her nostrils quivered as at a subtle fragrance. A school always made her blood tingle. She looked up to see if Grandfather was noticing the fine building, but his eyes were straight ahead, and her brief excitement subsided into fresh misery.

The farm which Dr. Dix rented for his son was near the southernmost end of town. They turned into its rutted drive, drove for perhaps a half mile down through a heavily wooded section toward the river, coming finally to a stretch of cleared fields. Unlike those of other farms they had passed, they remained unplowed, rank with last year's grass. The small unpainted farmhouse was at the end of the long rough drive, its two wheel tracks barely discernible. Grass swished against the wheel hubs as they rode through.

"Guess the Elder's been too busy preachin' this spring to do much farmin'," commented the driver apologetically.

Grandfather made no reply. Only when his small horse-hair trunk and saddlebags were on the ground and the driver had turned his wagon did he speak.

"Have a good saddle horse here in the morning," he ordered curtly. "I'll want to leave for the hills by daylight."

They went into the house. Dorothea gasped in dismay. It was even worse than she had feared. Mother must be having another of her sick spells. Smells of stale food, stale air, stale dust leaped to greet them. The room, a combined kitchen and living room, was incredibly untidy. Dirty dishes stood in the sink and on the table, clouded with swarms of flies. Clothes were draped over chairs or lay in heaps on the floor.

"Dorthy! Dorthy!"

A three-year-old child ran toward them, his dress soiled and torn, hair uncombed, face dirty, but a handsome little fellow, with his sister's sensitive features and fine silky hair. "Joey!" she cried, snatching him in her arms.

Grandfather's face softened momentarily, and he actually smiled. "Well, well, my grandson Joseph! How you've grown!" But the hardness returned at sight of the woman in the bedroom door.

Now in her late forties, Mary Bigelow Dix still retained vestiges of the fragile beauty which had so captured the heart of a young student almost twenty years her junior that he had sacrificed family approval and a professional career. With one hand she clutched the sagging folds of a faded wrapper and with the other vainly tried to tuck straying wisps of hair under a ruffled cap. She looked as frightened as Dorothea felt.

"I — we — didn't expect you — so soon —"

"Where is my son?" demanded Grandfather bluntly.

"He — he went away on a preaching tour — over a week ago — he —"

"When is he coming back?"

"I — don't know. He — isn't always sure. One place — leads to another, and —"

"Didn't he know I was coming? I wrote the name of the vessel and its approximate time of arrival — weeks ago."

"Yes, but — he wasn't sure just when. The boats — so uncertain —"

Grandfather's face had been white. Now suddenly it turned fiery red, like a tomato ripe to bursting. It was far more frightening than the whiteness. For a moment he swayed and clutched at his side. Then words came, harsh, bitter, but a little disconnected, as if he were choking.

"My son — sent him here to do my business — sell lands — run this farm — and where is he when I need him most? Running around the country — preaching!"

"He's a good preacher," said the woman with a brief display of dignity and defiance. "Everybody says so."

"And preaching what?" The man might not have heard. "Not the proper theology he would have learned at Harvard. Some — some hell-fire damnation spouting he picked up from an ignorant circuit-rider! Doddering ne'er do well! Put him here to do a job, and look at him! Look at these fields! If they've seen a plow in two years, I'll — swallow a dose of my own medicine. And if he's been near that settlement out on my lands or sold a single farm in the last six months, I'll — I'll —"

He staggered toward a chair and sat down, breathing hard. Forgetting her fright, Dorothea went to him. "Grandfather! Are you all right?"

The flush in his cheeks slowly faded. He patted her head. "Sorry, Pet. None of this — your fault. Just give me a minute. I'll be — fine."

The woman stood in the door uncertainly, both fright and defiance giving way to a more habitual expression of peevishness and complaint. "I know things are all upset, but I couldn't do a thing. Been having one of my sick spells. I'm sure I don't know how you'll manage. I'll try to get some supper later, but — oh dear, right now I feel so faint!" She vanished into the bedroom. Dorothea, following, helped to settle her, moaning and sighing, into the unmade bed. Even now, at seven, she sensed that these recurrent fits of sickness were one method of coping with problems which seemed insoluble. Already she herself had discovered another method, and she employed it now.

She took off the new dress and bonnet, put them away carefully, and donned an old but clean calico. To her relief Grandfather seemed to have recovered his usual abounding strength and aggressive efficiency. Already he had kindled a fire in the cold stove and put water on to heat. She picked the clothes off the chairs and floor, folding the clean and putting the soiled in a basket under the sink. She washed little Joseph's face and hands and found a fairly clean dress for him. When the water was hot she washed the dishes. She cooked a simple supper out of the scant food in the house and made cornmeal gruel for her mother. She made a bed for Grandfather on a straw mattress upstairs with the cleanest bedding she could find. It was no more than she had often done before when her mother was indisposed. She had to finish her work by the light of a dim candle, since there was no whale oil for the lamp.

The riding horse arrived before daylight, but Grandfather was ready, his saddlebags packed. He would pick up the necessary provisions at the new little store at the settlement in the center of his lands. Their population growth to over three hundred in the last ten years had been the largest increase in that part of the county. And not much credit to his son, he might have commented. It had been registered as the town of Dixmont, the 169th to be created in the District of Maine, just two years before, in 1807. Already it boasted a post office and a church. From the center he would head north into the wilderness, he told his son's wife, who had recovered sufficiently to prepare a decent breakfast. He could find men there to accompany him, he commented with deliberate sarcasm, men willing to work, especially when they were paid for it; men like Friend Drake and Elihu Alden and David Porter, who had gone in by bushpath on horseback and cleared their own land when not a tree had been felled. If any one wanted to know his whereabouts, he added significantly, he could inquire of anybody at the center.

He lifted little Joseph high over his head making him crow with delight, then turned to Dorothea, lips tender, eyes dancing. In that moment the anger, the bitter words of the night before, were forgotten. Here again was the grandfather she had always known.

"Good-bye, Dolly, my pet. You're a good girl, a credit to the name Dix — yes, and to Dorothea, which means 'Gift of God.'"

She clung to him, unable to keep from weeping, unable to speak the words that were crying to be spoken. "Oh,

Grandfather, I love you, better than anyone else in the world!"

He swung himself on the horse and turned to wave before riding away along the road between the fields and up the long hill into the woods. Always she would remember him so, straight and sturdy as one of the tall oaks lining the path, head upflung, arm gallantly waved in farewell.

Joseph Dix returned a few days later, bone weary, but eyes aflame with fanatical zeal. He had traveled more than a hundred miles, preached at least twice each day, sold or given away a thousand of his tracts and sermons, and, please God, added many saved souls to his Lord's diadem of glory.

"Your father was here," interrupted Mary tartly.

The light died out of his eyes. "He — he was? I — must have lost track of time. Had no idea he would — would get here so soon. Where is he?"

"Up in that godforsaken wilderness, where you ought to be."

Joseph's face showed a conflict of emotions, shame, guilt, worry, but mostly indecision. After a few hours sleep he saddled his horse, still as weary as he was himself, and set out for the fifteen miles of forest trail leading west.

The days passed. May drew toward its end. In spite of the bleak emptiness following her Boston visit Dorothea caught brief glimpses of Paradise. Spring, always late in Maine, burst into a repetition of the rebirth in Boston gardens. Willows shimmered from pale to deep gold on the river bank. The new lime-green leaves on birches and poplars burgeoned overnight into bright emerald. Pink and white apple blossoms gave way to the delicate mauves and lavenders of lilacs. On the stone walls along the roads a few wild roses sprang into bloom. Life still held beauty and anticipation. Grandfather would be back for at least a few hours, perhaps days, before returning to Boston.

Then one day the horseman who carried mail to the little post office at Dixmont rode into town. He brought news which swiftly found its way to the small house on the Isaac Hopkins farm. While surveying farm lots on a remote section of his lands Dr. Elijah Dix had collapsed. He had been carried to a friend's house situated on the north side of the road leading from Dix Corner to Bangor and had died there. His son had been with him. He had been buried in the small cemetery nearby.

The bright colors of spring turned suddenly gray. Now the gates of Paradise had really closed.

2

"I never knew childhood," Dorothea was to say long afterward. Except, she might have added, for those brief halcyon visits to Boston! The five years following Grandfather's death resembled the murky twilight of the Dark Ages, and they seemed like as many centuries.

There almost might have been no Boston family. True, an occasional letter came from Madam Dix to her son Joseph, brief, perfunctory, replete with caustic criticism and advice. Administration of the Dixmont land tracts had been put in other, more capable, hands. Now that Grandfather's patient subsidizing of his son's poor stewardship had ended, the family was dependent on the scant donations from Father's itinerant preaching and the proceeds from sales of his printed sermons and tracts. He produced these endlessly, words flowing from his quill pen with as glib fervor as from his lips. His few hours at home were spent bent over the rough board table, surrounded by Bibles and commentaries and foolscap, working often far into the night by the light of the whale oil lamp or a guttering candle. Then he would be off to the printer's in the neighboring town of Bangor, returning with stacks of loose printed sheets.

"Here! This is one of my best, I think. It should save hundreds of souls. Take time to read it, Daughter, while you and your mother do the stitching. And read it aloud to little Joseph. A child is never too young to repent of his sins and be saved."

"Yes, Father," she would promise, then help him load his saddlebags with big bundles of tracts already neatly stitched, watch him mount and ride away, to be gone perhaps for days, perhaps for weeks, fulfilling his vow "to carry the gospel to the farthest settlements."

Back into the house then, into the one small main room with all its unfinished work and clutter, its wooden sink filled with unwashed dishes, its bare puncheon floor crying to be swept, its small windows covered with oiled paper which kept out the cold in winter but the sun also in summer, and the fresh air at all times. More often than not Mother would feel too ill, or at least too tired, to make more than a pretense of helping. It was often Dorothea who must fill the pails from the well, keep the fire stoked with wood, scrub the dirty clothes in the big tin washtub and hang them out, cook the meals, wash dishes, sweep, make a grim attempt to maintain as much cleanliness and order as possible for both house and occupants.

However, these tasks were but preliminaries. One must get through them with feverish haste, rising often long before dawn, in order to spend more hours on the day's important stint, the cutting and pasting and sewing of those tracts and sermons. Even Mother left her sick bed and staggered to the table to help with this task, knowing that their living depended on it. They would bring little cash income at best, many given in exchange for Father's lodging or for horse's fodder, potatoes, maple sugar, yarn, and other commodities, all welcome but useless as tender for rent and flour and calico. It took most of his meager funds received from preaching to pay his printing bills.

The work was sheer torture. Hour after hour the child sat on a straight, hard chair, cutting, folding, pushing a big needle through thicknesses of coarse, heavy paper, pull-

ing the threads taut, pushing . . . pulling . . . Arms and
shoulders ached, head throbbed, legs prickled. The tips of
her right thumb and forefinger became first red and raw
then ridged with calluses. But there were compensations,
for the hateful bulky pages held the magic of words, and
had not Father bade her read them? Snatching moments
here and there, she hungrily absorbed them. Then later, as
he had also bidden, she read some of the more eloquent
passages to young Joseph, trying to inject into her soft,
childish voice something of the burning intensity which
held Father's audiences spellbound, made them blench
and tremble over their sins, brought them weeping and
repentant to the altar.

Dorothea had heard Father preach. He had taken her
with him when he had spoken in a schoolhouse in a
nearby settlement. With amazement she had watched his
thin delicate body assume towering strength. In the flaring
lamplight his eyes had blazed like live coals. His usual
mild voice had whipped like a lash. Seeing the listeners'
intent faces and sensing their aroused emotions, she had
felt wonder, pride, and, a new sensation, respect.

"The Lord is known by the judgment which He exe-
cuteth," she read solemnly to young Joseph. "The wicked
shall be turned into hell. Upon the wicked He shall rain
snares, fire and brimstone, and an horrible tempest.
Brothers and sisters, children, these words from Holy Writ
are meant for all of us. For is not even the youngest child
among us conceived and born in sin? To be lost forever, to
lie down in eternal burnings, how dreadful! It was when I
lay, a lost and condemned sinner upon the brink of hell,
just ready to be plunged into its fiery billows, that Jesus
saw me, ran to my help, and saved me. . . ."

The terror in young Joseph's eyes stopped her short.
"Let's go outdoors," she said hastily. "Let's look for wild
flowers and see if you can tell me their names. We might
even go down to the river and see if there isn't a sloop or a
schooner coming."

Obedient but still sober, Joseph ran with her down the

path through the grove of tall pines and oaks and beeches to their favorite perch atop the huge granite ledges sloping precipitously to the swirling water. Grasping the child's ragged little shirt, Dorothea succeeded in diverting his thoughts of hell fire to less fearsome prospects.

"That's Orrington over there. Father says that once Jesse Lee, the Methodist preacher, swam his horse across the river from Orrington to Hampden and preached in our meeting house. . . . Oh, look, there comes a schooner! You can tell it from other vessels because it has two masts and square sails on the foremast . . ."

But she did not forget. Why, she wondered, must Father talk all the time about God's being angry? There were plenty of verses in the Bible that told about his love; she had read them. It was the same with the preachers who came to the meeting house where she went every Sunday, both morning and afternoon, and sat in the pew that Grandfather had bought for them. When Mother did not feel well enough to go, which was often, Dorothea put on the gray poplin dress and the bonnet made in Boston, dressed Joseph in his carefully darned and patched best clothes, and together they trudged the two miles of dusty road to the meeting house.

These were the high hours of the week. She was part of the life of the thriving little town. She *belonged*. No need to be ashamed of her clothes, as she often was during the week. Even the stuffs and styles worn by the Crosby and Emery and Dudley women were no better than those produced by Aunt Mary's dressmaker. The Crosbys might have the finest house and the Dudleys the first piano in town, and the Emerys a living room big enough to be used as a ballroom, but they should see Dix Mansion in Orange Court!

Sundays! They were prison doors flung wide, no cutting, pasting, stitching; a cold dinner cooked on Saturday, clean clothes, fresh air. And time, most precious of all — time to think, to walk, perhaps to write a poem, to read, even though all the books in the house were the Bible, a hymn book, and a few theological textbooks from Father's college days. She could not remember when she had learned to read, certainly before the few terms she was able to attend the little one-room school down the road when Mother was well enough to do the housework. Probably Father and Mother had taught her, though it had taken little teaching. The days in school were high points, like Sundays, even though she must always hurry home to cut and sew and paste, never loitering along the road or stopping to play with children named Ellingwood or Higgins or Snow or Hopkins.

Perhaps the rare flashes of pleasure were brighter for their drab setting. An errand to Nathan Hopkins's big house just down the main road and on the other side was an adventure remembered for days. It was a beautiful house, built in 1783, sturdy, resting on solid granite blocks and inside great hand-hewn beams the color and texture of brown velvet. Unlike many in Hampden the Hopkins family did not seem to look down on the poor Dixes, though they might well have felt superior, Nathan being a direct descendant of Stephen Hopkins who came over from England on the Mayflower and when it landed at Plymouth was one of the signers of the Colony Pact. And their young daughter Elizabeth never looked askance at a faded outgrown dress or shoes broken at the toes.

There were other square, sturdy houses in the southern part of town, some even more imposing than the Hopkins's, but Dorothea had never been inside them. As they trudged past them to church or store, she would regale Joseph with gossip she had overheard.

"See! General Herrick's house up that road. They say it has a winding staircase and eight fireplaces!" . . . "Jesse Libby built that three-story house they use for a tavern. No wonder he needed a big one, with a wife and seven children!" . . . "A man named Martin Kingsley lives there. He's a big man, a judge. They say it has fifteen rooms!"

21

Joseph was duly impressed. "Are they bigger than Grandfather's Dix Mansion?"

"No!" Dorothea felt bleak homesickness. "Not near so big, or so beautiful. I just wish you could see —" No use wishing. The gates of Paradise had banged shut forever.

A trip for flour or sugar or molasses to Crosby's big brick store, with its tantalizing smells of spices and pickles and new clothing and fresh lumber, was almost as exciting as a journey to the West Indies. Once in an unusual mood of leisure Father took her and Joseph down to the end of Shore Street where a ship was being built, a great white skeleton getting ready, like Ezekiel's dry bones, to come to life. Many ships and schooners and sloops had been launched at Hampden, as at other towns along the Penobscot, destined for southern cities and foreign ports with cargoes of butter, cheese, potatoes, dried fish, bricks, lumber, hay, cord wood; returning with pitch, tar, turpentine from the south; sugar, rum, molasses from the Indies; calicos, woolens, cambrics from Britain — all to swell the considerable wealth of Crosbys and Wheelers and Herricks and Emerys.

But these were precarious days for American shipping. Relations with England were growing constantly more tense. After the repeal of the Nonintercourse Act and the lifting of the Embargo, shipping had flourished for a while, but in 1811, wooed by false promises of Napoleon, President Madison again declared nonintercourse with England. To the dismay of northern merchants the fiery Henry Clay and other southerners interested in agriculture pressed for war. True, there was enough provocation — seizure of sailors flying under the American flag, harassment of ships, supplying of arms to Indian tribes in the west. But grievances were becoming less acute, and peaceful settlement of differences seemed possible. To the merchants of the north Atlantic seaboard, including those of Hampden, the declaration of war in June, 1812, came as a stunning blow. It also aroused in many of the Hampdenites a sense of panic. Some remembered the Revolution and the occupation by the British of Castine. Once more the river towns would be easy prey, especially for troops coming down from Canada. Some families left immediately for places farther inland. Others surreptitiously packed a few valuables and necessities in readiness for enforced evacuation.

"Fools!" scoffed Harding Snow, one of Joseph Dix's neighbors, whose family had settled their farm in the 1780s and who himself had fought in the Revolution. "This here's my property, and I'm sartin sure no Britisher is goin' to drive me out. Jus' lct 'cm try."

Perhaps Joseph Dix found the fever of exodus contagious, or perhaps he had long resisted the urge of itching feet. Less likely, sensations of guilt may have stirred him to seek more lucrative fields of labor. He had another son now to support, Charles Wesley. One day he appeared, riding not astride his horse but in a two-seated wagon, once rather elegant but now obviously decadent.

"We're going to leave this place," he announced. "There are places farther west where the Gospel is needed more — yes — and where the Lord's emissary need not peddle his sermons for a few crusts of bread." They were to take only what could be packed in the back of the wagon. There would be better furniture where they were going.

"And where is that?" demanded his wife with a mixture of hope and resignation.

Joseph was vague but exuberant. She would see. He had been told of a town where a man with his education and abilities could not only preach but run a successful business. In fact, he had the offer of a store —.

Mary Dix was bluntly skeptical. She had heard such promises before. And while his family lived in a shack and half starved, she reminded tartly, his own mother was wallowing in luxury, spending all kinds of money on her other worthless sons. If his spine were made of hard bone instead of gristle —.

Joseph's lips tightened. His thin, slightly stooped shoulders straightened. For one of the few times in his life he looked very much the son of Dr. Elijah Dix. Never as long as he lived, he declared with asperity, would he ask his mother for a penny.

Dorothea was aghast at the thought of leaving. Suddenly the shabby little house seemed beautiful in its snugness and security. Never again to sit in the hard but familiar pew registered in the name of Dix, to dream of a future in the wonderful Academy, to hunt for the first wild flowers in the farm's uncultivated fields, to walk by the river and watch gulls flying and ships lifting white wings to the sky, yes, even to carry the heavy pails of water, dripping liquid diamonds in the morning sunlight!

But there was no time for mooning. Food must be cooked for the journey, the wagon packed. What to choose, with room for so little? Neighbors were kind, more so than in all the years past, bringing provisions, wishing them well. But when they finally rode up the long winding rutted trail between the tall oaks, there were none to see or say good-bye. Sitting on the backseat beside Mother, little Charles squirming in her arms, Dorothea kept looking back — and back — long after the shabby little house had disappeared.

"Like us," she thought with a wisdom beyond her ten years. "It won't be long before people will have forgotten that we ever lived here."

She could not know, of course, as the creaking old wagon left the trail to turn into the road that over that very spot nearly a century and a half later a beautiful stone archway would bear the words, DOROTHEA DIX PARK ... or that on Independence Day, 1899, the whole town of Hampden and many distinguished visitors would celebrate the dedication of the park, festive with flowers, booths, tents, flags, bandstand; roam the graveled path to the site of the old house by the river; listen to speeches and songs and poems honoring the memory of the town's most famous daughter. "Wave out," a poem of many stanzas, would apostrophize the day's proud symbol:

Wave out, wave out, O starry flag!
  O banner of the free!
Wave o'er the valley of her birth,
  Dear flag of liberty!
Wave till the river to the sea,
  The sea unto the shore
The story of her helpful deeds
  Shall tell forevermore.

3

The next two years were as shifting as a kaleidoscope, mostly without color. A few weeks or months in one place; then they were on the move again. The wagon became a more familiar shelter than a house. The offer of a store proved to be a temporary clerkship selling groceries. It ceased abruptly when Father refused to confine his preaching expeditions to weekends. There was a short sojourn in New Hampshire. Then in Barnard, Vermont, the kaleidoscope pattern burst into color. Father rented a small cottage near the meeting house. He opened a little shop and began to sell books as well as tracts and sermons, advertising for sale "a handsome and useful assortment of miscellaneous books, also schoolbooks, single or by the dozen, at Boston prices. Cash or produce taken in payment."

Books! Dorothea was in heaven. Whenever she could be spared from household duties (seldom enough) she was allowed to help in the shop. Merely handling the smooth cloth covers was fascinating, but to dip into their contents was bliss indeed. She devoured them greedily, indiscriminately, in every spare moment. But this paradise also was shortlived. Produce was far more forthcoming than cash, and that little enough. Rent was in arrears. The ambitious residue of stock had to be shipped back to Boston.

The Dixes prepared to move again, this time to Worcester, Massachusetts, Joseph's birthplace and early home. As the decrepit wagon clattered and crawled over the stony dusty road, constantly threatening a preview of the "One Hoss Shay," Joseph became increasingly hopeful and voluble.

"Father was a big man in Worcester. After studying medicine there for three years with Dr. John Green, then three more years with a pharmacist in Boston, he began practicing medicine in Worcester in 1770, eight years before I was born. Dr. Sylvester Gardner was his partner, and Gardner took the British side during the Revolution. Worcester became too hot for him, and he escaped to England. You know what Father did?" Joseph paused for effect.

"No," prompted Dorothea excitedly. "What?"

"After the war he went to England, found his old partner, and gave him all the money that was due him. That was the kind of man he was. Not only honest but public spirited and aggressive. He planted Worcester's first shade trees, when everybody there thought trees were men's enemies like bears and Indians. He promoted the first good road between Worcester and Boston, when people thought mud roads like this were ordained by the Most High. Oh, he'll still be remembered in Worcester, all right."

Dorothea swelled with pride. It was almost like hearing psalms of praise to deity. But all of Joseph's reminiscences were not so flattering.

He chuckled. "And not only for his good deeds. Oh, Father was bossy, and he had a temper. It got him enemies. Some of them plotted once to do him violence, maybe drive him out of town. One evening a man called at his house, asking him to come to the sick bed of a fake patient, some miles out of town. On the road they had planted an attacking party. Father suspected the plot, and you know what he did?" This time Dorothea did no prompting. Grandfather with enemies? She swelled now with anger instead of pride. "Surely, he said, he was willing to go. Then he opened his window and called out in a loud voice to his manservant: 'Bring round my horse at once; see that the pistols in my holsters are double-shotted; then give the bulldog a piece of raw meat and turn him loose to go along with us!' Ha, you can believe there was no more trouble. The men vanished."

Dr. Elijah Dix was indeed still remembered in Worcester. Dix Street, marking the southern line of the extensive property he had owned, extending westward into Main Street, beyond Harvard, bore his name. The elms he had planted, already impressive, would endure for a century. The house to which he had taken his bride, Dorothy Lynde, in 1771, though he had left Worcester in 1795, was still spoken of as "the Doctor's." And the name of Lynde was equally well known. The town's fine water came from Lynde Brook in Leicester. The four daughters of Joseph Lynde, who had escaped to Worcester after the burning of Charlestown by British troops, were spoken of as "among the most reputable and worthy of the ladies who made up Worcester society at the end of the last century." Sarah, one of Dorothy's sisters, was the wife of William Duncan; another had married into the wealthy Wheeler family; a third had become the wife of the eminent Judge Bangs.

But if Joseph hoped for a revival of his personal fortunes in his native city he was disappointed. He had inherited at least his father's independence. He refused to seek favors or even casual intercourse from relatives who had disapproved of his marriage. He moved his family into a crude house on the edge of the city, in an almost deserted area, and, because he knew himself a failure at other pursuits, turned again to his first love and only talent, preaching. Again for Dorothea there were the cutting and pasting and stitching, the loading of saddlebags, Father's long absences, the dirt and clutter, the long days of work never done.

"We might as well have stayed in Hampden," Mary Dix

Dorothy Lynde Dix, Dorothea's grandmother.
From an oil painting made about 1780.

chided her husband bitterly. "Things couldn't have been any worse there than they are here."

But in September of that year 1814 Joseph returned from one of his trips with a report that for a brief time silenced her complaints. He had met a former Hampden resident who had heard the latest war news from the District of Maine. The British had indeed reoccupied their old fort at Castine, then sailed up the Penobscot, capturing, or at least terrorizing every town as far as Bangor. They had landed 750 troops at Bald-Hill cove about a mile and a half below Hampden Corner and started their march toward Hampden meeting house. There a battle had taken place, and the defending troops had been obliged to retreat. The enemy had commandeered all public property and shipping. Hampden had suffered more than other towns. Almost every house had been plundered, and much of value stolen. It was reported that General Crosby had lost property amounting to twenty or thirty thousand dollars. But all the townsmen had not capitulated.

"Remember our old neighbor Harding Snow?" Joseph chuckled. "Well, he was sawing wood down on the river bank when a British officer ordered him to go kill his cow and bring the soldiers some meat. 'I shan't, sartinly,' shot back old Harding. 'I command you to do so,' said the officer. 'I shan't sartinly,' repeated Harding. 'I guess you don't know who you're talking to,' retorted the officer. 'You never saw a British soldier before.' 'Oh, yes, I have, and I've seen 'em run.' said old Harding. 'Well, where did you see them run?' 'At Bunker Hill,' Harding calmly replied. And he didn't kill his cow!" Joseph turned triumphantly to Mary. "Now do you still wish you were back in Hampden?"

Mary was silent. It was Dorothea who felt like retorting, "It couldn't be any worse." As the weeks passed, frustration turned to despair, despair to panic. She was twelve years old. The world, with all its precious knowledge, was spinning past her. Never to go more to school, to discover how and where those impatient wings she felt folded inside her were meant to fly? The years ahead, as far as she could see, stretched endlessly, like the thread pushed and pulled through the heavy papers. And her brothers — what would become of them? Little Joseph was eight. He should be sent to a good school. She had taught him to read and write, starting when he was not much older than baby Charles and spelling out words with a twig in the sand. But she knew so little!

An idea leaped into her mind, so wild that she jammed the big needle into her finger and, to her horror, made a big blood spot on one of Father's sermons. It was impossible, of course. Who would cook and wash clothes and sweep and dress baby Charles and sew sermons? Mother was more of an invalid than ever, spending almost every day in bed or on the couch. Yet when she knew Great-aunt Sarah Duncan was coming for a duty call she had got up, swept and scrubbed furiously, spread the table with the best linen, baked little cakes for tea. Cannily, Dorothea sensed that retreat into invalidism was Mary Dix's remedy for frustration. She could do many things if she had to. Still, the idea was impossible, unless . . . Dared she suggest it to Father? No. He would just be sad and sympathetic and — helpless. Whatever was done she must do herself. But how? Then something happened. It was a Sunday morning. The scratching of Father's quill pen suddenly ceased, and he stared at her, frowning.

"Is that the best dress you have?" he demanded. "It isn't fit to walk the streets in, much less attend divine services!"

She flushed. "I tried to mend it. I know it's faded, it's had so many washings. It's the one Grandmother and Aunt Mary Harris had made for me."

"But that was five years ago!" He reached into his pocket. "Here. Take this. We'll postpone the printing of this sermon. Go up to your Aunt Duncan. You remember where she lives, that big house on the hill? I showed it to you once." She nodded. "Ask her to get some cloth, the best this will buy, and have a dress made. We can't have you looking like a vagabond."

Heart hammering, she looked down at the silver piece. It would buy so many things, food, new clothes for the boys, or, perhaps, two dresses. Mother needed one as much as she did. Yet she knew what she must do. She planned carefully. Father left on a short preaching tour. He would be back, he promised, in three days. "And don't forget that dress, Dolly." No, she would not forget. Such a short time, three days! She washed and ironed. She cleaned the house. Never had it been so neat. She cut and stitched and pasted at night until she dared not burn another candle. And then she wrote a long letter, placing it on top of the finished pile of sermons where Father would be sure to find it as soon as he came home. The third morning she rose earlier than usual, cooked extra food, fed the family, washed the dishes, saw the children properly dressed, made her mother comfortable. Then she put on her best dress and bonnet.

"Where are you going?" demanded Mary anxiously.

"To spend my silver piece." She tried to smile as she leaned over to kiss her mother. "Remember, Father told me to go to Aunt Duncan and see about getting a new dress? If — if I shouldn't be back by dinner time, there is a pot of stew on the back of the stove."

"Be good," she told little Joseph, "until I see you again, and take care of Mother and baby Charles." She hugged them both so hard they squirmed in protest.

The stage driver gave her a long doubtful look. "Boston, you say, little miss? You alone? No mama? No papa? I'm not sure —"

She drew herself up to her full less than five feet and returned his look with one of pleasant but remote dignity, the same look which would insure her entrance past hundreds of such barriers in the next three quarters of a century. "It's quite all right, sir. My grandmother lives in Orange Court, in Boston, and I'm going to visit her."

He nodded. She held out the silver piece, inwardly trembling. Suppose it was not enough! But he gave her back a few coins. "Thank you, young miss. Have a good journey."

Grandfather may have been responsible for the road she was traveling, but it was not an easy one. The rattling wheels, however, were not all that kept her tense and trembling during the long forty miles. She was terrified. What had she done! Would Father be terribly angry? Would she be able to find Grandmother's house in that huge city? And would Grandmother take her in? She would travel hundreds of thousands of miles in the next seventy years, over roads far worse than this, but this was the longest and hardest journey she would ever take.

4

Madam Dorothy Lynde Dix, of Dix Mansion, Orange Court, off Orange Street (later an extension of Washington) was entertaining her daughter Mary, wife of the Reverend Thaddeus Mason Harris, at afternoon tea.

"A waif you say, Jennie?" She regarded the house maid with annoyance. "A girl? At the front door, not the servants' entrance? What impudence! But you know what to do. If she's hungry, take her to the kitchen and give her some bread and milk."

"But — she didn't ask for food, ma'am. All she said was, she must see you."

"Humph! A bold little begger! Probably a thief, too. I hope you didn't let her into the house, Jennie."

"Oh, no, ma'am. She's still outside on the stoop."

"Perhaps," suggested Mrs. Harris, "she has brought a message from one of our friends. Go and ask her what she wants, Jennie."

The maid soon returned. "She wouldn't tell me, ma'am. She just says how as she has to see you."

Madam Dix yielded reluctantly. "Very well. Bring her in. But watch her every step of the way."

The slight figure stood very straight, just inside the door. She was not prepossessing. Her dress, though of good cut and material, was soiled and rumpled and far too short. The wisps of hair escaping from what was obviously a child's bonnet were limp and dust colored. Her shoes were badly scuffed. In fact, she looked exactly as the maid had described her, a waif.

"Well, child," snapped Madam Dix. "Who are you, and what do you want?"

Mrs. Harris gave a little scream. "Mother! It's our Joseph's Dorothea!"

"Yes," said Madam Dix after a long, slow perusal. "I see. You may leave us, Jennie," she told the gaping house maid. "Now come here, child. Let me look at you."

There was no softness in her voice, and her expression did not change. She might still have been addressing a stray waif instead of a grandchild. "So," she continued, "you are my granddaughter, Dorothea Lynde Dix. My namesake, in fact. How did you get here?"

"I ran away, Grandmother. I came on the stage from Worcester."

"Does your father know you are here?"

"He should by now. He was coming home today, and I left a letter."

"And why did you come?"

"To beg you to take me in, Grandmother. I couldn't stand it any longer, living the way I did. I want to grow up to know things, to be somebody. I want to learn, to go to school."

Madam Dix was a formidable figure. The features beneath the close-fitting white cap — brilliant dark eyes, aquiline nose, unsmiling lips — were stern and, at first glance, forbidding. Even the crisp snowy ruching at the neck of the black dress seemed to have acquired its starch from the firm chin. Her seven sons and one daughter had often quailed before her, and with reason, for her unswerving devotion to family was conditioned by an inflexible will and a puritan perfectionism.

The twelve-year-old girl now facing her did not quail. Her eyes, a softer color but equally brilliant, looked straight into the other's without wavering. The small chin, just as firm, remained lifted high above an unusually long slender neck.

"They are two of a kind," thought Mary Harris, unable to suppress a smile. "She's more my mother's child than any of her own children."

It was Madam Dix whose eyes wavered. She turned to her daughter with unaccustomed helplessness. "What — what shall I do with her?"

Mary Harris continued to smile. It was one of the few times in her life when she had dared to advise her mother. "First," she said, "we will give her a substantial tea. She probably has had nothing to eat since early morning. Then I shall take her upstairs and see that she has a good washing and combing and brushing. The clothes will have to be attended to later. I'll tell the maid to make my old room ready for her."

Madam Dix's helplessness was only temporary. She despatched a message to Joseph saying that his daughter had arrived safely and would remain in Boston for the present. Within hours she had assumed the molding of her granddaughter's body, mind, and spirit with as conscientious and sacrificial thoroughness as she had attempted to shape the destinies of her own eight children, with only partial success. She was no longer young, nearly seventy, and twelve years of careless upbringing must be counteracted by intensive and rigorous tutelage. Her code was that of the finest New England gentlewoman of her day: industry, inflexible dignity, economy, perfection in manners, spartan discipline, puritanical piety.

"Never waste a moment," was her frequent admonishment to youth. "No task must be performed in a slipshod manner. Never raise your voice in anger." (A husband with a fierce temper had made this rule difficult to enforce!) "A lady or gentleman never gives vent to emotion in public."

Dorothea slipped into the rigid routine with at least outward meekness. She was too grateful to be accepted, given a chance to learn, to reveal any rebellion she might feel. And here was the site of her ancient paradise, even though bereft of its presiding deity. Grandfather's robust figure still seemed to dominate house, garden, and stable, his hearty voice to exclaim over his luscious pears, recite the names of flowers, scold the gardener, cluck and nicker to his thoroughbreds. She loved every feature of the great red brick house with its plate glass windows, its cupola, its carved wainscotings, its high scrolled ceilings. Its furnishings too were reminiscent of Grandfather, for he had brought many of the tables, desks, chairs, bureaus and poster beds from England after the revolution, solid specimens of Hepplewhite, Chippendale, Sheraton. Even the small treasures thronging the house brought back memories.

"See, Dolly, these beautiful bits of coral brought by one of my ships from the Indies? All built by tiny little sea creatures! And this conch shell — lift it to your ear and hear the roar of the ocean! . . . Feel the soft wool of this shawl from Kashmir, and this silk from Smyrna, all woven by hand. . . . These brasses are from India. . . . These tablets with British coats of arms are called hatchments. Very old. They used to hang them outside the door at time of death."

Was it Grandfather who had instilled in her the desire to know things, everything possible there was to know, or had she been born with the yearning? No matter. To her delight Grandmother also approved of education, even for girls, and she enrolled her new charge in one of the best private girls' schools in Boston.

"You must fit yourself for some occupation to earn your bread, and what can a woman do except teach?"

Since that was exactly what Dorothea wanted to do, especially in order to teach her young brothers, she assented eagerly. The coachman took her to the school and brought her home each day in the carriage. She absorbed the new nourishment with the eagerness of a newborn baby, but soon sucked the source dry. The proper education of a young gentlewoman of the day consisted of the three R's, plus a smattering of French and music, with liberal doses of manners, embroidery, and drawing. Dorothea supplemented this meager fare with Grandfather's library, which offered viands ranging through medicine, poetry, religion, botany, philosophy, for his interests had been legion. Fortunately Grandmother approved of reading, and she need not know of all the candles smuggled from the kitchen and burned to their butts long after the rest of the household was asleep.

But Grandmother's rigid disciplines were not all so congenial to her taste. A young woman must learn to sew, make jackets and shirts, hem endless seams in sheets and pillow cases, knit socks. And Grandmother's eyes were even sharper than her tongue. Every stitch must be like every other and so fine as to be scarcely discernible. There was one and only one correct way of cutting and fitting the neckband of a man's shirt, as Dorothea found to her grief when attempting to make one for Uncle Henry Elijah, the only one of the seven sons still living at home. One woman, so the story went, as a special reward for excellence in moral conduct, had been allowed to make an entire shirt under the stern tutelage of Madam Dix. "And all my life," she stoutly claimed, "I felt its benefit."

Had there been one word of commendation Dorothea could have suffered the long hours of apprenticeship with less reluctance. The tiny stitches were certainly less wearisome than pushing a great needle through folds of heavy paper. But Grandmother was too much the perfectionist to give praise which she believed undeserved. It was her duty to correct error, whether in the category of imperfect sewing or of uncouth manners or of heretic theology instilled by a vagrant from the orthodox Congregationalist fold. Dinners, when one might have basked in the loveliness of snowy linens and frail china and tall silver candlesticks, were orgies of admonition. Sundays had few leisure hours after the long services at Hollis Street Church around the corner, and they must include inquisitions on the catechism and Cotton Mather. Life in the big sumptuous house was joyless, as bereft of affection as in the poor cabin on the Penobscot. Her pillow was often wet with tears.

Aunt Mary tried to compensate for this lack as well as her own undemonstrative upbringing would allow, but she was busy with her own two daughters, Sarah and Dorothy, her two sons John and James, and her husband's church in Dorchester.

"Your grandmother really loves you," she assured the lonely child, "that's why she tries so hard to correct your faults." She smiled ruefully. "Somebody said once that Mother would gladly die at the stake for her children, but nothing would betray her into the weakness of kissing them good night!"

Dorothea sometimes gazed at the portrait of Grandmother painted by a Swedish artist some thirty years before in Worcester. It showed a handsome, keenly intelligent woman of forty, dressed in a tight blue satin bodice with huge sleeves, and surmounted by a vast lace headdress. It was startling how little she had changed in thirty years. Her cheeks were still smooth and the wings of hair beneath her cap just as black; yes, and the same needle-sharp eyes and firm mouth betokened the same iron will.

But her granddaughter had inherited that same will, and as months passed there came rebellion, silent but seething. It was inevitable that open conflict should one day arise. "But what *difference* does it make if the stitches are not all alike?" . . . "I hate samplers! Why should I have to make one when I'd rather read?" . . . "*Why* must I keep quiet when the Reverend Doctor from Hollis Street comes to call? I have so many questions . . ."

Seventy, Madam Dix concluded, was too old to attempt the remolding of a headstrong teenager. To the girl's dismay Grandmother decided to send her to her sister, Mrs. William Duncan, in Worcester. What now! The Worcester aunts and cousins had shown little interest in her when she had lived there. True, her father had removed his family to a small town farther north, but she could easily be sent to join them. She retraced the long stage journey with foreboding.

5

For the first time in her life Dorothea knew acceptance and contentment. Great-aunt Sarah Duncan assumed her new responsibility with gracious cheerfulness. She ran her household with orderly but relaxed discipline. While her expectations were no less demanding than those of Madam Dix, her methods were far more flexible. Dorothea soon became eager to acquire the skills and manners which in the chill atmosphere of Dix Mansion she had found so irksome and distasteful. Even the pursuit of tiny stitches seemed worthy of painstaking effort, since success elicited praise more often than censure, and criticism was always mild.

"Good, child, you're improving every day. Though I must say I'm amazed at your upbringing. Twelve years old before you started your first sampler! Why, your Cousin Sarah made her first one when she was three!"

"Yes," agreed her daughter with a good-humored laugh, "but I believe I got a blow for every stitch in it."

Cousin Sarah, the wife of Dr. Oliver Fiske, a woman of great beauty who had never been known to raise her voice

Runaway

in anger, was one of the Worcester relatives who brought
sympathy and zest to the new life. Dorothea became almost as much at home in the Fiske and Wheeler and Bangs
households as in the big Duncan house on North State
Street. There were numerous cousins. For the first time
she had companions near her own age. They walked with
her up and down the long main street with its stone em-
bankment, pointed out the mansions built by the city's
wealthy families, took her to parties and on picnics, to
rowing expeditions on nearby Lake Quinsigamond. But
she felt no real affinity with these cousins of her own age.
They seemed like carefree children playing at the serious
business of living. It was with the older cousins that she
came to feel the closest rapport — especially one.

Edward Dillingham Bangs, the son of Judge Bangs, who
had married Grandmother's sister, was fourteen years her
senior. He had studied law with his father and was already
embarked on a promising legal and political career. At
twenty-eight he was still unmarried and the quarry of half
the Worcester debutantes as well as their designing
mothers. But he bestowed upon all of them the same intently personal but whimsical interest with which he first
greeted his young cousin Dorothea.

"Little sobersides! Well, well, we must remedy that immediately. I shall make it my personal responsibility to
kindle some glints of laughter in those big pretty dark
eyes."

He proceeded to do just that, making her his willing
protégée and introducing her to the gayer facets of Worcester society. But Edward Bangs, in spite of his fashionable
dress, impeccable manners, and merry eyes, was no dilet-
tante. To her delight Dorothea found him as well versed in
literature and the arts as in law, and to his obvious surprise
he found her far more conversant with subjects of scholarly
interest than most of the frivolous young women of his
acquaintance. Grandfather's library and Father's sermons
had done their work well. They were soon discussing Cal-

vinist theology and Mr. Madison's war. She was teaching him the names of wild flowers in the neighboring fields, and he was reading to her poems by Byron, Wordsworth and a new young poet, Shelley. It was inevitable that the handsome, debonair, yet highly intelligent cousin, her first real friend, should quicken the heart beats of the impressionable fourteen-year-old.

But in spite of new glints of laughter the inner soberness remained. She would not, must not, continue a life of idle dependence. She must work, earn money to send presents to her brothers, make it possible for them to escape as she had done. And there was only one way to do it.

"I want to teach," she dared broach to Cousin Edward. "Do you think I could?"

He looked into her flushed young face and laughed indulgently. "Of course. You'll make a wonderful teacher — sometime."

"But you don't understand. I mean now."

He laughed again, this time with genuine amusement. "My dear Dolly, you're joking. Why, you're nothing but a child yourself!" Dorothea said no more, but her lips tightened. The next time Edward came to the Duncan house he was met by a slim young woman in ankle length dress, erect and dignified, hair sedately coiled at the neck, on her face an expression of stern composure. His eyes widened in startled admiration.

"Dolly! I wouldn't have believed it. Child into woman, and — what a beautiful one!" His laughter this time was sheepish. "All right. You've proven your point. You win."

He helped her persuade the family. Private schools were few and most young children were taught the rudiments at home. Teaching was a highly respectable occupation for a young woman — in fact, almost the only one — and the relatives welcomed the idea both as an opportunity for their own small children and as a beneficial outlet for Dorothea's abundant energy. At fourteen she was fully capable of teaching the necessary subjects: reading, writing, numbers, manners, and sewing — yes, even the latter two, so much had she improved. But — could a half-grown girl handle problems of discipline? Only time would tell. The uncles began looking for a place in a suitable building.

For a short time she conducted her classes in a room in a public schoolhouse on Main Street near the head of Central. Then — "I've found just the right place!" announced Judge Bangs. It was a vacant store which had once been a printing office. The family helped to clear and scrub the room. Benches and a desk were installed.

She had no difficulty in securing pupils. There were enough younger children among the relatives for a sizable class, and the family had many interested friends. Among the pupils were Levi and William Lincoln, whose father would later become governor. Francis Blake sent his son Chandler and his daughter Elizabeth. The Joseph Wheelers, distant cousins, sent their two daughters, Frances and Nancy. There were Ann Bancroft, destined to become the wife of Dr. Charles Ingalls of Jackson College, and Lucy Green, who would give years of distinguished service as a teacher in New York.

Problems of discipline? The family need not have worried. From the first day Dorothea not only exerted, she *was* authority. "She was tall, erect, slight, good looking," one pupil was to remember, "neither very dark nor very light with a round face and a very stern decided expression."

"Like her old grandfather," one of the older relatives might have added with a chuckle.

Strangely enough, the severity which had aroused rebellion against her grandmother's regimen was now accentuated in herself. Whipping was the accepted procedure in the education of the era, and no Worcester child under her tutelage should be spoiled through the sparing of the rod. One mischievous pupil, William Lincoln, destined to become a general, never missed a day without a whipping. "I

don't know that she had any special grudge against me,"
he was to recall, "but it was her nature to use the whip,
and use it she did." "But he deserved it," another pupil
was to comment. "He was never still, and a whipping a
day was a necessity."

With girls she used different but equally severe punishments. One was made to walk to and from school during
courthouse week wearing on her back a placard stating "A
Very Bad Girl Indeed."

Dorothea's brother Joseph, who to her delight was permitted to come and live with the relatives and be her
pupil, was no exception. Indeed, she was even more severe with him. "He had to eat, drink, sleep, and wink at
her direction," someone commented later with amusement. But severity was far exceeded by devotion. Finding
him much behind other children of his age in attainment,
she worked with him constantly and with the utmost patience.

Her methods of inculcating knowledge were equally
rigid. In addition to the daily lessons in reading, writing,
and manners each child was expected to memorize a chapter of the Bible every week. On Monday morning they
were marched to the front of the room, and, toeing a ruled
line, arms folded and faces upturned, like cherubs, they
recited their passages in turn. Even the sewing of samplers by the little girls, bane of her own childhood, did not
escape insistence on perfection. One struggling young
seamstress, no doubt equally rebellious, could not have
guessed that seventy years later, at age eighty, she would
proudly exhibit that very sampler made when she was a
pupil of the famous Dorothea Dix.

There was affection as well as fear in her pupils' response, for whatever aspects of severity they discerned in
her action and appearance were already imbued with the
potency of a rare charm and a magnetic personality. For
the three years during which she taught in Worcester the
foremost families sent her their children, and she was ex-

tremely popular as a teacher. But she cared nothing for popularity, only for achievement. The whip with which she spurred her pupils was a mere feather beside the one with which she drove herself. It was as if she must atone for all the failings of a weak generation. The years were a battleground of conflicting impulses and motivations — her grandfather's ambition and aggressive will, her father's zeal to drive evil from the human soul. But there was another desire equally strong, which conflicted with both.

"Don't take life so seriously, my sweet Dolly. A pretty forehead like that wasn't meant for frowning. Here, let me smooth out the wrinkles. And how about a row on the lake tonight instead of that interminable studying? Or shall I escort another Worcester damsel not half so beautiful?"

Long before the three years were past she knew that she was in love with Edward Dillingham Bangs, utterly, desperately, as she could never again love any man. Fourteen years difference in their ages? At seventeen she often felt far older than he seemed at thirty-one. "My sweet Dolly." His speech was full of such endearments, but how much did they mean?

It was both relief and torture when Grandmother sent word that she wanted her in Boston. Better to end the relationship now than to suffer such pain of uncertainty. Edward gave her a cousinly kiss in farewell. "I'll be seeing you often, my lovely Dolly. My law work will be taking me to Boston."

Once more she rode in the lumbering stage over the dusty turnpike which Grandfather's progressive energy had brought into being. She was welcomed by Madam Dix with surprised and obvious satisfaction. The transformation was astonishing. She had left Boston a noisy, disorderly, unruly child. She had returned a neat, poised, well mannered, ambitious, yes, and beautiful young woman.

Two

Teacher

*What greater bliss than to look back on days spent in usefulness
... in fitting young spirits for their native skies ...!*

1

IN 1820 BOSTON was in intellectual upheaval. Theology,
philanthropy, philosophy, literature — all were struggling to put down fresh roots in the resistant Puritan soil.
The hardheaded pragmatism of Federalist bankers and
merchants and shipbuilders was being challenged by Jef-
fersonian Republicans supporting the disquieting theory
of the equality of man. Across the river in Harvard University, where a young student named Ralph Waldo Emerson was sitting under the aegis of a liberal president, and
where a divinity school had just been founded, a philosophy known as Transcendentalism was rearing its head.
And in his new church on Federal Street the eloquent
William Ellery Channing was raising the hackles of his
brother ministers, heirs of Calvin and Cotton Mather, with
his concept of a loving rather than an avenging deity. The
status quo was being threatened. A Renaissance was in the
making.

Dorothea entered this intellectual arena with as keen zest as her grandfather had explored the uncharted wild lands of Maine. Fortunately Grandmother, proud of her attainments, encouraged every effort at self-improvement, paying for tutors to supplement classes at public school. There were subscriptions for public lectures given by Harvard professors. Dorothea took lessons in French, considered a must for the proper education of young ladies, though most things French were taboo to conservative Boston Federalists. But books were her most avid delight. Once more she delved into Grandfather's excellent library and that of Uncle Thaddeus Mason Harris, pastor of the Meeting House Hill church in Dorchester. She borrowed books from the Boston Library in a room above the central arch in Bulfinch's Tontine Crescent in Franklin Place and from the American Academy of Arts and Sciences. She went to read at the Athenaeum in the Amory house on Tremont Street, next to King's Chapel Burying Ground. Her favorite subjects were history, science, and literature, and she absorbed knowledge like a thirsty sponge.

"Until I was nearly twenty," she confessed long afterward, "I was determined to live to myself and to enjoy only literature and art."

Living to herself did not preclude the blissful possibility of sharing this intellectual euphoria with a kindred spirit. The bonds of understanding with her cousin Edward Bangs had been strengthened rather than broken. They corresponded often and at length. His visits to Boston "on legal business" grew more and more frequent. They took long walks together along the Mall by the Common and across the long bridge to South Boston, and she smiled to herself, remembering how she had assured Grandfather that she would never walk here with a lover. That Edward was beginning to return her love she did not doubt, for he showed it in a thousand ways. He lured her away from serious pursuits into lighter pleasures, taking her to dinner at the fashionable new Tremont House or to

Dorothea Dix, in 1822, age 20

Mrs. Elijah Dix, May 6, 1822, age 76.

concerts and fireworks displays at Washington Gardens at the corner of Tremont Street and Temple Place. She took girlish pride in the admiring glances at her handsome escort, faultlessly clad in plum colored coat, vest of beige velvet, cambric cravat trimmed with lace, and tall beaver hat. She had no idea that she also was a focus of admiration with her graceful slender figure, rich wavy red-brown hair framing her cheeks beneath the flowered bonnet, cheeks flushed and dark eyes brilliantly glowing.

She was indeed nearly twenty when the years of self-centered absorption ended. In 1821 Joseph Dix died, leaving his wife and two sons without support. Dorothea was jolted awake as from an idyllic dream. She had responsibilities. The boys must be brought to Boston and educated. Though Madam Dix began sending regular generous donations to her unloved daughter-in-law, it was Dorothea, not Grandmother, who should be supporting her family. The years of study and self-improvement had prepared her for this new role, and she knew what she must do.

"I want to teach," she announced resolutely. "My school in Worcester was successful, and now I am older and much better qualified."

It was a practical proposition. No child was admitted to a public school in Boston unless he had first learned to read, and girls were permitted to attend only from the end of April to the end of October, when the numbers of boys decreased. The famous Boston Latin School, founded in 1635, was restricted to boys over ten years. The public grammar schools were notorious for their tyrannical cruelty. The "dame" or "marm" school, as it was called, offered an excellent solution. Classes were held sometimes in an empty store or other building, but more often in the teacher's own home. Dorothea dared not suggest holding her school in Dix Mansion — not yet. She could picture Grandmother's horror at the thought of small boots grinding dust into the velvet carpets and twining about the legs of her Chippendale chairs, of books and slates spread on the gleaming surface of her mahogany dining table. She suggested the use of a small vacant house on the premises.

Madam Dix did not approve even this plan. Though the family fortune had shrunk appreciably, due largely to the dissipation and extravagance of her sons, there was sufficient for their needs. Moreover, she had become increasingly dependent on her granddaughter's companionship, her early posture of criticism and harsh discipline having long since mellowed into pride and approval. Except for an occasional excess of stubbornness the girl fulfilled all her expectations. The stubbornness was predominant now, and all of the old woman's arguments were refracted like barbs against steel armor.

"You're not strong enough," she appealed as a last resort. "You know you have a delicate constitution, all those colds and coughing. And no wonder! A father with no backbone and a mother a whining invalid!"

Dorothea had her way. The school was an immediate success. Beginning with a small class of day pupils, it soon outgrew its limited quarters and, with Madam Dix's reluctant permission, was removed to Dix Mansion. Joseph and young Charles became members of the household. She plunged into the venture with all the vigor of her intense and energetic nature. Never had she felt such self-fulfillment. Her pupils should be introduced to the whole vast world of knowledge which she found so enthralling, not merely the fundamentals but poetry, astronomy, mineralogy, botany and other sciences. Days were not long enough for the study and other preparation required. In the summer she was up at four, in the winter at five, to have her hour for devotions and then have time for studies before breakfast. Midnight usually found her still at her desk. But the rewards were immeasurable.

"What greater bliss," she wrote one of her friends, "than to look back on days spent in usefulness, in doing good to those around you, in fitting young spirits for their native skies! The duties of a teacher are neither few nor easy, but they elevate the mind and give energy to the character."

It was not only in teaching that she was finding self-fulfillment, or even in the fact that Edward Bangs had at last declared his love and that they were secretly engaged. As she watched the spring winds blow white gulls over the Common, across the hill, up into the blue and out to sea, her spirit soared with them to new dimensions of freedom. There were many fresh winds blowing in the intellectual climate of Boston in those early years of the 1820s, but her liberating inspiration had but one source.

When Dorothea first saw William Ellery Channing, she was not impressed. He was short, spare, stooped, pallid of complexion, thin to the point of emaciation. She had come to his Federal Street church to discover for herself what qualities made him the most popular yet controversial figure in a Boston pulpit. Even when he started to speak, she still wondered. Why his great appeal? Then his voice, low and a bit toneless at first, assumed all the flexible subtleties of a fine organ, ranging through dulcianas, flutes, gambas, swelling to a climactic diapason. He seemed to grow in stature. His deepset eyes glowed with intense fervor. But it was his message which penetrated her instinctive reponse to his magnetism as a preacher, for she had never heard its like from any pulpit. Instead of warnings of hell fire or stern admonitions of piety, he stressed the fatherhood of God, his infinite goodness, his benevolence and mercy; instead of man's depravity, his dignity and competence. Dorothea went to hear him again and again. Always shy at first with new acquaintances, she slowly made friends with members of his parish, attended small group meetings in the Channing home. She avidly read his published sermons, discovered in them an expression of her own intense feeling of oneness with all creation.

"The Christian," Channing had once written, "Beholds *unity* in the midst of variety. He looks round on the changing scenery, and in every leaf of the forest, every blade of

William Ellery Channing, 1839.

grass, every hill, every valley, and every cloud of heaven, he discovers the traces of Divine Benevolence. Creation is but a field spread before him for an infinitely varied display of love."

She knew the joyousness of release after long imprisonment. Here was a faith which both her keen mind and her questing spirit could accept, neither the fiery vengeance of her father's fear-rousing sermons nor the cold rigidity of Calvinist orthodoxy. It was like flinging open windows and letting clean air and sunshine into a stuffy room.

The opened windows revealed new sights and sounds, for Dr. Channing was a quickener of the human conscience. For twenty years he had concerned himself with social problems, reasonable housing for the poor, associations for working men, economic help for Boston's free Negroes and Irish immigrants. "Christ preached to the poor," he had told the newly organized Congregational Unitarian Society in 1819, "and I think that no system bears the stamp of his religion, or can prevail, which is not addressed to the great majority of men."

Now suddenly Dorothea saw people through new eyes. One sabbath she noticed children going by the house to the Mason Street Sunday School, established by the "Society for the Moral and Religious Instruction of the Poor." They were ill-clothed, hollow-eyed. The purpose of the school was to teach them the scriptures. On inquiring, she learned that of the school's 336 children a quarter of them could not read words of one syllable. What could they possibly learn in just an hour a week! They had no money for a "dame" school, and without private instruction they could not enter the public schools, which required knowledge of reading. If only she could teach some of them in the afternoons after her pupils went home!

She could imagine Grandmother's reaction to such a proposal. "What! More hours of work when you're already half killing yourself! Bad enough to have all those respectable little feet tramping through the house without letting in all the dirty riffraff!" It was not that Grandmother was unkind or uncharitable, but she preferred to render her good works at a distance, like providing a Bible for every young married couple in Dixmont and Dixfield and giving the land for a meeting house in Dixmont. Very well. Let her perform this charity at a distance also — a short distance, to be sure, but at least removed from her eyes and ears. After long thought Dorothea composed a letter.

"My dear Grandmother," she wrote, "Had I the saint-like eloquence of our minister, I would employ it in explaining all the motives, and dwelling on all the good, good to the poor, the miserable, the idle, and the ignorant, which would follow your giving me permission to use the barn chamber for a schoolroom for charitable and religious purposes. You have read Hannah More's life, you approve of her labors for the most degraded of England's paupers. Why not when it can be done, without exposure or expense, let *me* rescue some of America's miserable children from vice and guilt and dependence on the Almshouse, and finally from what I fear will be their eternal misery? ... I can, without loss of health, do more for them; and God has placed us here to serve himself in serving the children of earth. Do, my dear Grandmother, yield to my request, and witness next summer the reward of your benevolence and Christian compliance. Your affectionate Granddaughter, D. L. Dix."

And how could Madam Dix refuse? The barn loft was cleared and cleaned. The charity school was opened. Dorothea gave fully as much energy to these waifs of the street as to her more fortunate pupils, often more, for their needs were so much greater. She called the school "The Hope."

She tried to share her new insights and concerns with Edward Bangs, but he was unresponsive. Her health was likely to suffer from the extra work, as well as from unnecessary exposure to slum dirt and disease. And, like Grandmother, he did not approve of her infatuation for such theological dissenters as Dr. Channing. His family had always been strict Calvinists. But her health had never been better, she assured him. She awoke each morning rested, eager for the day's work, and the coughing spells were much less frequent. As for Dr. Channing — she hesitated, wanting to be honest — she was not one of his adherents. Not yet, that is, she amended silently. She attended the Hollis Street Church each Sunday morning with Grandmother and would continue to do so. Edward appeared satisfied.

"Have your way, Dolly," he lifted her firm chin a bit higher for a kiss, then, his merry eyes twinkling, "at least until we're married."

2

It was well that she soon had a confidante with whom she dared share all her deepest thoughts and emotions. She was calling in the Channings' home when she was introduced to Anne Heath, one of their young parishioners. The two girls felt instant rapport.

"It was in winter that we first met," Dorothea was to write Anne. "I shall ever love the chilly old season the better for that."

Anne invited Dorothea to visit her at Erica Farm, her home in Brookline, and a close intimacy developed which was to endure for fifty years. In the rambling white house on a hill overlooking a broad valley Dorothea was welcomed into the big Heath family, Anne's parents, her sisters — Hannah, Abby, Susan, Elizabeth, Mary — and her two brothers Charles and Fred. And in the shy, sensitive, deeply spiritual Anne she found the sister she had always longed for, responsive to her every mood and need. They were soon writing letters to each other, sometimes three or four a week, often little notes on three sides of a single sheet, folded and sewed together with needle and thread, delivered, not by post, but by relatives or friends traveling the five miles between Boston and Brookline. They wrote on a vast variety of subjects — poetry, sermons, a beautiful sunset, philosophy, religion — sometimes with an effusive sentimentality and always intended for no other eye to see. Theirs was a pure and exalted friendship between two kindred spirits, one of them exceedingly lonely and hungry for affection and understanding.

"Anne, my dear friend, if ever you are disposed to think your lot an unhappy one or your heart desolate, think of her whose pathway is yet more thorny, and whose way is cheered by no close connections. You have an almost angelic mother, Anne; you cannot but be both good and happy while she hovers over you, ministering to your wants, and supplying all that the fondest affection can provide. Your sisters, too, they comfort you. *I* have none."

Yet even with this most intimate of all friends Dorothea was never quite able to break the shell of reserve which had been her self-imposed defense in a lonely childhood. However thin it was, Anne must have felt its restraint. For, though Dorothea often addressed her as "Ann," "Anne," "Annie," and signed herself "Thea," seldom in all the fifty years did Anne begin her letters with a given name. It was usually "My dear friend," or "Dear Miss Dix."

It was often midnight when Dorothea found time to compose such letters. All day she was like a racehorse driven by whip and spurs. Grandmother was becoming increasingly feeble. After the death of a sixth son, Henry Elijah, in 1822, from an epidemic in Norfolk while performing his medical duties in the marines, her iron will seemed to weaken. Dorothea became the practical mistress of Dix Mansion. She was housekeeper, motherly elder sister, and teacher on fire with new concepts of education. When her pupils asked questions she was unable to answer, she flew to libraries, museums, scientific authorities. All this gave her an idea. If her pupils were curious, other children must be. She began a gigantic task writing such questions and answers into a book. She would call it *Conversations on Common Things.*

"Why, mother," she began Conversation One, "did you spend so much time in the factory the other day? I saw spindles whirl till I was tired. Do tell me why you looked so long at that pile you called machinery!"

There followed a thorough lesson on the machinery and techniques of cloth manufacturing. Once she had started, the questions and answers covered an astonishing variety of subjects, all treated with exhaustive and scholarly detail: time, clocks, manufacturing, architecture, printing, metals, stamps, banks, money, salt-making, cultivation of vegetables and fruits, animals, woods, sculpture, weather, government, and a hundred other subjects. It was veritably a children's encyclopedia, forerunner of what would be called a hundred years later a *Book of Knowledge.*

But the grueling labor took its toll. She grew thin, had bouts of coughing. Dr. Hayward, the family physician and friend, urged her to relinquish some activities. So did Edward Bangs. She was finding less and less time to give him on his visits to Boston, more frequent now since he was becoming actively involved in politics. On one of their rare walks they strolled along the Mall edging the Common, stopping to watch the grazing cows; turned up Park Street past the church on Brimstone Corner, so-called because brimstone, used in making gunpowder, had been stored in the church basement during the War of 1812; stopped to admire Bulfinch's State House and marvel at the engineering feat by which John Hancock's heirs had carted away the summit of Beacon Hill to fill the old Mill Pond; then sauntered down Beacon Street, once "Poor House Lane" but now lined with mansions of the élite.

"Do you realize, Dolly, this is the first strolling you've found time for, at least with me, in many months?"

"I know." She was contrite. "I'm sorry. I've been so busy —"

"Much too busy." His voice sharpened. "It's utter nonsense your spending so much energy on other people's children, especially those young hoodlums. And you must not continue this book writing. I forbid it."

She stopped short and looked up at him. "Did — did you say — *forbid*?"

"I certainly did. I can't permit you to jeopardize your health. Of course when we're married all this teaching business will stop, anyway. You'll have all you can do fulfilling the duties of my wife." When she made no reply, only continued to stand motionless, he went on, voice suddenly charged with eager excitement. He might have a surprise for her soon. There was talk of his being in line for a very important position. In fact, she might one day be living in a fine house here on the Hill, not a mansion like this one of Nathan Appleton's, of course, but one suitable for entertaining the Commonwealth's leading citizens. "Wouldn't you like that, my pet?"

She might not have heard the question. "You say — I'm not to teach?"

"Of course not." He laughed indulgently. "You'll have other things to do."

"What things?"

"Why — just being my wife. Look beautiful, as you always do. Entertain my friends and clients. Preside over my table. And don't worry, my pet, you'll have a chance to teach — your own children."

He took her arm, and they walked on, down Beacon Street to Charles, along the river between the ropewalks and the Common; turned south, passing the old burial ground and Boylston Market, then into West Orange and so to the Dix house in Orange Court, just opposite Harvard Street. Edward was his usual merry self, chatting about events in Worcester and apparently not noticing his companion's unnatural silence.

Soon afterward Dorothea wrote him a letter, finished long after midnight for it had taken hours to compose it. Was he sure that she was the wife he really wanted? She would never be content merely running his household, furthering his career — no, not even in confining her teaching to their own children. She was a *person* with her own abilities and responsibilities. She must somehow make herself useful to society, using all her God-given talents, however small. He must not tell her what she could or could not do, like teaching poor children or finishing writing her book. And she hoped he would understand, because she loved him with all her heart. But he must consider himself free and not bound by any promises. She sent the letter and waited in an agony of hope, then as weeks passed in a torment of foreboding, for his answer.

It came. One day Grandmother looked up from a letter written by a relative in Worcester. "Well, well, here is news! Edward is to marry Mary Grosvenor, a young Worcester woman. It seems likely that he will be appointed secretary of state in the near future. His family is very happy and proud." Her sharp eyes probed her granddaughter's face. "I thought for a while there might be a union between you and Edward, you seemed so fond of each other. But I suppose it was only cousinly devotion."

Dorothea's nails dug into her palms, but her features remained unperturbed. "That's right." Her voice betrayed no emotion. "Cousinly devotion."

Only with Anne did she share the bleakness of her hurt and desolation, and her friend's gentle sympathy was all that helped ease the pain. Once she expressed her gratitude in the verse which came so easily to her pen.

To A. E. H.

In the sad hour of anguish and distress
  To thee for sympathy will I repair;
Thy soothings sure will make my sorrows less
  And what thou canst not soothe, thou wilt share.

Though many are to me both good and kind
  And grateful still my heart shall ever be,
Yet thou are to me a more congenial mind.
  More than a sister's love binds thee to me. Thea.

3

As an antidote Dorothea plunged into even greater activity, finishing her book and submitting it to a publisher, attending lyceum lectures on astronomy, giving lessons two afternoons a week to some of her more gifted pupils on mineralogy, taking more French lessons from a private teacher. Most of all she took solace in the spiritual challenge of Dr. Channing, and to her grandmother's displeasure she left Hollis Street Church and became a regular attendant at Federal Street, finding new purpose in his teaching that "the supreme good of an intelligent and moral being is the perfection of its nature."

Grandmother, who had been the belle of Worcester, could not understand her disdain of social pleasures. To Anne Dorothea confessed, "I have little taste for fashionable dissipation, cards, dancing; the theater and tea parties are my aversion and I look with little envy on those who find enjoyment in such transitory delights, if delights they must be called. I am reading Adams and Wilson on Astronomy and exploring the encyclopedias in search of architectural knowledge."

Even when Lafayette, one of her heroes, came to Boston in August, 1824, she contemplated a reception in his honor with mitigated pleasure. "This evening I am to be presented to the Marquis," she wrote Anne. "I dare not think what I may appear like, but fear very like a simpleton. . . ." Perhaps a part of her dread lay in the possibility of meeting Edward Bangs, who had been married in April and was now Secretary of State for the Commonwealth. But she found the day as exciting as did her pupils. Early in the morning 1200 horsemen proceeded to the Neck to meet the General, who entered the city in an open barouche drawn by four white horses. Bells were rung, guns fired. Boston's entire population of 43,000, it seemed, was gathered outside the Amory House at the corner of Park and Beacon. As he crossed the Common he passed between a double row of school children, Dorothea's among them, who welcomed him with cheers and cast flowers in his path. After he entered the house, even his shadow cast on a window shade was greeted with cheers.

"I have been presented," Dorothea continued her letter to Anne, "but cannot tell how I felt. At a little after seven we were ushered into Mrs. Hayward's drawing room. The General was announced and from a tumultuous assembly we were transformed into mutes. He paid his compliments with ease and dignity." It was exaltation, not her usual shyness and reserve, which dispelled all other emotions. Here was the one man, next to Washington, most responsible for her country's freedom. Even the meeting with Edward Bangs and his wife, so long dreaded, was of minor importance. She acknowledged the introduction with both dignity and cousinly cordiality.

"What is the matter with you?" asked one woman curiously. "Why do you look so solemn all the evening?"

"Because," she replied, "I feel and am only thinking of what has been."

"Do you think the General handsome?" probed the woman.

"I did not criticize his features. I was thinking only of his deeds."

It was well that the meeting with Edward Bangs and his wife was charged with this other intense emotion, or her determined poise might have wavered. She would never recover completely from the heartbreak of this first love. She would burn his letters, try to sublimate human passion in the ardor of useful service, yet never quite succeed. No other man would ever arouse her serious romantic interest, though many would try, and friends would help press their suits. Even Anne suggested that the tendency of young Mr. Wentz, Dorothea's French teacher, to linger in the Dix drawing room after her lessons was not prompted solely by the attractions of a substantial tea and Madam Dix's company.

"Your suspicions concerning L. W.," Dorothea was forced to admit, "are not unfounded, and I must learn patiently to endure all things."

She was outraged when she heard that an acquaintance, Miss Bellows, had reported her engaged to Mr. Wentz. "Oh, Anne, is it not vexing to be so ridiculously spoken of. Mr. Wentz, my former French master, never had a line of my writings except my grammatical exercises and a note to request his discontinuance at my study, alias my grandmother's parlor, while I was out of town for my health."

Such unwilling concessions to health were becoming more and more frequent. Her weakness was lung congestion, diagnosed by Dr. Hayward as rheumatism of the lungs. He prescribed cantharis. She developed a tendency to hemorrhage. Her voice grew weak and husky. Sometimes, teaching, she was forced to support herself by holding to the desk with one hand while she pressed hard to her side with the other to suppress the sharp pain. At intervals she was obliged to take to her bed and temporarily close her school. But even then she refused to rest. The time was spent in writing.

Her *Conversations on Common Things,* published in 1824 by Munroe and Francis, was well received. The *American Literary Gazette* commented, "We are gratified with finding an American writer who duly estimates the importance of giving to American children knowledge as will be actually useful to them, instead of filling their minds with vague, and therefore useless, notions of subjects not accommodated to their age." It was selling widely not only in New England but all over the country and would continue to sell through many years, until in 1869 it would have gone through sixty editions.

In 1825 she published two more small books, *Hymns for Children* and *Evening Hours*, meditations written during her own late evenings. Some of the hymns were original. Dorothea wrote wryly, "Grandmother, who is never ready to give me credit for solidity and seriousness of feeling, read one of my hymns. She said something in its favor; then, discovering it was my writing, was sorry!"

Dorothea never rested. When forced to take to her bed or to visit relatives for a vacation her mind was busy making plans, reading, composing poems even when too ill to write them down. She would say the lines over and over, committing them to memory until able to write or dictate them. Continuous labor was a matter of conscience. She wrote to Anne, "There is in our nature a disposition to indulgence, a secret desire to escape from labor, which unless hourly combated will overcome the best faculties of our minds and paralyze our most useful powers. Protracted ill health is often suffered to become the ally of this hidden disposition, and there is hardly anything so difficult to contend with and conquer. I have often entertained a dread lest I should fall victim to my besieger, and that fear has saved me so far."

Even Dr. Channing, who was largely responsible for her dedication to a life of usefulness, failed to temper her zeal. "I look forward to your life," he wrote her, "not altogether without solicitude. Your infirm health seems to darken your prospect of usefulness. But I believe your constitution will yet be built up if you will give it a fair chance. You must learn to give up your plans of usefulness, as much as those of gratification, to the will of God. We may make these the occasion of self-will, vanity and pride as much as anything else. May not one of your chief dangers lie there?"

But willpower and obstinacy yielded finally to exigency. In 1826, advised by Dr. Hayward that her life was in jeopardy, she gave up her school. She must spend her winters in a warmer climate. Grandmother also was insistent. Dorothea's greatest worry was in leaving Charles. Though in public school, he still needed constant help. "Nonsense!" scoffed Grandmother. "He should teach himself and learn to do without you."

"Because of him," Dorothea confessed, "I am bitter in sickness. Oh, Anne, if that child is but good, I care not how humble his pathway through life. It is for him my soul is filled with bitterness when sickness wastes me; it is because of him I dread to die."

She spent that winter boarding with friends in Washington and Alexandria. It was not defeat. She would not let it be. She refused even to remain spiritually quiescent.

"Dear Annie," she wrote, "I am never less disposed to sadness than when ill and alone. Sometimes I have fancied that it was the nature of my disease to create a rising, elastic state of mind, but be that as it will, the hour of bodily suffering is to me the hour of spiritual joy. It is then that most I feel my dependence on God and his power to sustain. The discipline which has brought me to this has been long and varied; it has led through a valley of tears, a life of woe. It is happiness to feel progression and to feel that the power that thus aids is not of earth."

4

She could scarcely believe her good fortune. Returning to Boston in the spring of 1827, she was invited by Dr. and Mrs. Channing to go with them to their summer home at Portsmouth, Rhode Island, as their children's tutor. She had envied Elizabeth Peabody, Dr. Channing's brilliant but unapproachable secretary, for her intimate association with the family. "Such an experience might be set down," Miss Peabody had said, "as the first year of one's intellectual life." Now a similar opportunity was to come to Dorothea Dix.

There were other possibilities. It was suggested that she become joint editor of a new magazine with her friend Lydia Maria Francis (later Child). It was a flattering offer, but after some deliberation both declined. She could have found a good position teaching, possibly in Dr. Fowle's famous Monitorial School, where she had previously taught for a time in addition to carrying on her own school. But her health, while improved, prohibited a rigorous schedule. Anyway, she would have sacrificed the most tempting opportunities to be with the Channings.

"Oakland," the Channing summer home on Narragansett Bay a few miles from Newport, was an ideal spot for physical and mental invigoration. Her duties as governess were light. Mary, nine, and William Francis, eight, were bright if by no means docile pupils, Mary already sharing her father's interest in history, William turning a deaf ear to all subjects unrelated to science. Years later Mary was to describe the children's reaction to their young tutor:

"She was tall and dignified, but stooped somewhat, was very shy in her manners, and colored extremely when addressed. This may surprise you who knew her only in later life, when she was completely self-possessed and reliant. . . . She was strict and inflexible in her discipline, which we her pupils disliked extremely at the time, but for which I have been grateful as I have grown older and found how much I was indebted to that iron will from which it was hopeless to appeal, but which I suppose was not unreasonable, as I find my father expressed great satisfaction with her tuition of her pupils. . . . I think she was a very accomplished teacher, active and diligent, very fond of natural history and botany. She enjoyed long rambles, always calling our attention to what was of interest in the world around us. I hear that some of her pupils speak of her as irascible. I have no such remembrance. Fixed as fate we considered her.

"We all became much attached to her, and she was our

dear and valued friend, and most welcome guest in all our homes. She was a very religious woman, without a particle of sectarianism and bigotry. At the little Union Meeting House which adjoined Oakland Miss Dix always had the class of troublesome men and boys, who succumbed to her charm of manner and firm will."

Dorothea felt she was learning far more than her pupils. A whole new world of nature surrounded her. She collected hundreds of specimens — flowers, shells, seaweeds, algae, and other marine life. She listened with as rapt enjoyment as the children to their father's salty tales of his boyhood life in this seaside setting, how he had climbed the tall masts of ships bound for far places, wrestled with his playmates, become a champion at pitching quoits. Hard to connect such activities with the frail, shrunken figure usually seen on Boston streets wrapped in a long cape, face half hidden beneath a broad brimmed hat! She rose early to tramp with him and the children and the dogs, rode with the family in the rough farm wagon drawn by his horse, Old White, went bathing with them all on the beach, where, holding each other by the hand, they would walk down in a long line into the surf, letting the waves roll over them. On stormy days or in the evenings there were long conversations, poetry reading, charades. Dr. Channing was adept at this sport, one of his masterpieces having become almost legendary.

"My first and third my middle bear, my whole takes ladies through the air. What? Of course. Horsemanship!"

The summer's therapy was spiritual as well as physical and mental. No one could feel the impact of Dr. Channing's life-style day after day without much soul searching.

"Do you know," she wrote Anne, "that I think the duty of self-examination one of the most difficult which we are called to perform as Christians. It is so flattering to our pride and it ministers so agreeably to our vanity to assign praiseworthy reasons for our conduct that the investigation we ought to make into our motives and rules of action is far from bringing us to a knowledge of ourselves."

When she tried to express appreciation for the summer's benefits, Dr. Channing would have none of it. "You have no burden of gratitude laid upon you, for we feel that you gave at least as much good as you received. If you should think another summer's residence would be beneficial to you, Mrs. C. and myself would be glad to engage your services for our children."

She could hardly wait for winter to pass. She spent some of it in Philadelphia, where she was confined for weeks with a lung attack, and where she made lifelong friends of Dr. and Mrs. Joseph Hare. He was a noted scientist and she a former schoolmate of Mrs. Channing. Then she went farther south with Miss Sarah Gibbs, Mrs. Channing's sister. No time was wasted. She read, studied, wrote.

Several of her stories had been published in magazines during the previous year. Now ten of them were collected in a book, *American Moral Tales for Young Persons*. They were intended to entertain, instruct, develop habits of neatness, honesty, industry. After the literary fashion of the times her heroes and heroines were models of perfection, her "villains" young transgressors of the accepted mores and virtues: William Montague, the "dainty boy" who complained about his food; Marrion Wilder, the "passionate little girl," pretty but selfish and ungrateful; George Mills, who unlike his industrious brother Henry had no use for learning. "I trust," the author concluded with the usual moral, "that those children who read this story will not hesitate which of these two boys they will take for their pattern." The virtuous were always rewarded, the guilty punished and often redeemed from error. But the stories were entertaining, action swift, dialogue natural and pungent. They contained much local color, playing on the Common, walks to South Boston, a visit to the iron casting foundry.

She was at work now on a book about flowers, to be called *A Garland of Flora*. According to the flyleaf:

In Eastern lands they talk of flowers,
And they tell in a Garland their loves and cares,
Each blossom that blooms in their garden bowers
On its leaves a mystic language bears.

It was a compendium containing name, genus, description, history of, and literature pertaining to almost every plant known to man. The list ran the alphabetic gamut from almond to willow, covered every possible variety from common daisy and dandelion to rare *Houstonia cerulea* and mezerion, a hundred in all. Legends and customs were detailed from old England, Greece, Italy, north Africa, France, India. She collected quotations by the hundreds ranging from Virgil and Plutarch to Spenser and Wordsworth, and varying in number from one quote (Thyme — Inconstancy: "Gadding thyme with mosses spread," from the Spanish of Navagero) to ninety-two about the rose, covering eighteen pages.

But it was in her religious writings that she most revealed herself. *Meditations for Private Hours,* published in 1828 and later appearing in many editions, was a collection of devotional readings for each day of the week, morning and evening. Though she wrote for others, it was her own soul baring itself.

Here in a world of doubt,
A sorrowful abode,
O how my heart and flesh cry out
For Thee, the living God!

"Has my conscience been awakened," she demanded for Sunday morning after public worship, "to a more lively sense of its duties and obligations?" and at the end of day, "My soul, pause and consider well how thou hast improved the day...."

Always there was the unquenchable yearning after perfection; always the battle yet the terrible frustration.

"If I have full measure of health and strength, may I not waste it in self-indulgence; if languor and disease have invaded my earthly frame, let me still keep in mind that I have work to perform and duties to fulfill. Let me remember that, so long as life is spared, it is spared for some good use; and may I take diligent heed to know what that use is."

Yes, *what?* Life seemed to be always marking time. Even the second summer with the Channings became a trial in patience — teaching two children when she yearned for at least thirty, receiving when she longed to give. Dr. Channing also was fighting ill health, but he could afford to be patient. His work was being ably performed by his young assistant, Ezra Stiles Gannett. Her winters, unsuccessfully attempting to teach, wandering about the south in search of sunshine and warm air, were far worse. Though she knew that Grandmother was being well cared for and her brothers fast becoming self-sufficient — Joseph well launched in business and Charles a promising student in the Boston Latin School — nevertheless she felt the guilt of shirked responsibility.

Then in 1830 came new hope and a promise of high adventure. Dr. Channing, still in search of better health, was taking his family to the island of St. Croix for the winter. Would Dorothea go with them as instructress of his children? *Would* she!

They sailed from Boston on November 20 in the schooner *Rice Plant.* The beauty of the island was overwhelming, with Blue Mountain rising over a thousand feet above the long green emerald expanse set in glimmering sapphire. Dorothea drew long breaths. The weight seemed lifted from her chest. Boston fogs no longer clogged her throat. Here, she was certain, she could become free from pain. Free also, she discovered, to her dismay and mortification, from the desire and ability to act. When she attempted to go out exploring, her limbs literally refused to carry her. Getting up in the morning was an almost impossible chore. The indomitable will with which she had gritted her teeth and kept teaching was suddenly powerless. It was a shattering and humbling experience.

Dr. Channing, familiar with tropical languor, treated the phenomenon with humor. "My dear," he jested to his wife, "where can Miss Dix be? But I need not ask — doubtless very busy, as usual. Pray, what is that I see on yonder sofa; some object shrouded in white? Oh, there is Miss Dix! Well, well, tell it not in Gath! How are the mighty fallen!"

"All this I bear," Dorothea wrote her friend Mrs. Torrey, a member of Dr. Channing's congregation, "but I am rising above it in more than one sense. I am really getting well — or well over this vexatious no-disease that does nothing, thinks nothing, is nothing."

Recover from it she did and used the six months in St. Croix not only to improve her health but to increase her already near-professional knowledge of flora and fauna. The island was a paradise of trailing vines, palms, bananas, rare birds, shells, marine plants. She collected hundreds of specimens and sent many to scientific friends, Dr. Benjamin Silliman, a specialist in algae, John James Audubon, her cousin William Harris. She read profusely, filling notebooks with extracts from religious writings of all ages and all lands.

Though the estate where they lodged was on the north side of the island among high precipitous hills, they took trips to Christianstadt and Bassin. In the former city they attended an Episcopal church, where Dr. Channing, always the individualist, put up his umbrella to avoid a draft. Though she came to love and respect the family more and more, she was often amused by their eccentricities.

"When we ride in a little wagon," she wrote home, "nobody would think we were not three ladies, for Dr. C. wears a white straw hat lined with green tied by a black ribbon to keep it from blowing away, a gown around his shoulders like a shawl. The equipment for our drives is amusing — two umbrellas, three parasols, five or six shawls, plus a large bundle containing a pelisse and coat. We are prepared for all emergencies as for a week's travel."

She was fascinated by the human life of the island, with its 500 whites and 3300 slaves. Slavery? At first it did not repel her. "You have no idea how interesting the Negroes are here." So beautiful, so graceful, so merry and musical in their dancing, so innocent in their unmorality did they seem that her rigid New England standards of judgment suffered temporary lapse. She declared she would not change them, even to teach them the difference between right and wrong. Then she visited a boiling house on a large estate where slaves were employed, a furnace of torturing heat, and her eyes were opened. When a slave ran away and was seized, she learned, he was conveyed to the judge of the King's Court at Bassin and when identified by his owner was invested with a collar of iron riveted about his throat, to remain there three, six, nine, or twelve months at the pleasure of the judge. Projecting from the collar were three spikes, forked, and about eighteen inches long. He must sleep sitting on the floor of his hut.

It was Dr. Channing who put her shocked confusion into words as they walked a half mile from the house that evening, meeting slaves all along the way who greeted them with cheerful, "Good night, missee," and, "How d'ye, sir?"

"Every human being," he said thoughtfully, "has in him the germ of the greatest idea in the universe, the idea of God; and to unfold this is the end of his existence. Is it possible that such a being is meant to be owned as a tree or a brute? No. All men, however poor or ignorant or despised, are possessed of sacred rights, inseparable from their human nature."

5

Dorothea returned to Boston in the late spring so restored to health that immediately she made plans for a new school, one that should embody all her mature concepts of an ideal education. Grandmother was so relieved to have her back that she made little protest, even at the prospect of pupils living in the house. Dix Mansion in Orange Court, now Number 495 Washington Street, was easily transformed into a day and boarding school. Its many chambers made excellent dormitories. Again classes would be held in the dining room.

"The arrangements of the school were very primitive," one of the pupils was to write later, "no desks for the girls, only a long table through the middle of the room, at which we sat for meals, and at which it was very inconvenient to write. The merit of the school was not in its elaborate equipment but in the supervision of its accomplished mistress."

It required an accomplished person for the task Dorothea Dix set for herself. She must be not only teacher but also housekeeper, dietitian, matron and mother to girls of varying ages away from home for the first time, disciplinarian, nurse, religious mentor. Her goal was perfection in all these roles, and she flung herself into the herculean task with all the fierce energy and dedication of her intense idealism.

Boston was in the full vigor of renaissance. Channing, Ralph Waldo Emerson, Edward Everett, Horace Mann, Margaret Fuller, Elizabeth Peabody — all and many more were prime movers in the currents of change. And the fresh winds which had long been blowing away dusts of tradition in religion, philosophy, literature, social prejudice, were now agitating new ideas and trends in education. Public schools were opened to girls in that same year of 1831. George Barrel Emerson, whose lecture on the "Education of Females" had just been delivered and published, was principal of a girls' school opened in 1823. Mr. Cummings was holding classes in Latin for the young ladies of his school. Dr. Fowle's Monitorial School, where Dorothea had briefly taught, had pioneered in the teaching of music, dancing, and scientific studies, as well as gymnastics. Elizabeth Peabody was already experimenting with theories which would distinguish her as the founder of the kindergarten.

In spite of such competition Dorothea's school flourished. Her writings were popular and her reputation as a teacher well established. Pupils came to her from as far away as Maine and New Hampshire. Her most unique contribution to the curriculum was in natural history or general science. Other teachers in her school taught the fundamentals of French, and a smattering of Latin. But her major emphasis was always in the formation of character. High morals, religious faith based on a joyous not frightening concept of God, a stern sense of duty, unflagging industry, complete self-mastery — in short, the qualities so painfully nurtured in herself — were the goals, rather the requisites, of her pupils' training.

Discipline, while for the most part kindly, was as rigid as in her former schools. Lines were toed, scripture verses learned. There was no rudeness, no running in the street, no laughter or loud talk in public. Each afternoon the pupils sallied forth for beneficial exercise, two by two, neatly dressed, hair meticulously braided, Miss Dix leading the procession holding the youngest by the hand. Yet far more important in their training than manners, she felt, was their spiritual development. Knowledge must be accompanied with the desire to use it in the service of mankind.

Even the youngest were encouraged in the art of soul-probing. On the mantel of the study room there was placed a large shell, sort of an "ear of God," into which letters might be dropped, preferably each day, giving the results of this self-examination, perhaps asking questions, and to these she would write answers, usually in the midnight hours. Each Saturday evening she encouraged pupils to come to her study for private interviews, when their spiritual progress would come under the most searching scrutiny, a kind of Protestant confessional. So precious were these scraps of soul-revelation that sixty years later the official biographer of Dorothea Dix would find a big bundle of them among her cherished possessions.

"Please write me a note, dear teacher," wrote one child. "I send you the paper in hopes that you will: do, please! The *casket* is ready, please fill it with jewels. Your child, Molly."

Another note indicated the teacher's ability to instill her own indomitable will into at least one of her pupils. "You know, dear Miss Dix, that I told you just now that I could not do my composition, and isn't it singular that I just read in Martha's letter Borridill's quotation from Mr. Gannett's sermon, 'An iron *will* can accomplish everything.' Dear Miss Dix, I *will have* this 'iron will,' and I *will do* and *be* all you expect from your child."

"I thought I was doing very well," another wrote, "until I read your letter, but when you said that you were 'rousing to greater urgency,' all my self-satisfaction vanished. For if you are not satisfied in some measure with yourself, and are going to do more than you have done, I don't know what I shall do. You do not go to rest until midnight, and then you rise very early."

Inevitably this intense introspection aroused silent rebellion in some children, emotional over-stimulation in others. But if there was fear, it was not of punishment, rather of a beloved teacher's displeasure.

"You may perhaps laugh," wrote one child, "when I tell you I have a disease, not of body but of mind. This is *unhappiness.* Can you tell me anything to cure it? If you can, I shall indeed be very glad. I am in constant fear of my lessons, I am so afraid I shall miss them. And I think that if I do, I shall lose my place in school, and you will be displeased with me."

It was remarkable that such implacable strictness could inspire so much affection.

One of her pupils, Mrs. Margaret J. W. Merrill of Portland, Maine, recalled long afterward: "I was in my sixteenth year, 1833, when my father placed me at her school. She fascinated me from the first, as she had done many of my class before me. Next to my mother, I thought her the most beautiful woman I had ever seen. She was in the prime of her years, tall and of dignified carriage, head finely shaped and set, with an abundance of soft, wavy brown hair."

Perils of emotional stresses and neuroses notwithstanding, most of her pupils seemed to benefit rather than suffer from the intensive regimen, like Ellen Hayward, who wrote her fifty years later: "To you I feel that I owe some of the most abiding of my religious impressions, a debt of gratitude which I can never repay, and my daily 'chapter' is always read from the Testament you gave me. I had it rebound a year ago, for it was fairly worn out with long service, and I value it more than I can tell you with the hymns, etc., on the fly leaf, written in your own hand."

Devotion was not confined to her pupils. One day a visitor brought Dorothea a bouquet when her pet dog Benjie was in the room. He registered uneasiness, soon slunk away, and presently returned with a large flower held carefully in his mouth. Hopefully wagging, he deposited it at her feet.

Time! There was never enough of it, even though she used every minute from five in the morning until midnight. The sands of each hour, each day, were forever running out. Her charity school, "The Hope," was as much a part of her concern as her paying project. She worried because there was no religious training on Sunday for the neighborhood poor, and finally in 1832 she found an ally in a young Harvard Divinity School graduate, Charles Francis Barnard, who had decided to dedicate his life to uncared for children. Together they gathered a class of three street waifs in the Dix parlor one Sunday afternoon. News of the little gathering spread fast. A good place to spend part of Sunday, even if one had to learn hymns and listen to Bible stories! A small price to pay for free food, warmth in winter, excursions to the country in summer! The class grew so large that Mr. Barnard moved it to Warren Street Chapel, where by 1836 it included over seven hundred waifs. Samuel Appleton, the merchant scion who had built himself a mansion on the corner of Beacon and Walnut Streets, became interested in the project and supported it financially. But the lifting of this burden gave Dorothea no more rest or leisure, merely made it possible to resume the Sunday School class she had previously taught at Federal Street.

School and church activities consumed her whole time. Though the shyness which had once been an unconfessed reason for eschewing social events was largely conquered, she had neither time nor desire for the parties, receptions, teas which her grandmother considered requisites for an attractive young woman with fading prospects of marriage. She conceived of the word "social" now in a far different context, Dr. Channing's credo that personal righteousness must be coupled with action for human betterment — relief for the poor, better housing and employment for Boston's Irish immigrants, temperance, improved education, prison reform. If there was energy to spare Dorothea expended it in such enterprises, an evening school for working young men and women in the church basement, her own charity school in the coach house, a class of ship boys from the Charlestown Navy Yard.

She was thrilled when in 1835 Dr. Channing endorsed the antislavery cause, scandalizing his parish so that many refused to speak to him on the street. Yet when William

Lloyd Garrison was dragged by a mob through Boston streets that same year, and when the Englishwoman, Harriet Martineau, who espoused the abolitionist cause, was besieged by a similar mob throwing mud against the windows of the house where she was speaking, Dorothea deplored the violence yet sympathized with the emotion causing it. As Channing believed, slavery should be abolished through moral influence, a slow healing process of the diseased body, not Garrison's bloody surgery.

"You're doing too much," chided Grandmother, wishing she could exert the same discipline over this inflexible woman of thirty-three as she had over the malleable, if rebellious, girl of sixteen. But grandmother and granddaughter seemed to have changed places in recent years. Though the hair under the ruffled cap was just as black, the patrician face almost as unlined, the iron will had somehow transferred itself from the old woman to the younger. Since the death of her last son, John, some seven years before, Madam Dix had only her daughter Mary and this beautiful, efficient granddaughter on whom she now lavished most of her fierce pride and love. Not that she revealed either emotion in word or action. It was too late to release the inhibitions of nearly ninety years. Yet, noting the return of the old symptoms which Dorothea was unable to hide — husky voice, hectic flush, hand lifted involuntarily to stifle pain, finally the frequent hemorrhaging — she tempered chiding with pleading.

"Please — take the doctor's advice, Dolly. You know Dr. Hayward is worried. For all our sakes, stop this mad, prodigal waste of your life."

"It's not waste, Grandmother. And I promise I will rest. As soon as this term is over, a good long vacation . . ."

It was neither chiding nor pleading but necessity which brought an abrupt end to her labors. In the spring of 1836 she suffered a complete breakdown. Dr. Hayward issued an ultimatum. "This is the end, my dear. You must never try to teach again."

The end? She knew by the gravity of his face, his whispered conversations with Aunt Mary outside the door, that he suspected it was not only the end of teaching. The sands were indeed running out, not only of hours and days, but of life. Well, at least she had accomplished what she had set out to do five years before, make herself independent, influence some young lives, fulfill her obligations to her family. Her mother she had made the recipient of her book royalties. Her brothers were self-sufficient, Joseph a successful merchant dealing in shoes and leather, Charles, who had graduated from the Boston Latin School in 1832, a trusted seaman on a merchant ship. She had accumulated sufficient funds to support her through whatever time of invalidism might remain. And she had no regrets.

"I don't feel that I did too much," she told Grandmother firmly, "nor have I the slightest belief that my health would have been better in our climate if I had done nothing at all. To have yielded to myself sooner would have been to fix lastingly the anguish of self-reproach. No, it was right not to tell you I was very ill,"

"Posh! Stubborn as ever." Grandmother's eyes, still so keen she could darn a linen handkerchief with invisible stitches, became even brighter with moisture. She blinked so rapidly that she pricked her finger.

Dorothea had one duty to perform. She did not worry about her regular pupils. Their parents could afford to send them to other good schools. But — The Hope! She wrote a letter to George Barrel Emerson, one of Boston's pioneers in education. They had much in common, a love of teaching, an exhaustive knowledge of natural history, a concern for the poor. She told him of her sickness. She believed her end was near. Would he take over "The Hope"? He assured her that he would, with such heartiness and sincerity that she knew she had found a true friend.

"You have shed a calm bright light on one in shadows," she wrote back. "You can't know the composing influence of your friendship, and the encouragement it has given me. Farewell. I cannot write much."

Farewell! Something in her rebelled at the sound of the word. "For myself," she had written Anne, "I feel that it is very possible I may never again enjoy the fragrancies of spring. . . ." She had known the comfort of a beloved hymn, "Come, said Jesus' sacred voice." But those words had been written fourteen years ago. Now she wanted to live. She *must* live. She *would* live. There was work for her to do.

Three

Invalid

*I am a wanderer in the land where
my fathers dwelt; a pilgrim where their
hearth fires blazed, an isolated being,
who walks among the crowd, not of it.*

1

I T WAS THE CUSTOM of elite Bostonians to take frequent
trips to Europe. Sons and daughters of shipbuilders,
heirs or founders of a far-flung mercantile empire, they
had the sea in their blood, and they were almost as much
at home in Piccadilly as in Merchants' Row, and in Naples
as in Newport. They traveled on business, for pleasure,
and for health. An ocean voyage, with a holiday in Italy or
the south of France, was considered a sure cure for every
ailment from dyspepsia to boredom. It was natural, then,
that Dr. Hayward should suggest for his patient a complete
change of scene and climate, a sea trip to England, where
she would spend the summer, then go to the south of
France or Italy for the winter. Arrangements were made.
Dr. Channing gave her letters of introduction to friends
whom he had met on similar therapeutic trips. Dorothea
faced the leavetaking with an unspoken but tacitly recognized fear that the farewells might be final.

"My resolves falter a little, but I trust will not fail," she wrote her new friend, George Emerson. "Pray for me that at the last rest may be found; and that the Most High may bring me out of darkness into the light of health. Yet His will be, He who hath smitten can heal. I will trust. I will believe that He will restore." And she hoped that they might meet "where all trials are unknown and where infirmity is exchanged for perfection."

She sailed from New York for Liverpool on April 22, 1836, under the tender care of friends, Mr. and Mrs. Frank Schroder and Mr. and Mrs. Ferrer. The ocean voyage of several weeks did not benefit her as hoped. Instead she grew steadily worse, the frequent hemorrhages leaving her so weak that she spent most of the time in her cabin. Arriving in Liverpool, she had barely strength to reach a hotel, certainly none for sightseeing or further travel. Far worse than the suffering was her guilt at interrupting the plans of her friends, who refused to leave her alone. Suddenly she remembered the letters of introduction given her by the Channings. Surely there was one to a family in Liverpool! Relieved, she found the name, a Mr. William Rathbone, and she despatched a letter to him with a note of explanation. Perhaps he could tell her of some convalescent home where she could be accommodated until she regained some degree of health.

Immediately Mr. and Mrs. Rathbone called on her at the hotel. "My dear Miss Dix, of course you must come to us at once. It will be a pleasure. No, no, not a word of remonstrance. Any friend of the Channings is our friend, too."

Within minutes these strangers had become acquaintances, the acquaintances friends. Within hours she was ensconced at Greenbank, the Rathbones' country estate about three miles from Liverpool, received as an honored guest. Within days she was a member of a loving, close-knit family and far more at home than she had ever felt in any house of her experience, including Dix Mansion. At first the hard core of independence with which she had steeled her loneliness resisted this encroachment. She was a giver, not a receiver. She felt guilt, embarrassment, humiliation. But she was too ill to protest, and so genuine was the concern of her new friends that resistance yielded, and for the first time in her thirty-four years she experienced the luxury of being pampered, protected, served instead of serving. Of course, she assured both them and herself, she would not burden them for long, just until she was well enough to rejoin her friends.

"But *we* are your friends," they insisted. "And how could you possibly be a burden when we are all enjoying you so much?"

She was like a tight, stubborn bud unfolding into luxuriant blossom in the warmth of kindness and affection. She might always have been a part of the family, so completely was she absorbed into the loving concern of every member: the scholarly and humanitarian William Rathbone and his strongminded, cheerful wife; their two beautiful daughters, Elizabeth and Mary; their son William, about eighteen, who brought quantities of flowers to her room each day, never permitting the presence of a faded leaf. There were three other children, Sam, Agnes, and Henry, the first away at boarding school, the other two spending the summer at the seashore with their governess. Then there were Dr. Reynolds, Mrs. Rathbone's brother, and his wife at nearby Woodcroft.

"You know I am ill," she wrote home after she had been at Greenbank for some months. "You must imagine me surrounded by every comfort, sustained by every tenderness that can cheer, blest in the continual kindness of the family in which Providence has placed me. . . . I write from my bed, leaning on pillows in a very Oriental luxury of position, one which I think will soon fall into a fixed habit."

She could write only a little each day, and she knew her writing was not easy to read. Grandmother, she urged, should ask Uncle Harris to help decipher it. She went into rhapsodies about her apartment, which received the morning sun, had plenty of fresh air, a jasmine with lovely starlike flowers trained against the windows, birds singing from morning to night. In fact, one larch tree was so full of birds that she was wakened at dawn with a cacophony of sound.

She was inundated by letters from devoted pupils: Fanny and Juliana Aspinwall; long sheets of very thin paper from Sarah Waters, describing in small, neat handwriting Cambridge and the university on a public day; Mary Haven, who remembered quarreling with Ella Abbott over who should give teacher her favorite crust. Concerned because she could not answer them, Dorothea wrote Grandmother, "When any come to see you, give them my love and charge them to weary not in well doing. I never forget them. I so wish I could see Adie. That child was too dear to me, and Mary Curtis, too. Marisa must let me know how she gets on in study. And Sarah Coffin."

Though confined to bed, she was seldom alone. Members of the family were in constant attendance. She exchanged poems with Richard, Mr. Rathbone's nephew, who lived at Woodcroft. In September she wrote a long poem to Elizabeth, who was traveling in Wales, Ireland, and Holland.

> I don't remember, Bessie, love,
> If since confined in bed — above —
> I've told you how affairs proceed
> In this gay refuge; . . .
> But as I musing quiet lie,
> A gentle knock bids silence fly;
> Into my bedroom Willie comes,
> With luscious peach or ripened plums,
> Or gathered, wet with morning dew
> Sweet buds and flowers, to renew
> The cheerful aspect.
> Soon Sarah comes . . .

and so on for many stanzas.

The therapy was as much mental and spiritual as physical. Each evening William Rathbone spent an hour with her in conversation, and she found him as stimulating as that other William who had so influenced her thinking. "I have never seen such a man," she wrote Grandmother, "so embracing all the qualities of the mind and heart." Fifth to bear the name, William Rathbone was inheritor of a long line of Quaker forebears, though he himself had become a Unitarian. Dorothea found his religious concepts thoroughly in harmony with her own. But far more exciting was his family's participation in social and political reform. He told her of his father's zealous efforts against the slave trade. Though a prosperous and wealthy merchant himself, he was vitally concerned with conditions of poverty, bad housing, disease among the workers in the fast-growing industrial plants of Liverpool. There had been scarcely a great social question in the last twenty years in which he had not been an outspoken exponent of liberty and justice: Catholic emancipation, repeal of the corn laws, national education, penny postage, a home for sailors. First donating a tenth of his income to charity, he was now giving at least half. Not that he told her all these things. It was no member of the family who showed her the handsome service of plate, worth twelve hundred pounds, which had recently been given him for his invaluable service in promoting parliamentary and municipal reform. In fact, she learned of his achievements largely from the constant stream of visitors flowing through Greenbank.

They came from America, Boston intelligentsia like the younger Channing, the Ezra Stiles Gannetts, Professor Ticknor of Harvard, Dr. Wainwright, the Tuckermans. Writing to Grandmother, Dorothea called it "The Travelers' and Strangers' Home." And it was a meeting place for liberal and cultured Englishmen. Reverend John Hamilton Thom, the Unitarian minister in Liverpool, was a frequent visitor with whom she had many earnest discussions — though she suspected his visits were inspired as much by a romantic interest in young Mary Rathbone as in dutiful attendance on an invalid. There were Robert Owen, the socialist founder of New Lamarck, Father Mayhew, the temperance reformer, Blanco White, the Spanish priest and author. She met Dr. Samuel Tuke, son of the noted William Tuke, the Quaker who, shocked by the barbarous treatment of the insane at York, had founded York Retreat, an experiment in more enlightened care of the mentally ill.

To her astonishment Dorothea was accepted by the Rathbones and their British visitors as an intellectual peer. While she had been somewhat acquainted with the great scholars of Boston — Emerson, Theodore Parker, Edward Everett, George Bancroft — and was respected as a teacher, she had never been invited to participate in any of the erudite discussion groups, not even Channing's small clique of intimates. When opportunity afforded, she had always been too shy and modest to take part in religious or philosophic discussions. Here she found expression easy. Her opinions were respected, her mind constantly expanding.

The new insights into social and religious problems stirred her profoundly. She wished she could contribute more facts about social betterment in America.

"Is the condition of the poor improved?" she begged Grandmother to tell her. "What is the condition of the ministry, and how do affairs stand in the religious world? How about the farm school and the houses of correction?" She remembered to ask also about Grandmother's health. What was she doing? Knitting? Could she send her a pocket handkerchief or a cambric ruffle? "Your needlework is so beautiful. You called it useless to try and teach me."

Presently Madam Dix's censure was directed at conduct even more shocking to her Puritan sensibilities than irregular stitches. Was Dorothea still lolling in luxury, taking advantage of those complete strangers, eating their bread, playing the sycophant, without any possibility of giving anything in return? It was disgraceful! Did she have no shame? Grandfather and a dozen others of her respectable forebears must be turning in their graves!

It was like an ugly serpent rearing its head in Eden. Dorothea was more hurt than angry. That the first experience of spontaneous family affection she had ever known should be sullied by such innuendos of impropriety was almost more than she could bear. Lolling, indeed! Of course Grandmother's idea of the correct way to die was sitting bolt upright in a straight chair! She wrote back a stiff little letter.

"I have felt the obligation to my friends in England so exclusively my own that it was not less surprising than painful to know you indulged so much solicitude on that point. There is a danger, perhaps, of my getting a little spoiled by so much caressing and petting, but I must try to do without it if I get better. So completely am I adopted into this circle of loving spirits that I sometimes forget I really am not to consider the bonds transient in their binding."

Mail across the Atlantic was slow, sometimes taking two months. It was so with a letter from Mrs. Hayward telling of the death of Dorothea's mother on September 28, in Fitzwilliam, New Hampshire. The news brought less of grief than of guilt — guilt most of all because she felt so little grief. Since her father's death in 1821 her mother had been well cared for, first through Grandmother's generosity, later from Dorothea's own earnings. As the letter reminded her, she should have no regrets.

"The remembrance of duties so faithfully performed, and the consciousness that you could have done nothing more had you been at home, will be a comfort to you. Your mother's departure was so unexpected that even those in the room were unprepared."

No regrets? What of the lost childhood, the loveless

home, the poverty and neglect, the long hours of back-breaking work, the happy and understanding family that might have been? The wound which had never quite healed was reopened. Perhaps it was coincidence that in November all the physical gain of the past months seemed lost in a sudden relapse. Not until the last of January was she able to write Anne, "I have been very ill from the middle of November till the past week, but have just now less pain in the side, diminished cough, and, on the whole, an accession of strength. This week, for the first time since September, the physician gave me permission to walk about the room several times daily "

Then came a genuine crisis of decision. Grandmother, now ninety-one, felt herself failing. She wanted to see her beloved Dolly once more before the end came. It was time for her to come home.

What to do? With the heralding of spring her health began to show marked improvement. She was able to go downstairs, to walk in the garden, even to make several trips to the homes of Rathbone relatives. But — another three to eight weeks of tossing, stomach-churning misery? The sea voyage recommended as a sure means of healing had been for her sheer torture. It was her attending physician who made the decision for her. No, she must not risk losing all the new health she was gaining. A few more months . . . She did not go.

It was on June 2nd that the letter came telling of her grandmother's death on April 29. This time grief was fully commensurate with guilt. Had she known the end was really near, of course she would have gone. But Grandmother had seemed so impervious to time and age, with her black hair and smooth cheeks and straight posture! It had seemed that she must forever be sitting there by her little table, back ramrod straight, keen old eyes measuring almost invisible stitches. In spite of the restraint and occasional friction between them, there had been deep, if unexpressed, affection. "I feel the event," Dorothea wrote to

Anne, "as having divided the only link, save the yet closer one of fraternal bonds, which allied me to kindred."

2

She returned to Boston that autumn. It was like the old expulsion from Grandfather's Paradise into the bleak exile of her childhood. She seemed to have left everything of interest behind her. For weeks she still lived the lives of her beloved friends, realities bounded by the news received in letters — William Rathbone's election as mayor of Liverpool, Mary's coming marriage to John Hamilton Thom, Dr. Reynolds's account of "philosophers week" at Greenbank, young Philip's trip to the zoological gardens, where he saw a dromedary, a llama, and a Bengal tiger. "How like a dream it seems," wrote Dr. Reynolds, "that for more than twelve months you were so mixed up with us!" To her it was no dream, but the only reality in a round of nightmares.

She had no home. Dix Mansion must be sold, certain valuable furniture and household articles bequeathed to her put in storage. Brother Charles was off on a ship bound for Africa. Joseph was helpful, but he had his business and a home of his own. Relations were strained with Aunt Mary and her daughters, who believed Dorothea remiss in her duty to Madam Dix. She should have been at her grandmother's side when she died instead of playing the invalid, as her mother had done. The rift between them would never be quite bridged. Of course there were many dear friends delighted to see her back — Anne Heath, Mrs. Torrey, her old pupils, the Channings. Yet never in her lonely life had she felt so completely alone. She visited for some time with the Channings at Newport. Anne begged her to spend the winter boarding near the Heaths in Brookline, but Dorothea did not dare risk a northern winter. Again she began a life of wandering — to New York, to Washington, to Georgetown, to Oakwood near Alexandria. She read constantly, visited historic shrines, would have spent long days in the Library of Congress, but "ladies were not supposed to spend time there, it was too public." A visit to an Orphans' Asylum roused all the old hungers to make herself useful, but — how?

"I trust," she wrote Anne in February, 1838, "I shall learn rightly to bear all the adversities of my lot and to make a practical use of troubles in whatever form they reach me. Perhaps it is in myself the fault chiefly lies. I may be too sensitive, too eager for that cordial relationship that exists not in mere outward forms or uttered sounds; I may be too craving of that rich gift, the power of sharing others' minds. I have drunk deeply, long, and how blissfully, at a fountain in a foreign clime. . . . But there are duties to be performed here, life is not to be expended in vain regrets."

Knowledge of the death of Edward Dillingham Bangs in April, 1838, startled her into a consciousness of further loss. For fourteen years he had been Secretary of State for Massachusetts, living in Boston, and, though she had seldom seen him, a sentimental nostalgia for this one romance of her life had never left her. Now it was as if somehow her own youth had died with him. She withdrew even further into the protective cloak of reserve. Though Anne was still her confidante and would remain so throughout their lives, she no longer signed her letters "Thea," but always "D. L. Dix" or "D. L. D." No one was permitted to call her "Dolly."

Winters in the South, summers visiting friends and relatives in Boston, Weston, Newport . . . a journey through Virginia, Pennsylvania, New York . . . a trip to New Hampshire to settle her mother's bit of property . . . a visit to the home of Reverend Ichabod Nichols, pastor of the Unitarian church in Portland, Maine . . . then on to her cousins who had long been settled in Dixmont.

The first time she went there it was like slowly digging a

grave into the past. With every mile the years slipped away, one by one. There were no railroads yet in Maine, and it was a trip of several days by stage, long enough to retrace more than a quarter of a century. From Augusta, which they left on a Wednesday, they followed the Kennebec River to Fairfax, then struck east, traveling all night through sparsely settled woods and farmlands. Dorothea did not sleep. The rattle of wheels over stones, the clop-clop of hooves . . . she was back in the old wagon with Mother beside her and baby Charles heavy against her shoulder.

"Unity! Unity!" shouted the driver. She roused to peer out the dust-flecked window. Lanterns, excited faces, a new passenger, baggage hoisted to the roof . . . then off again into the darkness, farther into the past. The horses began climbing. Forested hills loomed on either side. These had been Grandfather's lands. He must have ridden this road many times. She was a child again, watching him ride away between the trees, hand lifted in farewell.

It was still dark when they pulled up with a great flourish in front of a lighted tavern, the last hostelry before Bangor. Already the four fresh horses were being led from the adjoining stables. Dorothea straightened her body, adjusted her shawl. As she looked down into a confusion of blazing torches, milling horses, excited townsmen, familiar faces emerged, eager hands were lifted to help her down the step.

"Welcome, Cousin! Welcome to Dixmont!"

The two sons of Thaddeus Harris, John Alexander and James Winthrop, had settled on their uncle's property years before, married two sisters named Flynn, and become leading citizens of the growing community. For years John had been Madam Dix's secretary. His comfortable house had been built in the central settlement at Dixmont Corner, and nearby was the new Town House built on land donated by the family in 1836.

Grandfather's presence was pervasive — the roads he had surveyed, the church for which he and Grandmother had given the land, the five schoolhouses for which, in the last letter he had ever written, he had promised twenty dollars for every eighty raised, the small house near the watering trough where he had died, the granite monument dominating the little cemetery.

> In Memory of
> Doct^r. Elijah Dix
> who deceased in this town
> of wchich [*sic*] he was the founder
> May 28, 1809
> Aged 62
> A man distinguished
> by strength of mind
> active industry
> and arduous enterprise

She did not go on to Hampden. Here was all the past she wanted to remember.

She was free of all ties and responsibilities. Fortunately Grandmother had left her with a stipend which, with the royalties of her writings and the money earned from teaching, made her financially independent. But it was an empty freedom.

" 'The world is my home,' " she quoted in one letter. "I am a wanderer in the land where my fathers dwelt; a pilgrim where their hearth fires blazed, an isolated being, who walks among the crowd, not of it."

In Boston she often stayed with her friend Miss Sarah Gibbs at 85 Mt. Vernon Street, the house belonging to the Channing family. Boldly she determined to stay there during the winter of 1840. It seemed more like home than any place since Greenbank. One of the finest old Boston houses, built for Harrison Gray Otis by the noted architect Bulfinch, it sat high off the street on the ridge of Beacon Hill and commanded a magnificent view to the west, past the Common, the sweeping curves of the Charles River, over the new land formed by trundling thousands of ox-carts of earth from the top of Tri-mountain, on toward the countryside of Brookline. It was a little like Dix Mansion, with its rose-red brick, its towering three stories, its cupola, its high ceilings and full length windows. But best of all was the fact that Dr. Channing had built his home just across the cobble-stoned driveway at Number 83, a few short steps from Miss Gibbs's side entrance. Dorothea could spend long hours writing his letters, copying his sermons, reading to him.

But they were bitter hours as well as sweet. In spite of his increasing feebleness the "great little man's" every word, spoken or written, was a stimulus to achievement. Around him swirled all the tumultuous currents of thought and action which were stirring Boston at the beginning of the 1840s. Earnest and brilliant followers were garnering the harvest sown by Channing and others: Horace Mann, just beginning his revolution in the common school system as first secretary of the new state Board of Education; Emerson, Holmes, Longfellow, Hawthorne, Alcott, Parker, with their hopes for a more just society; George Ripley, propounding his utopian plan for Brook Farm; Samuel Gridley Howe, who had just moved his school for the blind to a big hotel in South Boston. Many of them banded into a Symposium for erudite discussion, meeting often at the Channing home. Elizabeth Peabody and Margaret Fuller were invited to join the Symposium. Not Dorothea. Nor was she included in the select little groups which met in Elizabeth Peabody's Bookshop on West Street, where every Wednesday the redoubtable Margaret Fuller conducted her "Conversations" for intellectual females on such subjects as "Woman and her place in society." Though Dorothea had exchanged a few long and introspective letters with Elizabeth Peabody, she had always detected a coldness in the other's manner, due, she suspected, to the fact that she had supplanted Miss Peabody as Dr. Channing's secretary and governess of his children.

She did not mind exclusion from the intelligentsia, al-

85 Mt. Vernon Street, home of Sarah Gibbs.

though the remembrance of those free and spontaneous months at Greenbank, where her opinions had been sought and respected, brought nostalgia. But she minded bitterly exclusion from the fellowship of hard labor that Dr. Channing's credo for a better world demanded. Teaching a Sunday School class of twelve boys, fifteen and sixteen years of age, was a palliative for enforced idleness, but only that. While the stream of worthy action rushed by, she floated helplessly in a backwater, waiting . . . for what? The early death that everyone expected?

Yet she was about to be swept into a flood which would embroil governments, batter ancient prejudices, reshape the contours of social organisms through almost half a century.

Home of William Ellery Channing at 83 Mt. Vernon Street.

Four

Crusader

If I am cold, they too are cold;
if I am weary, they are distressed;
if I am alone, they are abandoned.

1

"Miss Dix?" You may not remember me — John
Nichols."

"Of course. You are Reverend Ichabod Nichols's son. I
have often visited in your home in Portland, Maine."

"My mother suggested that you might be able to help
me. I have a problem."

Dorothea ushered the young man into Miss Gibbs's parlor. "What can I do to help you?"

John Nichols, studying for the ministry at Harvard Divinity School, was one of a group of students who had assumed the Sunday instruction of inmates of the East Cambridge jail. To his dismay all the women, twenty of them,
had been assigned to him.

"It took only one session," he confessed ruefully, "to
convince me that I was not the person for the job. They
need a mature woman to teach them, not a young man. I
talked with my mother, and she suggested that you might

know of someone who could take over the class. It's certainly a much needed service."

As she sat, obviously considering, his hopes waned. Would this woman have any acquaintances willing to associate with those wretched uncouth criminals? She was pure patrician from small, daintily shod foot to proudly lifted head with its crown of rich waving brown hair. Those soft blue-gray eyes had surely never looked on such filth and degradation as pervaded the East Cambridge jail! Blue-gray? He looked again, startled. For, suddenly brilliant, pupils dilated, they looked black.

"I will take them myself," she said decisively.

He protested. No, no, she must not. He knew she was in poor health. That was the last thing he had expected. He certainly had not meant to suggest . . .

She stopped him with a peremptory gesture. "I shall be there next Sunday."

She felt imbued with new life. Here was an opportunity to put her thwarted yearnings into action. Did not Dr. Channing teach that even the lowest of human souls was redeemable? It had been a long winter, her first in the hostile northern climate for many years. Like those women, she herself had been imprisoned in confining walls. Now spring had come. The paths across the Common were ankle deep in mud. At night one could hear the peepers in the Frog Pond. Outside the house yellow and purple crocuses were blooming. The March winds were sweeping the gulls across the Common, bringing the smell of the sea or of the Berkshires or of the cedars on Mount Monadnock. She would take springtime to those poor women icebound in sin.

But Sunday, March 28, 1841, did not feel like spring. The east wind was bitter cold. She had intended to take the omnibus, but Miss Gibbs insisted on sending her in the carriage with the family coachman. "If you *must* risk getting your death —!" Even in the closed vehicle, with a soapstone wrapped in a woolen bag at her feet, she shiv-

Dorothea Dix, taken from a daguerreotype
about 1840.

ered. They rattled across the bridge over the Charles, swollen and still fringed with ice, plowed through streets deep in mud. One could smell the prison area before arriving, whether from its human odors or the miasmas of its swampy environs, it was hard to tell. Dorothea's hands tightened on her Bible and hymnal, and she closed her eyes.

The twenty women were a motley group, some habitual offenders, chronic drunkards, prostitutes, thieves, others first offenders. Earnestly Dorothea delivered her prepared lesson. She told the story of Mary Magdalene. While most of the faces remained stolid, indifferent, even hostile, a few seemed eagerly responsive. She sang a hymn and was thrilled when a timid, quavering voice, then another, joined her. The lesson finished, she conquered natural fastidiousness sufficiently to move among them, pressing grimy hands, resolutely stifling the nausea aroused by fetid breath and unwashed bodies.

"God bless you, sister," she assured over and over. "I shall come again."

On leaving the group she decided on impulse to walk through the jail, much to the jailer's shock and displeasure. "No place for a woman, ma'am!"

"But you have women here. I have just been with them."

"Those uns, yes. But there's others. Not like you, ma'am. I can't let you —"

He might have been remonstrating with a cyclone. Had he but known it, he was the first of hundreds of similar protesters who would find themselves equally frustrated.

She was talking with some of the prisoners when she heard the scream. It sounded like nothing animal or human, long drawn and eerie, trailing away into plaintive gibberish. She turned to the jailer, alarmed. "What was that?"

"Just one of the mad uns, ma'am. There's no keepin' 'em quiet."

"You mean — there are insane persons here — in the jail?"

"Always have a few. But don't worry, ma'am. They're all shut up proper."

"But — this is a jail! There are institutions for the insane, asylums."

"Not for these uns. Not for paupers."

"Take me to them, please."

"But — ma'am —!" A look at her determined face, and he threw up his hands in resignation.

A barred door was cautiously opened a few inches, letting out a blast of chill air, heavy with a stench that almost made her faint. She forced herself to peer inside. It was a small bare room, unfurnished except for a few heaps of straw, its stone walls damp with moisture. In the small space were a half dozen figures, huddled close together for warmth, hunched within thin ragged clothing. Was it the windows rattling in the wind that she heard, or the sound of chattering teeth? Both, she decided. She tried to open the door wider.

"No, no! It's dangerous, ma'am. Some of 'em's quite violent at times."

Violent? These pitiful, shivering creatures? "But — they're freezing!" She exclaimed. "There isn't even a stove in there!"

He shrugged. "None needed for those uns, ma'am. Mad folk don't know hot from cold. Besides, it wouldn't be safe. They'd set theirselves afire."

Just then the screaming came again. "That was a woman," she charged. "Take me to her."

He was past remonstrating. The door to a smaller adjoining room emitted the same damp blast of noisome air, but within the stone walls two cages or pens of rough boards had been constructed. Inside one was the source of the screams, a raving maniac, wild eyed, disheveled, naked but for a few filthy rags. In the other was a young woman who, except for a slight vagueness in her eyes, might have passed for sane. As screams and blasphemies issued from the other's lips, the young woman cowered as if subjected to physical blows and covered her ears.

Dorothea forced herself to speak calmly. "How long have these two been together?"

"Oh, for months, ma'am. But, as you see, they aren't really together. If it weren't for the cages, the old un would tear t'other to pieces."

"Yes," said Dorothea. "I see." She held her temper until the door was closed, shutting out the appalling sounds. Then, still calmly but with a sharpness matching the steel in her eyes, she spoke her mind. She was shocked, horrified. The idea of putting insane persons in a jail with criminals was abhorrent, but she realized that was not the jailer's fault. However, some changes could be made, and at once. Of course mad people could feel cold. If some warmth was not provided in these rooms before she came again, she would go to the proper authorities. And — she was most certainly returning soon.

She did, even before the next Sunday, bringing with her warm clothes and blankets and food. Returning to teach her class, she found that nothing had been done. The jailer had regained his confidence, even acquired an armor of arrogance. After all, this was only a woman, formidable as she had first appeared. It was the commissioners who told him what to do, and they had prescribed no stoves. The blankets and clothes? She ought to know what mad folks would do to such things, tear them to rags. And as for the food, it would be like what the Good Book said, puttin' pearls in a pig's trough.

The commissioners! Dorothea learned their names, appealed to them for stoves. They only laughed. The East Cambridge Court was in session. Impossible, of course, for a woman to speak before it, but she could present the case in writing, and she did, in cogent language, describing the condition of the demented cases as she had seen them, the neglect, lack of sanitation, freezing quarters, promiscuous herding together without regard to state of health or degree of insanity. Her specific request for stoves was finally granted, but the sensational details of her protest reached the newspapers and aroused a storm of indignation. A woman meddling in politics? This Miss Dix was an interfering busybody! Peddling a pack of lies and stirring up trouble! She cared not a whit for the opposition except that it impeded progress in further reform procedure. A stove was a tiny palliative, welcome enough when cold weather should come again — *if* it was ever installed — but no remedy for the appalling distress she had uncovered. It was like applying a bit of salve to a malignant growth. She discussed the problem with Dr. Channing, who had grown so feeble that he could do little but give advice.

"See Sam Howe," he suggested. "Other possibilities are Charles Sumner and Horace Mann. You may recall that some thirteen years ago as legislator from Dedham Horace made an exhaustive survey of prisons, almshouses, and houses of correction in the Commonwealth and found that many persons 'furiously mad,' as he expressed it, were still committed to jails, even though in 1827 the law had been changed so that such persons should be committed to lunatic asylums instead of to jails."

"You mean," demanded Dorothea in shocked amazement, "that it used to be the law to send them to prison?"

"Yes. According to a statute of 1816 it was the duty of the supreme court of Massachusetts to commit to prison any person whom a grand jury refused to indict or a jury to convict by reason of his mental condition, and to keep him confined there until his health made it safe for him to be released, or until some friend or relative would assume responsibility."

"But — how horrible!"

"Horace Mann thought so. Wait a minute. I think I can lay my hand on something he said in his report." He rummaged in his desk. "Yes, here it is. 'Had the human mind been tasked to devise a mode of exaggerating to the utmost the calamities of the insane, a more apt expedient could scarcely have been suggested, or had the earth been searched, places more inauspicious to their recovery could scarcely have been found.' "

"I'd agree to that," Dorothea assented fervently.

"It was Mann, of course, who put through the appropriation for the new asylum at Worcester in 1830, but even with its enlargement in 1837 it was unable to care for all the mentally ill being lodged in prisons and jails. When Samuel Eliot became mayor of Boston in 1837 he became concerned about the insane persons and idiots in the city House of Industry and Correction. You see, according to the revised law of 1835, each county was required to provide for the paupers within its limits who were mentally ill and who could not be admitted to the asylum at Worcester because of its overcrowding. Through the mayor's efforts the Boston Lunatic Asylum was established two years ago."

"Still," Dorothea marveled grimly, "not an hour's walk away there are conditions such as I find in the East Cambridge jail!"

It was always a delight to visit the Perkins Institution for the Blind, of which Samuel Gridley Howe was founder and director. Dorothea had become interested in Laura Bridgman, the blind and deaf mute whom Dr. Howe had started to teach four years before when she was eight years old and who had learned to read and write in sixteen months. She had received a letter from the child, inscribed in neat slanting capitals. Now, as the sensitive fingers moved lightly over her features, she saw the bright little face turn radiant with happy discovery. "Miss Dix," the fingers wrote swiftly on a slate. Eagerly the child pointed out her new accomplishments, her hair braided with her own hands, the shirtwaist she had made, the doll she had dressed, about its eyes a green bandage like the one worn by all the pupils in the school.

"And you," Dorothea accused herself with sudden scorn, "who have eyes, ears, and voice, let a pair of weak lungs define the limits of your life!"

Always the ardent philanthropist, Dr. Howe was as sympathetic to the problems of the insane poor as to those of blind children or Greek revolutionists or Polish refugees. Yes, he would be glad to visit the East Cambridge jail and publish his findings. He would try to get Charles Sumner to accompany him. He was as good as his word. An article from his pen appeared in the Boston *Advertiser* of September 8, 1841, corroborating all of Miss Dix's findings. It was fiercely attacked. Then Dr. Howe appealed to Charles Sumner, who had accompanied him on the investigation, for confirmation. Sumner, already a champion of civil and political liberty and an outspoken opponent of slavery, wrote his friend an open letter of corroboration.

"My dear Howe — I am sorry to say that your article *does present a true picture* of the condition in which we found those unfortunates. They were cramped together in rooms poorly ventilated and noisome with filth." He went on to describe the two women in cages whose proximity Dorothea had found so shocking. "It was a punishment by a cruel man in heathen days to tie the living to the dead. Hardly less horrid was this scene in the prison at Cambridge. Ever faithfully yours, Charles Sumner."

Dorothea appealed to other prominent citizens for assistance, among them Reverend Robert C. Waterston and Horace Mann. She had been somewhat acquainted with Mann during her teaching days. Now he gave her an eager welcome, his deepset eyes in their cavernous sockets aflame with enthusiasm. Though his efforts at reform were now chiefly in education, the condition of the mentally ill was still a major concern.

"It's a long time since our committee made its investigation," he commented, running restless fingers through his shock of prematurely white hair. "At that time most of the insane were lodged in jails and poorhouses. We sent letters to every town and hamlet in the state, but failed to get answers. Even with the reforms we effected, the enlarged facilities at Worcester, the new Boston Lunatic Asylum, there is still little provision for the insane poor. With each town responsible for its own dependents, it's difficult even to know the facts. What is needed is a thorough survey of the state, not by letter, by person. But it would be a herculean task, and who could possibly be found to do it?"

"Yes," said Dorothea.

What is need*ed* . . . *Who* . . . As she returned to Mt. Vernon Street, the clatter of the horses' hooves on the cobblestones pounded the words into her brain. The idea they suggested was preposterous, yet she knew it had long been germinal in her subconscious thought, like a babe in embryo. Now suddenly it was pressuring, demanding to be born. Since that day in the East Cambridge jail she had visited other institutions, the Boston House of Correction, a city almshouse, a prison, and had found mentally ill persons, some violently insane, herded indiscriminately with criminals, idiots, paupers, or, worse yet, isolated in cramped cells or individual cages. If such conditions existed in enlightened Boston, what must they be in outlying towns and hamlets of the Commonwealth! Providing a little warmth for victims in one jail was a hard-won triumph, but nothing more than a first halting step up a mountain.

Who? Not I, every outraged instinct protested. She was a woman, a *gentle*woman bred in the Puritan tradition. A blessing Madam Dix could not know of the indelicacies her granddaughter had already perpetrated — challenging jailers, petitioning courts, publishing charges! Certain activities were permitted to ladies, teaching school, dispensing charities, improving their minds at lectures and concerts, even selling books like Elizabeth Peabody; certainly not gallivanting about the country accosting strangers, prying into local politics, prowling about noisome haunts of crime and disease and madness! Moreover, she was an invalid. This experimental winter in the north had almost proved a disaster. Doctors advised her not to attempt it again.

But the idea persisted and took shape. At her morning and evening prayers certain Bible verses seemed to leap at her from the page.

"No man, having put his hand to the plough, and looking back, is fit for the kingdom. . . ."

"I was in prison and ye came unto me. . . ."

"Whosoever will save his life shall lose it. . . ."

". . . and who knoweth whether thou art come to the kingdom for such a time as this?"

2

She was a scientist. Before going into the field to collect specimens, one made a thorough study of botany and zoology. She rode to Charlestown to visit the McLean Hospital, a private institution for the insane housing some seventy patients, and consulted with its superintendent, Dr. Luther Vose Bell. Surprisingly young, not more than thirty-five, he was one of the foremost authorities on mental illness in the country. The previous year he had visited a number of institutions in Europe. He had heard of her work in East Cambridge, and the keen eyes regarding her through steel-rimmed spectacles were bright with admiration. Yes, he would be glad to explain to her his methods of treatment. They followed very closely the theories of Pinel in France and of the York Retreat in England. He was delighted to learn that Miss Dix had met Samuel Tuke.

At McLean Hospital Dorothea found comfortable, uncrowded rooms, well heated, lighted, and ventilated. The patients were clean, decently clothed, well cared for. No restraints were employed except when absolutely necessary in the case of extreme violence, and even the most intractable were not confined in irons or in solitude. Occupations of various kinds were encouraged, and recreation, such as horseback riding, was provided for both sexes. Through soothing language, exercise, medicines, cures were often effected, and at least the malady in many cases was alleviated. What a contrast between these favored few who could afford such costly and exclusive treatment and the wretched victims crowded together with prostitutes, criminals, vagrants, drunkards in the prisons, jails, and workhouses she had visited!

"We are still barely emerging from the dark ages," agreed Dr. Bell, "in our concepts and treatment of mental illness."

And what were those concepts and treatments? Dorothea now spent her days in libraries in Boston and at Harvard, her nights poring over books, treatises, articles on insanity, devil possession, witchcraft. It was a long grim journey through the ages, from the casting out of devils in Bible times to the burning of witches in Salem to the caging of ersatz animals in the filthy unheated pens of the East Cambridge jail. Insanity, it seemed, in the popular mind had always been purely mental and moral, not physical. If not demon possession, it was an outbreak of the animal. It turned men and women into lions and tigers. They must be restrained like wild beasts in a zoo, by iron cages, chains, clubs. In the Middle Ages treatment had consisted of loathsome medicines, purgings, emetics, bleedings, duckings, not as an attempt to cure but to drive out devils. As Dr. Bell had observed, science itself had not long since emerged from these concepts, much less a largely ignorant and superstitious public.

As late as 1815 Bethlehem Hospital in London (Bedlam) had earned hundreds of pounds annually by charging admission of one penny for the exhibition of the most violent inmates, great amusement accruing from the antics of the raving, fighting maniacs, some of them chained, others guarded by jailers ready to club them into submission. Madmen were allowed to display madmen, and performances were organized in which they played the roles of actors, arousing mocking laughter. Since there was little provision for feeding them, the more harmless were turned out in the streets to forage, wearing black robes with white stars as their badge of identity, setting them apart like lepers.

Horrified, Dorothea learned that in Lille, France, the crazed had long lived underground; at Strasbourg, Germany, in tiny cells. In La Salpêtrière in Paris, near the end of the eighteenth century, the cells at the level of the sewers containing the more violent inmates became not only inundated in winter when the waters of the Seine rose, but infested with large rats. Madwomen were found with feet, hands, and faces torn by bites. Many were chained like dogs at their cell doors and separated from keepers and visitors by an iron grille through which food and straw were passed and the filth raked out.

Then to France in the 1790s had come Philippe Pinel, shocking the country by liberating the insane from their chains, insisting that insanity was a medical problem not a sign of moral degradation or divine punishment. Though the full application of his theories of treatment — kindness, nonrestraint, occupational therapy — was still far in the future, Pinel had introduced a new era in the philosophy of mental illness which earned him the title of "liberator of the insane." To England had come William Tuke the Quaker, father of Samuel whom Dorothea had met. Shocked by the conditions in public asylums and workhouses, he had established York Retreat, a private institution largely for members of the Society of Friends, following Pinel's methods of nonrestraint and humane treatment.

The Puritans of New England had been unreceptive to a rational or medical concept of insanity. Mental aberrations in earlier days had been given religious interpretation, marks of either prophetic gifts or of devil possession, the latter resulting in the witchcraft hysteria of Salem, when nineteen persons had been executed. Though this furor had soon passed, the idea that the mentally ill were either dangerous or inferior persisted. Brutal treatment, prompting animal-like behavior, created a vicious circle. The town, a governmental unit, was held responsible for its own paupers, including the insane. Often the victims were driven away, shunted from town to town, much as the deranged of Germany had once been set adrift like lepers or handed over to boatmen to be borne away in "ships of fools." Then as each town acquired its jail or work- or alms-house, this became its depository for every human derelict. The first workhouse, built in New York in 1736, was well called the "Poorhouse, Work-house, and House of Correction." It contained dungeons in its cellar for the mentally ill.

Hospitals of any kind were slow in coming to America. The first were the Pennsylvania and New York hospitals, antedating the Revolution. Both had strong rooms for the mentally ill. The first institution established solely for the care of the insane was at Williamsburg, Virginia, founded in 1773. Others followed until by 1841, when Dorothea began her delving, there were some eleven state or private asylums in the country.

Long before she had finished her intensive research her mind was made up. She discussed her plan with Howe and Sumner, with Dr. Bell and Dr. Butler of the Boston Lunatic Asylum, who had been closely associated with Dr. Samuel Woodward of the Worcester State Lunatic Hospital. They were at first wary and doubtful, but finally enthusiastic. Certainly such a survey was needed. If facts could be documented and presented to the legislature, they could not fail to make an impression. The times were ripe for reform, and proponents of varous causes were gaining followers everywhere — Ripley and Alcott with their Brook Farm, Garrison with his *Liberator*, Emerson with his Transcendentalism, Margaret Fuller with her gospel of women's rights. But — had Miss Dix considered the difficulties? A woman traveling alone, subjected to all the likely gibes, insults, possible ridicule? Her chin rose even higher above her long slender neck. She had. The hazards to her already delicate health? She was willing to take the risks. The expense? There was no money available from public funds. Fortunately she had a small income, plus savings from her teachings and royalties from her books. She was glad to expend it in such a cause.

There was no dissuading her from her purpose. Others tried. Her friends, like Anne Heath, Sarah Gibbs, Mrs. Torrey, in distress: "It's foolhardy, it will be your death, we can't let you!" Her relatives, Aunt Mary Harris and her daughters, the Duncans, the Bangses, the Fiskes, brother Joseph, with shock as well as distress: "What would Madam Dix say, you'll make us a laughingstock, think of us if not of yourself, do you think we want to see you dead, whoever heard of a woman, that is, a respectable woman —!"

Dr. Channing did not try. Looking at the upflung head, the brilliant, far-focused eyes, he nodded with satisfaction. He had long waited for this moment, as a father waits for the first sign of full maturity in a beloved child. At last she had found a dedication worth living for — or dying for, as it might well prove. Life was not measured in terms of length. These years of his own increasing frailty had brought fresh intellectual and moral vigor. Just last year he had written his strongest denunciation of slavery. Some of his most profound discoveries concerning the nobility and possibilities of mankind had come during these months when he knew his days were numbered.

"I rejoice with you, my friend," he said. "You have waited a long time for the trumpets to sound."

She had indeed. But now that she had heard them, strong and clear, she would be marching to their summons for the next forty years.

3

It was a crusade, inspired by as self-renouncing zeal as that ancient struggle to redeem the Holy Land, and attended by similar, if lesser, difficulties. To cover the Commonwealth of Massachusetts, to visit every city, town, village, and hamlet, to discover the existence and investigate the conditions of the mentally ill in every almshouse, jail, house of correction, and prison in the area of over 8,000 square miles — it *was* a herculean task! It would have been arduous a hundred years later for a team of trained statisticians. For a woman in the year 1841 it was unthinkable. For most women, that is. Not for Dorothea Dix.

"It should take no more than three or four months," she decided. That would mean she would be finished before the worst of winter and could spend the coldest weather in her comfortable rooms in Boston assembling her findings. Time passed. Autumn . . . winter . . . spring . . . She had covered but half the state. Summer . . . another autumn . . . well into the winter . . .

Travel was slow, long, difficult. There were three railroads in Massachusetts — Boston to Worcester, Boston to Lowell, Boston to Providence. Trains traveled no more than fifteen miles an hour, were often late, having many delays along the routes. The cars were uncomfortable, hard seats without springs, soot and cinders seeping dust through the cracks, reddening the eyes, grinding into the pores. Sometimes she had to sit up all night on a hard wooden bench in a cold bare station. But the railroads touched only half the towns she had to visit. She must take a stagecoach or hire a carriage to reach the rest, riding over roads which, if not deep in mud or ice or water, were often rough with stones and thick with dust. It took constant washing in tavern room wash basins to keep the white kerchiefs she wore with her plain dark dresses immaculate, vigorous brushings of her black bonnet and cloak to prepare for proper appearance at the next almshouse or jail or prison.

A woman traveling alone elicited curious glances which might easily have become bold, derisive, or even seductive, had it not been for the quiet, aloof dignity which commanded respect. Her approach to the objects of her investigation was circumspect. She called on the overseers of the poor in each community, presented letters of introduction, requested their cooperation. Jailers and other institutional heads, at first suspicious and resentful, found themselves yielding almost against their will to the tall woman with the brilliant eyes and the rich low voice which spoke with a quiet but powerful authority. Doors were opened, often to the creaking of rusty bolts, the bombardment of nauseating odors, moans, pleas, wails, imprecations, raucous laughter, sights which would have sent her fleeing in sickened horror had she not steeled herself to subdue all personal emotion. She questioned, sympathized, advised, dispassionately and meticulously entered facts in her notebook. As in Saugus . . .

It was December 24 when she visited the town. The thermometer was below zero. She drove to the poorhouse and was conducted by the master to his family room. Its walls were garnished with handcuffs and chains. She did not inquire how or to whom they might be applied.

"How many inmates have you?" she asked. There were thirteen paupers, she was told, one insane man, one woman insane, one idiotic man.

"Please, may I see them?"

The two men were led in. They appeared decently cared for and comfortable.

"Now may I see the other insane subject, the woman?" No, no, it was impossible. She insisted, kindly but firmly. Finally reluctant consent was given. She was led through an outer passage into a lower room occupied by the paupers, crowded, not neat. They ascended a low flight of stairs into an entry, entered a room completely unfurnished, no chair, table, bed. It was cold, *very* cold. Her conductor threw open a window, a measure imperative for the digestive stability of a visitor. On the floor sat a woman, her limbs immovably contracted, knees brought upward to the chin, face concealed, head resting on folded arms, body clothed with what looked like fragments of many discarded garments. They gave little protection, for she was constantly shuddering.

"Can she not change position?" inquired Dorothea. No, the contraction of her limbs was caused by "neglect and exposure in former years," before, it was inferred, she came under the charge of her present guardians.

"Her bed." As they left the room the man pointed to an object about three feet long and from a half to three-quarters of a yard wide, made of old ticking and containing perhaps a full handful of hay. "We throw some blankets over her at night."

Neglect? Abuse? Yes, but not intentional. People actually believed that the insane were insensitive to discomfort, hunger, cold, heat. Typical was the conversation she had with a man in Berkley when she asked the way to the almshouse and inquired if there were insane persons there.

"Oh, yes, plenty of insane people and idiots."

"Are they well taken care of?"

"Oh, well enough for such sort of creatures."

"Are there any violently insane?"

"Yes. My sister's son is there, a real tiger. I kept him here at my house awhile, but it was too much trouble, so I carried him there."

"Is he comfortably provided for?"

"Well enough."

"Has he decent clothes?"

"Good enough. Wouldn't wear 'em if he had more."

"Food?"

"Good enough. Good enough for him."

"One more question. Has he the comfort of a fire?"

"Fire! Fire, indeed! What does a crazy man need of fire? Red-hot iron wants fire as much as he!"

Up and down the state, back and forth, day after day, week after week, month after month. Occasionally she would return to Boston, consulting with Dr. Channing, Horace Mann, Dr. Bell, Samuel Gridley Howe, Dr. Butler of the Boston Lunatic Asylum. A new friend was Dr. Samuel Woodward, formerly of Hartford Retreat but now superintendent of the Worcester hospital, one of the finest institutions in the country for the treatment of mental disease. During his administration over a thousand patients had been received, nearly half of them restored to health. Dr. Woodward had not looked forward with pleasure to her visit, but she had immediately won his confidence and respect and was soon relying on his superior knowledge in the techniques of modern treatment. At Worcester there were no instruments of restraint save for occasional mittens and wrist bands. Amusements were provided, and there was an excellent library.

During occasional intervals in Boston she continued her study of insanity and its most recent treatments. Consultations with Dr. John S. Butler were revealing. Most of his patients at the Boston Lunatic Asylum were of the pauper class, many coming as hopeless cases, with the reputation of tearing their clothes, lacerating their bodies, giving vent to violent actions and filthy language. Now they were all neatly clad by day and comfortably settled in separate rooms at night. They read the papers, discussed news intelligently, dug in the garden, used edged tools, walked about the neighborhood with attendants. They attended religious services, participated in choral groups. Dr. Butler, who had worked closely with Dr. Woodward in Worcester for ten years, was a loyal disciple of that pioneer believer in the abolition of seclusion and restraint, the encouragement of occupational and recreational therapy.

In Boston also Dorothea provided herself with books, blankets, boxes of clothing, bundles of magazines, to give to patients and prisoners in the institutions she visited. One of her great concerns was the lack of good reading matter in the Massachusetts prisons. She wrote a letter, formal and in the third person, to Nathan Appleton, the wealthy merchant, soliciting books or money for permanent prison libraries at Middlesex and East Cambridge, where she had found moral and religious instruction neglected. Since many of the prisoners came from Lowell, where his mills were located, she felt assured of his concern and interest.

But her chief consideration was the condition of the mentally ill. Only a small fraction were accommodated in the three asylums. The rest, the responsibility of the various towns and villages, were of necessity cared for at home, in jails, almshouses, workhouses, or farmed out — sometimes auctioned off — to caretakers willing to assume the burden for a pittance. Conditions were even more appalling than she had feared. All over the Commonwealth she found insane persons "confined in cages, closets, cellars, stalls, pens, chained, naked, beaten with rods, and lashed into obedience!" Detail after detail came marching, a grim parade of horrors, through the pages of her notebook. Later she would rewrite the brief notes into a more continuous narrative.

> Dedham. In the almshouse, two females in stalls, situated in the main building; lie in wooden bunks filled with straw; always shut up. One of these subjects is supposed curable. The overseers of the poor have declined giving her a trial at the hospital, as I was informed, on account of expense....
>
> Newburyport almshouse. Eighty inmates, seven insane, one idiotic. Several of the partially insane apparently very comfortable; two very improperly situated, an insane man, not considered incurable, in an out-building, whose rooms opened on what was called 'the dead

room', affording in lieu of companionship with the living, a contemplation of corpses. The other subject was a woman in a *cellar*. I desired to see her; much reluctance was shown. She was "dangerous to be approached", said the Master of the House, "had lately attacked his wife", and was "often naked". I persisted. The outer doors were opened. As we descended the stairs, a strange, unnatural noise seemed to proceed from beneath our feet. A door to a closet beneath the staircase was opened, revealing in the imperfect light a female apparently wasted to a skeleton, partially wrapped in blankets, face furrowed by suffering. In that contracted space, unlighted, unventilated, she poured forth the wailings of despair. "Why am I consigned to hell? dark — dark — I used to pray, I used to read the Bible — I have done no crime in my heart." How long, how many days or years was she imprisoned there? For years! . . .

Groton. A few rods from the poorhouse is a wooden building on the roadside, heavy board and plain. One room, unfurnished but for a bundle of straw. Occupant a young man, declared incurably insane. He can move in his prison, so far as a strong, heavy chain, depending from an iron collar about his neck, permits. In fine weather the door is thrown open, giving admission to light and air, and affording some little variety to the solitary in watching the passers-by. But that portion of the year which allows of open doors is not the chiefest part. What is the condition of one who, for days and weeks and months, sits in darkness and alone, without employment, without object?

Shelburne. November. No poorhouse, few paupers. I had heard of the bad condition of a lunatic pauper. Reached a house of most respectable appearance. Concluding I must have mistaken my way, I prudently inquired where the insane person might be found and was readily answered, "here". After some difficulties I was conducted into the yard, where was a small building of rough boards imperfectly joined. This shanty, or shell, inclosing a cage, might have been eight or ten feet square. A narrow passage within allowed to pass in front of the cage. Very cold, air within burthened with most noisome vapors. All still save now and then a low groan. At last I saw a human being, partially extended, cast upon his back amidst a mass of filth. "He'll soon rouse up and be noisy enough," said the mistress. "He'll scream and beat about the place like a wild beast, half the time." "And cannot you make him more comfortable? Can he not have some clean, dry place, and a fire?" "As for clean, it will do no good. He's cleaned out now and then, but what's the use for such a creature?" "But a fire, there is space even here for a small box stove!" "If he had a fire, he'd only pull off his clothes, so it's no use." I made no impression. "How do you give him his food? I see no means of introducing anything here." "O," she pointed to the floor, "one of the bars is cut shorter there, we push it through there." "There? Impossible! You would not treat your lowest dumb animals with that disregard to decency!" "As for what he eats or where he eats, it makes no difference to him, he'd as soon swallow one thing as another."

It was November when she came to Danvers. In the almshouse were three insane, one in close confinement at all times. Dorothea found the mistress and was conducted to the "home" of the forlorn maniac, a young woman in a condition of extreme neglect and misery. She had once been "a respectable person, industrious and worthy." Disappointments and trials had shaken her mind. She had been at Worcester hospital but had been returned to the town as incurable. When at Worcester, the mistress had been told, the woman had been "comfortable and decent." Not now! Here she stood, clinging to or beating on the bars of her caged apartment, the size of which afforded space only for increasing accumulations of filth, arms naked, hair disheveled, unwashed body clothed in unclean rags, the air so offensive, in spite of ventilation on three sides, that one could remain only a few moments before retreating for recovery. Irritation of body, produced by filth and exposure, was making her tear off her skin by inches.

"We can't help it," explained the caretaker. "Half her skin is off sometimes. We can do nothing with her. And it makes no difference what she eats, for she consumes her own filth as readily as the food which is brought her."

In the poor farm at Sudbury screams and imprecations, amazing blasphemies apprised Dorothea of her goal long before she reached the place. In a stall, built under a woodshed on the road, was a naked man, defiled with filth, furiously tossing through the bars and about his cage portions of straw, the only furnishing of his prison. The mass of filth within diffused a most noisome stench. She hastened to the house overwhelmed with horror. Ten days since, the mistress informed her, the man had been brought from Worcester hospital where the town did not choose any longer to meet the expense of maintaining him. "He's been dreadful noisy and dangerous ever since. He's a dreadful care, worse than all the people and work on the farm beside."

"Have you other insane persons?" asked Dorothea.

"Yes; this man's sister has been crazy here for several years. She does nothing but take on about him, and maybe she'll grow as bad as he."

Dorothea found the sister in an adjoining room, sitting on a low chair, hair uncombed, her whole mien one of unmitigated woe. When Dorothea spoke to her kindly, she grasped her hand and burst into a passionate flood of tears. "O, my poor brother, my poor brother; hark, hear him! Hear him!" Then she lapsed into apathy, still weeping, but neither speaking again nor moving.

Leaving, Dorothea avoided the maniac's cage. But there, staring with avid curiosity, was a group of little boys and girls, pointing, giggling, eagerly exclaiming.

It was late in December, four degrees above zero, when she visited the almshouse in Bolton. It was a neat, comfortable establishment. There were two insane women, one in the house, the other "out of doors." Dorothea asked to see her. Following the mistress through the deep snow for several yards, numbed with cold, she came to a small building in the rear of the barn. There was a cylinder stove with a rusty pipe. Uttering an exclamation at finding no fire, the caretaker started to light one, while Dorothea explored in the poor light the cage occupying part of the building.

"Oh, I'm so cold, so cold," came a plaintive cry.

And well she might be! thought Dorothea, shivering. The driver of her sleigh had complained that it was too hard to stand the wind and snow that day, yet here was a woman caged without fire or warm clothes, not naked, for one thin cotton garment covered her, and part of a blanket was gathered about her shoulders.

"Well, you shall have a fire, Axey," comforted the caretaker. "I've been so busy getting ready for the funeral!" One of the paupers, it seemed, had died.

"Oh, I want some clothes!" begged the woman.

"Well, Axey, you shall have some as soon as the children come from school. I've had so much to do."

"I want to go out, do let me out!"

"Yes, as soon as I get time."

"Why do you keep her here?" asked Dorothea. "She appears harmless and quiet."

"Well, I mean to take her up to the house pretty soon. The people that used to have the care here kept her shut up all the year. But it *is* cold here, and we take her to the house in hard weather. The only danger is her running away."

The smoke from the kindling fire became so dense that a new anxiety struck the captive. "Oh, I shall smother! Don't fill that up. I'm afraid!"

As Dorothea moved away, she held out her hands, crying piteously. "Do take me with you, do, I'm so cold. Do let me go!" Shivering with eagerness to get out, she rattled the bars of her cage.

It was not cruelty, Dorothea knew, but ignorance which inspired such neglect and atrocities. People actually believed that mental aberration was synonymous with physical insensibility. Most caretakers, jailers, wardens, almshouse masters were not intentionally unkind. In fact, they had no conception of the efficacy of cleanliness, good food, some kind of employment, in many cases lack of restraint, in restoring theinsane to at least partial normality. Over and over in her travels she saw the beneficial results of simple kindness.

In Barre, where paupers were disposed of annually to families, she saw a young woman, neat, well clothed, quiet, employed at needlework. A year before, auctioned to another family, where she had been caged, chained, beaten, she had been a raving madwoman. Now, with a more understanding family, she was no longer chained, caged, beaten; only, if she became overexcited, a pair of mittens were drawn over her hands. What would she be like next year, after the annual sale?

In Sandisfield was another young woman, for years a raging maniac, uncontrollable, it was said, except by chains, cage, and the whip. She also had been put up for auction. An old man had come forward to apply for her. He was derided. What would he and his old wife do with such a mere beast? She was given to his charge. She was washed, neatly dressed, placed in a decent bedroom opening into the kitchen. At first the chains were not removed. She was restless, at times violent, but the kind ways of the old couple wrought a change. "After a fortnight," said the old man, "I knocked off the chains and made her a free woman." She was not cured, at times excited but not violently so. They were careful of her diet, kept her clean. She called them "father" and "mother" and, when Dorothea saw her, was a safe and comfortable inmate of their home.

The practice of herding together all types of mental aberration seemed especially deplorable. In a miserable outbuilding of the almshouse in Ipswich were three individuals confined in stalls or pens: one apparently insensible to his environment; a second one a former newspaper editor, then a state senator and a judge in the Court of Errors, now pitiably confused yet not so lost to propriety but that the condition of his stall embarrassed him. When she had gone on, he asked earnestly, "Is the lady gone — gone quite away?" Dorothea returned. "Did you wish to see me?" "And have you too lost all your dear friends?" he asked. Perhaps he had noticed her black dress and cloak. "Not all," she replied. "Have you any dear father and mother to love you?" He sighed, then laughed, and began pacing his limited stall. Adjacent to his cubicle was another occupied by a *simple* girl, "put there to be out of harm's way." A madman on one side of her, another almost opposite, and no screen!

Equally deplorable was the practice of housing the insane with other indigent persons or with prisoners. Instead of being asylums for the aged, homeless, and orphans, almshouses were transformed into perpetual bedlams. In prisons it was a two-edged evil. Not only must the mentally ill be mingled indiscriminately with criminals, but prisoners were subjected to ravings, blasphemings, furious shouts, almost around the clock. Said one warden of a crowded prison near Boston after the admission of insane persons according to the Revised Statute of 1835, "The prison has often more resembled the infernal regions than any place on earth!" Hospitals, Dorothea became more and more firmly convinced, not prisons, jails, almshouses, were the proper places for the mentally disturbed.

She was sure of it one day near the end of 1842, encountering a patient in the Worcester hospital. For two years the woman had been the dread of the jail where she was confined, pouring forth torrents of obscenity, subjecting sounds of her violence and passion to all in the vicinity: the warden and his household, attendants, men and women waiting trial, the neighborhood, almost the whole town. Then finally, importuned beyond the possibility of refusal, the judge had granted a warrant for her transfer to Worcester. Dorothea found her there, orderly, neatly dressed, capable of light employment, eating her meals with the other patients. But a change which might not be lasting! With the limited facilities for hospitalization in the Commonwealth she was liable to be returned at any time to prison.

The march went on inexorably . . . weeks, months . . . mud, snow, dust, stones and deep ruts . . . jolting cars, cinders, cold stations, noisy taverns . . . sly glances, muttered gibes . . . racking cough, pains in the chest which never became quite unbearable . . . cities, towns, hamlets. Line after black damning line, words marched across the pages of her notebook, words which in the writing became human flesh.

> Taunton, one woman caged. . . .
>
> Plymouth. One man stall-caged, from Worcester hospital. . . .
>
> Barnstable. Four females in pens and stalls. . . .
>
> Ipswich prison. In the common room, occupied by a portion of the lunatics not furiously mad, I heard someone say, "I know her, I know her," and with a joyous laugh John hastened towards me. A simple boy whom I had met in the East Cambridge House of Correction. Most of the idiotic subjects in the prisons of Massachusetts are unjustly committed, being wholly incapable of doing harm. . . .
>
> Wayland almshouse. Man caged in a woodshed, fully exposed on the public road. Confinement and cold have so affected his limbs that he is often powerless to rise. . . .
>
> Westford. Young woman fastened to the wall with a chain. . . .
>
> Newton almshouse, a cold morning in October. I ascended the stairs in the woodshed, and passing through a small room stood at the entrance of the one occupied. With what? The furniture was a wooden box or bunk containing straw, and something I was told was a man. Protruding from the foot of the box was — it could not be feet!

Yet from these stumps were swinging chains, fastened to the side of the building. The master told me his history. The old man had been crazy above twenty years. As until recently the town had owned no farm for the poor, he had annually been put up at auction. A few winters since, being kept in an out-house, the people "did not reckon how cold it was", and so his feet froze. "Are chains necessary now?" I asked. "He cannot run." "No, but he might crawl forth, and in his frenzy do some damage." . . .

Fitchburg almshouse, November. A man in an outbuilding returned from hospital as incurable. "Is he violent or dangerous?" "No." "Is he clothed?" "Yes." "Why keep him shut in this close confinement?" "O, my husband is afraid he'll run away, then the overseers won't like it." He raised himself from the floor and came unsteadily toward me. "Give me those books, oh give me those books!" "You could not use them, friend. You cannot see there." He raised his hand and bent a little forward, lowering his voice. "I'll pick a little hole in the plank and let in some of God's light." . . . The master came round. I asked, "Why cannot you take this man abroad to work on the farm, he is harmless? Air and exercise will help to recover him!" He replied, "I've proposed getting from the blacksmith an iron collar and chain, then I can have him out by the house." "An iron collar and chain!" "Yes, I had a cousin up in Vermont, crazy as a wild-cat, and I got a collar made for him, and he liked it." "Liked it! How did he manifest his pleasure?" "Why, he left off trying to run away."

By the end of December, 1842, Dorothea had visited at least once every almshouse, workhouse, jail, and prison in Massachusetts, many of them several times. She returned to Boston tired, heartsick, angry, griefstricken because of Dr. Channing's death the preceding October, but with a whitehot purpose already hardening into steel.

The crusade was not over. It was just beginning.

4

"I didn't write you about his death for fear of upsetting you," said Mrs. Channing. "I knew he would not have wanted your work to be interrupted. He spoke of you just a little while before he died. Tell her to persevere, he said."

Never one to reveal her deepest emotions, Dorothea had become even less demonstrative in the past months. She had learned to observe hideous barbarities without betraying anger or horror, descend to the depths of human suffering with an expression of sympathy undiluted by the sentimentality of an extremely sensitive nature. Now she said simply, "I shall never cease to mourn him."

There was no time for indulgence in grief. She had work to do, and quickly. The Legislature of Massachusetts would be meeting in January. Samuel Gridley Howe had volunteered to present a memorial. When Mrs. Channing offered the use of her husband's study, next door to Dorothea's rooms at 85 Mt. Vernon Street, she accepted gratefully. There, surrounded by his books and papers, sitting at his desk using the same pen which had probed the mystery of the universe and found it good, sensing his presence as pervasively as if he were looking over her shoulder, she began her work.

MEMORIAL TO THE LEGISLATURE OF MASSACHUSETTS

I respectfully ask to present this Memorial, believing that the *cause*, which actuates to and sanctions so unusual a movement, presents no equivocal claim to public consideration and sympathy. Surrendering to calm and deep convictions of duty my habitual views of what is womanly and becoming, I proceed briefly to explain what has conducted me before you unsolicited and unsustained, trusting, while I do so, that the memorialist will be speedily forgotten in the memorial. . . .

I tell what I have seen — painful and shocking as the details often are. . . .

I proceed, Gentlemen, briefly to call your attention to the *present* state of Insane Persons confined within this Commonwealth, in *cages, closets, cellars, stalls, pens! Chained, naked, beaten with rods,* and *lashed into obedience!* . . .

Though she was obliged to refer to persons and to indicate localities, she explained, no indictment was intended of individuals or places. She believed most wardens, keepers, and other officers erred not through hardness of heart and willful cruelty but through lack of skill and knowledge. It was the system which was at fault, the Commonwealth which was accountable for most of the existing abuses.

Without ornate diction yet with vigorous and lucid detail she cited illustrations from her journal, mentioning some forty towns which she had visited ranging from Cape Cod to the far Berkshires, some meriting but a single line or a couple of sentences.

Lincoln. A woman in a cage.

Medford. One idiotic subject chained, and one in a close stall for seventeen years.

Williamsburg. The almshouse has several insane, not under suitable treatment. No apparent intentional abuse.

Granville. One often closely confined; now losing the use of his limbs from want of exercise.

Other towns, among them Danvers, Newburyport, Saugus, Ipswich, Sudbury, Groton, Fitchburg, Bolton, Shelburne, Newton, were cited in several paragraphs, even long pages, detailing graphic descriptions of individual cases, occasionally but only rarely indulging in personal comment or impassioned appeal.

I have been asked if I have investigated the causes of insanity? I have not; but I have been told that this most calamitous overthrow of reason often is the result of a life of sin; it is sometimes, but rarely, added, they must take the consequences; they deserve no better care! Shall man be more unjust than God, who causes his sun and refreshing rains and life-giving influence to fall alike on the good and the evil? Is not the total wreck of reason, a state of distraction, and the loss of all that makes life cherished a retribution, sufficiently heavy, without adding to consequences so appalling every indignity that can bring still lower the wretched sufferer?" . . .

Toward the end she quoted comments from the sheriffs of various counties who heartily seconded her contention that the occupation of prisons and houses of correction by such persons was under all circumstances an evil.

"We have in jails," stated the Sheriff of Plymouth county, "no conveniences to make the situation of lunatics and idiots much more decent than would be necessary for the brute creation."

Said the Sheriff of Hampshire: "This feature of our law seems to me a relic of that ancient barbarism which regarded misfortune as a crime and those bereft of reason as also bereft of all sensibility."

Similar statements were quoted from sheriffs of other counties, Berkshire, Middlesex, Dukes, and from prison wardens and masters of almshouses. She closed with a brief but cogent appeal.

Gentlemen, I commit to you this sacred cause. Your action upon this subject will affect the present and future condition of hundreds and of thousands.

In this legislation, as in all things, may you exercise that "wisdom which is the breath of the power of God."

Respectfully submitted,

85 Mt. Vernon St., Boston   D. L. Dix
January, 1843.

Samuel Gridley Howe read the completed manuscript with both delight and awe. He was amazed at its clarity and dramatic forcefulness. It was rushed to the printer, an impressive document of some thirty pages, and on the day that he presented it to the legislature copies were distributed to all the members.

"I presented your Memorial this morning," he wrote her, "indorsing it both as a memorial and a petition. Your work is nobly done, but not yet ended. I want you to select some newspaper as your cannon, from which you will discharge often red-hot shots into the very hearts of the people; so that, kindling, they shall warm up the clams and oysters of the house to deeds of charity. When I look back upon the time when you stood hesitating and doubting upon the brink of the enterprise you have so bravely and nobly accomplished, I cannot but be impressed with the lesson of courage and hope which you have taught even to the strongest men."

The memorial exploded like a bombshell. Years later a commentator would refer to it as "the greatest sensation produced in the Massachusetts legislature since 1775." Another would call her investigation "the first piece of social research ever conducted in America." News of it reverberated through the Commonwealth with almost the traumatic shock of that shot at Lexington "heard round the world."

"Incredible! Incredible!" was the dismayed reaction of sensitive and humane souls both in the legislature and among the populace. Hastily the matter was referred to a committee of which Dr. Howe was the chairman.

But the voices of shocked humanitarians were drowned in the more vociferous outrage of town selectmen, almshouse masters, jail keepers, private citizens who felt their personal reputations along with that of their towns maligned.

"Lies! Slander! Meddlesome tomfoolery! Trumped-up sensationalism!"

Even some newspapers, supporters of the cause at first, were pressured into registering opposition. "There are some," one stated, "and Miss Dix may be one of them, who are always on tiptoe, looking for something more marvelous than is to be discovered in real life; and because the things themselves will not come up to this pitch of the imagination, the imagination is brought down to them, and has a world of its own creating."

Over and over she protested that it was not persons or localities but a cruel and outdated *system* which she was castigating. Hospitals were the only places where insane persons could be properly treated. The only solution was for the Commonwealth to build more state hospitals or enlarge the only one at Worcester. No use! Some insisted on taking her statements of hard cold fact as personal affronts.

An imposing list of friends rallied to her support.

"I have felt in reading your Memorial," wrote Horace Mann, "as I used to feel when formerly I endeavored to do something for the welfare of the same class — as though all personal enjoyment were criminal until they were relieved."

"I trust," wrote Lucius Manley Sargent, "that you will not suffer a moment's disquietude from a consideration that there is a morbid sensibility abroad, which may question the propriety of such an investigation by one of your sex. . . . Woman was last at the cross and first at the tomb, and she is never more in her appropriate station than where placed precisely as you are at this moment."

Dr. Bell of McLean Asylum, Dr. Butler of the Boston Lunatic Asylum, Dr. Woodward of Worcester, all substantiated her findings.

"I have read over very carefully the account of the visit to the four almshouses," reported Charles Sumner, referring to Sudbury, Wayland, Westford, and Groton, "and I am obliged to add that it accords most literally with the condition of things at the time of my visit. Even the vivid picture of Miss Dix does not convey an adequate idea of the unfortunate sufferers in the almshouse in Wayland. The correctness with which Miss Dix has described the four almshouses I have seen leads me to place entire confidence in her report."

Several of the towns' officials made public their indignant protests. Danvers sent a long list of affidavits affirming that her statements about their almshouse were untrue, and she entered into a lengthy correspondence with a gentleman from that town, replying to his accusations firmly but with dignified restraint.

"I could not have made a mistake as regards fact, for, as I always have done, I took notes on the spot. . . . If the parties assuming to be aggrieved are disposed to subdue passionate excitement I do not doubt they may receive all the evidence they desire of the correctness of my statements."

In answer to the fiercely indignant protests of the town of Groton concerning the young man in the almshouse confined with chain and iron collar, she merely published a letter received from Dr. Luther Bell who hàd seen the young man in the same almshouse in 1840, confined in the following manner: "A band of iron, an inch wide, went round his neck, with a chain six feet long attached. His hands were restrained by means of a clavis and bolt (of iron), appropriated to each wrist and united by a padlock." In this bondage he had been brought to the asylum, where his shackles had been immediately knocked off, his swollen limbs chafed gently, whereupon the delighted patient had exclaimed, "My good man, I must kiss you." During his residence at the asylum he had shown no violence and improved so markedly as to seem well on the way to recovery. But after four months the overseers of the poor had sent for him, unwilling to pay for his continued support at the asylum. Dr. Bell's record had closed with the words, "Reluctant to go, for fear they will again chain him."

"How much now, my dear madam," Dr. Bell's letter

ended, "do you suppose the charge to the large and thriving town of Groton was for this poor man under the care of this department of the Massachusetts General Hospital? Precisely three dollars a week for every expense of support, care, and comfort; perhaps a third or a half more than his present cost."

The report of the legislative committee strongly endorsed the memorial and recommended additional buildings for the Worcester State Lunatic Hospital to accommodate 200 more patients. Since there were listed 958 pauper insane and idiotic persons in the Commonwealth, to say nothing of about 800 in private charge, and the entire provision for the insane was not adequate for 500, this was a moderate proposal. However, the furor of opposition had its dampening effect on the legislature's first fires of purpose. An editorial in the *Courier*, which had been an ardent supporter, advised that it would be wise to accept only half of Miss Dix's report as truth. Dr. Howe's and Charles Sumner's answers to this accusation, together with Dr. Bell's quotes from his notebook, only partially blunted the edge of its damaging effect.

Dorothea invited some of the legislators to call on her and learn the truth from her own lips. Some came. At first she believed their promises of support. As action on the bill was delayed, Dr. Howe became less sanguine.

"I do not like to indulge in feelings of distrust, but have been irritated by the cold, pecuniary policy of these men," he wrote Dorothea. "A friend overheard one of those very men who talked so pathetically to you, say, 'We must find some way to kill that devil of a hospital bill!' "

On February 22 he moved that resolves relating to the State Lunatic Asylum be taken up and that nine o'clock on Saturday, February 25, be set aside for action. There was opposition, but the motion carried.

On Saturday morning Dorothea left 85 Mt. Vernon Street and crossed the driveway to spend the hours of waiting in Dr. Channing's study. If ever she had needed the supporting assurance of his spirit, it was now. Understanding, Mrs. Channing left her there alone. She sat at his desk, a copy of the Memorial held tightly in her hands. It was not just paper that she held, but human flesh. She could feel it quivering in the imprisoning clasp of her fingers. It seemed to have a pulse quite apart from the quickened tempo of her own heart. It was the tortured composite body of all the helpless souls whose suffering she had made her own.

After what seemed an eternity she heard the rattling of carriage wheels on the smooth stone tracks of the driveway, the pounding of hooves on the cobblestones between. A few moments later Dr. Howe appeared in the doorway. She dared not look up for fear of the disappointment his face might betray.

"Miss Dix," he announced joyfully, "your bill has passed."

5

"Now," said Anne Heath with fond satisfaction, "it's over, and you can take a long rest. Why not stay here for a while? Or would a trip south be beneficial? March can be very raw indeed."

Dorothea smiled to herself, comparing the fresh salty breezes which already held a breath of spring with the icy blizzards, the knee-deep snows, the bone-chilling winds and rains, the unheated tavern rooms and depots encountered during the preceding marathon. It was good to be back in this beautiful normal home after many months of absence. Though Anne's saintly mother had been gone ten years, the same mutual love and concern bound together the brothers and sisters. Now for the first time Dorothea felt no envy of Anne for this close family relationship which she herself had never had, no reluctance to return to her own lonely orbit. In fact, she became impatient for the days of her visit to end.

"I hope you've decided to go south for a little trip," urged Anne, worriedly watching her preparations for departure.

"Yes," said Dorothea. No need to tell her anxious friend that her crusade, far from ending with the victory in Massachusetts, had only begun. She was going south, yes, but not in pursuit of more healthy and balmy environs, and not to Philadelphia or Washington or Baltimore. Only to Rhode Island.

During the Massachusetts crusade she had frequently crossed the borders into Rhode Island, Connecticut, New York. Her brief visits to institutions there had convinced her that need for reform in other states was equally imperative. Letters were beginning to come to her from ministers, physicians, humanitarians concerned with conditions in many different areas. One from the Reverend Edward Hall in Providence told of a case in a small village on Narragansett Bay which he felt needed immediate attention. He begged her to investigate it. She took the train for Providence from its Park Square station and, arriving some hours later, went to the minister's house.

Louisa Hall was in the nursery when her husband came to tell her that Miss Dix was below. "It's you she has come to see," his wife replied a little curtly. "There's no need of my going down."

"She's coming up," returned her husband. "She is staying the night and would like to see you in the nursery."

Mrs. Hall frowned her displeasure. She was already prejudiced against this woman who went about, a "self-appointed critic," and who had the reputation of being "cross" when she kept school. But, she was to recall later, "One look at that calm, gentle face had its effect. Then only a word of sweet ladylike apology in a sweet low voice, and I began to feel the gift she had. I was mending my boy's socks, and she quietly took one up and began darning with a skillful hand and talking most pleasantly of the beautiful city of Providence and of some Boston ministers we both knew. For two hours we sat together and not one word about the insane or her 'mission.' After dinner she said to my husband, 'Now I am at your service.' "

Soon after her arrival in Providence Dorothea set off by stage coach for the village of Little Compton, accompanied by an interested friend of the Halls, Thomas Robinson Hazard, who had brought the case in question to the clergyman's attention. They went at once to the almshouse, and, as usual, her quiet but authoritative insistence won access to the cells where two or three insane persons were in close confinement. "Is this all?" she inquired. "You have no other patients?"

There was one other, she was told. But she must not go into his cell. He would surely kill her. "Please," she insisted, "let me see where he is." Very well. She should see. "But stay outside till I get a lantern."

Having explored cells and dungeons in the cellars of dozens of almshouses and prisons, Dorothea concluded that the insane man was confined in some such dark, damp retreat. Weary and oppressed, she leaned against an iron door which closed the sole entrance to a queer stone structure, rather resembling a tomb, in the courtyard of the almshouse. Soon she heard smothered groans and moans issuing from the place, as from something buried alive. The mistress came from the house with keys and a lantern.

"He's here," she said, unlocking the strong iron door.

Dorothea followed her down one step, around a turn and through a narrow passage to the right. Here was a second iron door, equally solid. The woman unlocked this also, and it swung open a few inches. Immediately such a stench filled the passage that Dorothea choked and was forced to retreat. "Wait," she gasped. "I'll be back." Out in the air she drew long deep breaths before forcing herself to return.

"He's used to me, but you're a stranger," warned the woman. "He's like to kill you if you go near."

Dorothea groped her way in. The lantern gave only a dim glow and there was no window or source of other light or ventilation. The room was perhaps seven by seven feet, six and a half high, all, even the ceiling, of stone. An iron frame interlaced with rope was the sole furniture. The inmate stood near the door, motionless and silent, tangled hair about his shoulders, bare feet pressing the filthy, wet stone floor. He was thin as a shadow and bore gruesome resemblance to a disinterred corpse. Never had she seen such a pitiable object. Disregarding the woman's warning, she went toward him, took his cold hands, tried to warm them by gentle friction. She spoke to him of release, of liberty, of care, of kindness. "Come away, he'll kill you," the woman kept warning. But the man showed no signs of violence. He spoke no word, made no movement. He might not have been conscious of their presence except that a tear stole over his hollow cheek. Moving slightly, Dorothea struck against something which sounded sharp and metallic — a length of ox-chain, connected in the middle to an iron ring which encircled the man's leg. At one end it was joined to a solid chain, bars of iron perhaps two feet long, linked together, and at the other end it was connected by a staple to the rock overhead.

"Why, he didn't even try to hurt you!" the woman exclaimed in amazement as they left the cell, again securely double-locked, and returned across the muddy swamp to the almshouse. "My husband," she continued companionably, "sometimes rakes out of a winter morning half a bushel of frost, and yet the creature never freezes! Sometimes he screams something dreadful, and that's why we had the double wall and two doors in place of one. His cries disturbed us in the house."

"How long has he been there?" asked Dorothea.

"Oh, above three years. But then he was kept a long while in a cage first. But once he broke his chains and the bars and escaped, so we had this built, where he can't get off."

Get off! Dorothea clenched her teeth to keep from

crying out. As well might a buried corpse break out of a tomb! Yet again, she knew, it was not cruelty but ignorance which prompted such brutal treatment. This woman and her husband actually believed that the mental patient had ceased to be a human being. And the more enlightened citizens who had power to correct such injustices were ignorant, also, of their existence. Well, that was why she was here, to tell them.

Thomas Hazard was her active and concerned ally in making the facts known.

"In the course of her investigations," he wrote to a friend, "she has ferreted out some cases of human suffering almost beyond conception or belief — one case in a neighboring town, of which I was yesterday an eye-witness, which went beyond anything I supposed to exist in the civilized world, and which, without exaggeration, I believe was seldom equaled in the dark ages, the particulars of which she will describe."

She did, not only to this friend of Thomas Hazard but to other concerned citizens. The case of Abram Simmons was blazoned across newspapers, discussed in hushed tones by shocked and embarrassed selectmen, made the subject of heated debate at numerous town meetings. In August Thomas Hazard would be able to write Dorothea that Simmons had been transferred from his stone dungeon to a wooden structure and that the town would become responsible for having him placed in an asylum at the modest stipend of three dollars a week and a decent quantity of clothing.

But there progress came to a dead end. There was no proper asylum in Rhode Island. Dexter Hospital in Providence, established through the gift of a public-spirited individual for the benefit of the poor, was totally inadequate to meet the needs of the indigent, least of all the insane. A law passed over a hundred years before still empowered town councils to make whatever provision they saw fit for their vagrants and "mad persons." Justices of the peace continued to commit insane persons "dangerous to safety" to county jails and almshouses. During the rest of the spring and summer Dorothea pursued her thorough investigation of all almshouses, jails, and prisons, and, finding the same shocking conditions as in Massachusetts, she prepared to present her findings in a Memorial to the legislature meeting the following January in Providence. However, a new development changed her plans.

Nicholas Brown, founder of Brown University, who died in that same year of 1843, left a will bequeathing $30,000 for the erection of an insane hospital or retreat. Dorothea, now involved in investigations in New Hampshire, Vermont, and New York, wisely decided to postpone her own activities until the Rhode Island General Assembly should take action on the bequest. Meeting in January, 1844, the assembly issued a charter incorporating the Rhode Island Asylum for the Insane, to be named, if desired, for any individual who might contribute the additional funds necessary for such an institution. Returning to Providence, Dorothea immediately plunged into the task of seeking such funds. What wealthy persons were there, she asked Edward Hall, who might be approached for donations? He mentioned the millionaire Cyrus Butler.

"But getting money out of him is like milking a stone," he discouraged. "He's all get and no give. I doubt if he has ever given a dollar away."

"He is human," returned Dorothea, "and every human being has a heart."

Still skeptical, Mr. Hall accompanied her to the Butler mansion. "Only to the door," he insisted. "It might be a bit harder for him to refuse a woman. But, please, my dear Miss Dix, don't get your hopes up."

She rang the bell, and a servant came to the door. She gave her name, asked to see Mr. Butler, and, by the same alchemy which had won her admittance to barred prisons, was conducted to the parlor. Presently a man in his late seventies entered, face stern, manner austerely polite.

"Ah, Miss Dix. I believe I have heard your name. You're from Massachusetts, I believe." His tone managed to endow her presence in Rhode Island with questionable propriety.

She smiled. "Yes, sir, but I have spent much time in your beautiful state, at Dr. Channing's summer home in Newport."

"So? And how do you find our weather compares with that of your own delightful state?" There followed a conversation on the diversities of weather and other trivialities which might have jogged on for hours if Dorothea had not finally taken the reins into her own hands.

"Mr. Butler," she interrupted with quiet but commanding dignity, "I want to bring before you certain facts involving terrible suffering to your fellow-creatures all around you, suffering you can relieve. My duty will end when I have done this, and with you will then rest all further responsibility."

Simply but with cogent clarity, suppressing her own emotion, she related the facts as she had found them, telling the story of Simmons and a hundred other cases, managing somehow to give the impression that the parlor was a hall of judgment presided over by a just but avenging God. The man listened to the end without comment. Then he demanded abruptly, "Miss Dix, what do you want me to do?"

"Sir," she replied calmly, "I want you to give fifty thousand dollars toward the enlargement of the insane hospital in this city."

He wrote a check for $40,000, given on the condition that forty thousand more be raised within six months from April 1st of that year. Dorothea rose and thanked him. As the eminent psychologist Dr. Pliny Earle was to remark years later, "She walked forth the marvel of Rhode Island which had always been hearing how Moses smote the rock but had never witnessed such a miracle."

Dorothea felt satisfaction but not triumph. There was

still the other $40,000 to be raised. And Abram Simmons was still bound in chains in his wooden prison. She wrote a newspaper article called "Astonishing Tenacity of Life," which appeared in the Providence *Journal* of April 10, 1844. It was unsigned, as usual, and she kept herself in the background, reporting the experience of others, in this case of Thomas Hazard.

> It is said that grains of wheat, taken from within the envelope of Egyptian mummies some thousands of years old, have been found to germinate and grow. . . . Even toads and reptiles have been found alive in situations where it is evident that they must have been encased for many hundreds, if not thousands, of years. It may, however, be doubted whether any instance has ever occurred in the history of the race where the vital principle has adhered so tenaciously to the human body under such a load and complication of sufferings and tortures as in the case of Abram Simmons, an insane man, who has been confined for several years in a dungeon in the town of Little Compton, in this state.

She went on to describe her own experience but as though reported to her by another visitor. The final paragraph gave vent to all the bitter irony so carefully repressed during face-to-face encounters.

> Should any person in this philanthropic age be disposed, from motives of curiosity, to visit the place, they may rest assured that traveling is considered quite safe in that part of the country, however improbable it may seem. The people of that region profess the Christian religion, and it is even said they have adopted some forms and ceremonies which they call worship. It is not probable, however, that they address themselves to poor Simmons's God. Their worship, mingling with the prayers of agony which he shrieks forth from his dreary abode, would make strange discord in the ear of that Almighty Being, in whose keeping sleeps the vengeance due to all his wrongs.

She went immediately to Newport, where the General Assembly was in session, not to address it in person, but to approach legislators who might seek her out to discuss funds for the proposed hospital. With each one she stressed the urgency of Abram Simmons's case. Eight months before, the town had promised to remove him to a hospital, yet nothing had been done. Surely the legislature could compel the town to act.

One legislator, a Mr. Updike, became fired with concern. He made an impassioned speech urging the assembly to take action and remove Simmons at once. Before a vote could be taken, however, a member from Little Compton rose and announced that the action proposed had come too late. Simmons was dead.

Though the legislature was shocked into appointing a committee of investigation to inquire into other cases of maltreatment, no appropriation was made for enlarging the hospital. Mr. Butler's donation might well be lost by default. Appeals to the conscience of legislators were too often ineffectual. Could they perhaps be shamed into action?

There was another pitiable case in Little Compton, a violently insane young girl who had often tried to commit suicide by cutting her throat, setting fire to her clothes, jumping into a well. Nothing could be done for Abram Simmons, but this girl with proper hospital care might still be helped. True, there was no hospital in Rhode Island, but there was in Massachusetts. Dorothea wrote to her friend, George Emerson, and arrangements were made for the girl's admission to the McLean Asylum in Charlestown. She provided clothes for the girl and accompanied her personally on the eighty mile trip to Boston. George Emerson met them at the train and took them to McLean. Dorothea made certain the deficiencies of Rhode Island as compared with Massachusetts were well publicized.

Wounded pride proved a more effective stimulus to action than a wounded conscience. Before the six months were up Mr. Butler's donation was more than matched. A large addition was made to the Dexter Hospital in Providence, and the new institution was renamed Butler Hospital. Dr. Isaac Ray, whose work Dorothea had commended on her visit to the Insane Hospital in Augusta, Maine, was to become for many years its eminent and highly successful head, superintending the building of the hospital and its opening in 1847.

Some years later Dorothea Dix was receiving guests in a hotel room. One gentleman remained after the others had gone. She remained standing, expecting him to leave.

"Would you please sit down?" he requested. He introduced himself as Alexander Duncan. He had married the niece and heiress of Cyrus Butler. "How," he asked curiously, "did you manage what no one else was ever able to do, get Mr. Butler to make a contribution to a public cause?"

She told him the story. It was no superior persuasion on her part, she was careful to explain, merely a statement of fact which had aroused the humanitarian concern which was latent in every human being.

"Thank you, Miss Dix. You have aroused mine also. I would like to give twenty-five thousand dollars to whatever public institution you think could make the best use of it."

She had a ready answer to that. Why didn't he buy land adjoining the Butler Hospital and make the addition that was again so badly needed? He did so, and at last, after many years, she had the satisfaction of seeing her work in Rhode Island really completed.

6

"I encounter nothing," Dorothea wrote George Emerson on November 13, 1843, "which a determined will, created by the necessities of the cause I advocate, does not enable me to vanquish."

She was traveling by the Steamer *Chautauqua* on Lake Erie, bound for a place she called Barcelona, during ten weeks of uninterrupted travel which had taken her from one end to the other of the state of New York. Traveling, she continued, had been indescribably bad, chiefly plunging through mud sloughs in carriages and lumber wagons, or breaking roads through snowdrifts in sleds, in all sorts of weather except sunny skies, journeying both day and night in order to count a little progress. "I have about sixteen or eighteen hundred miles more to go over," she added, "then I return to Utica to meet the trustees of the State Hospital."

George Emerson and his family had become increasingly valued among her friends. She visited his home on her infrequent trips to Boston. She prized his counsels, listened to his cautions about overwork, though she never heeded them. "Your pleasant voice," she wrote after one such visit, "rest in your cheerfulness, always does me good. You seem to be of those really happy." In another letter she confessed, "You have taken the place of Dr. Channing as guiding friend in my respect and affection."

She had needed guidance and support this year. Sensitivity to others' suffering had been honed to sharpness by personal grief. Her brother Charles had perished with his ship off the coast of Africa. She felt more than ever alone.

In January of 1844 she was back in Albany writing her Memorial to the Legislature of New York. Much of her report was commendatory. The state had made liberal appropriations for its curative asylum at Utica. Her visits to Bloomingdale Asylum and to the Blackwell Island hospital resulted in only a few criticisms: insufficient attendants, lack of enough employment and outdoor exercise, architectural defects. She commended the almshouse at Bellevue and the farm schools on Long Island. Fortunately

New York laws prohibited the commitment of the insane or mentally deficient to prisons or jails.

But the fifty-two county almshouses she had visited, some of them several times, were another matter. Some, like Rensselaer at Troy, Schenectady, Franklin at Malone, she characterized as "excellent." Each of the fifty-two merited a separate paragraph, many of them whole pages, in the memorial, and its good and bad features were presented in detail. Every county house had its "crazy house," "crazy cells," "crazy dungeons," or "crazy cellars." In some she found insane and mentally deficient women exposed to vice becoming mothers "without consciousness of maternity." Again and again she reported confinement by chains and heavy iron balls, unlighted and unheated cells, exposure to frost and cold, shocking neglect.

Her first visit to the almshouse at Albany on a severely cold November day consumed four full pages of the printed report. They presented a grim graphic picture.

> Inquiring of the master who held charge of the establishment the number of the insane then in close confinement, I was answered, "There are plenty; somewhere about twenty."
>
> "Will you let me see them?"
>
> "No, you can't, they're naked, in the crazy cellar."
>
> "Are all in the same apartment, then?"
>
> "No, not all, but you can't see them."
>
> "Excuse me, but I must see the women's apartment. It is to learn the condition of the insane that I have come."
>
> At length a direction was given, and I was conducted by the mistress of the house into a court-yard . . . entered an apartment not clean, not ventilated, and over-heated. . . . several females, decently dressed . . . hot air, foul with noisome vapors. . . . I asked to be conducted to the dungeons.
>
> "Dungeons?" repeated the attendant, eyeing me closely.

"Yes, I have heard there are dungeons here; I am in haste. Oblige me by losing no time. . . ." We emerged on a yard enclosed by a high board fence and opening on the left upon still another enclosed space, surrounding a wooden building. . . . at length induced the turnkey to produce his keys . . . ascending a flight of steps found myself in a passage on each side of which were "the dungeons" or cells . . . totally dark and unventilated, no provision for drying or warming them . . . horrible stench. . . . I affirm that the dungeons of Spielberg or Chillon, and the prisons of the Court of the Inquisition before their destruction, afforded no more heartrending spectacles than the dungeons of the Albany alms-house. . . .

Turning from the dungeons, the keeper said, "Come to the crazy-cellar, you'll get noise enough there." . . . Reaching the cellar, the keeper entered and "for the sake of exercise" began knocking one down, and so went on to rouse the whole company; there were twelve or fourteen men here, sufficiently clothed for decency, some extended on the floor, others chained to their beds.

But on a second visit a year later she had found a new overseer, and, considering the very crowded state of the house, a surprising degree of orderliness and cleanliness had been secured. There were bunks, beds, and bed clothing in the dungeon cells, improved accommodations in the "crazy cellar." Yet all such measures, while beneficial, were but palliatives, not cures of a virulently evil system.

"There is but one remedy," she asserted, "prevent the possibility of such monstrous abuses by providing hospitals and asylums where vigilant inspection and faithful care shall protect and minister to those who, in losing reason, can no longer protect themselves."

The New York Memorial was only partially successful. Though it recommended the building of at least four new hospitals, the legislature voted only a larger appropriation for the asylum in Utica. Dorothea was not discouraged. Like the seventy sent out on a mission to Galilean towns, she had already shaken the dust of one locale from her garments and moved on to others. Indeed, long before the New York Memorial had been submitted, she was at work in New Jersey, Pennsylvania, and even other states.

On December 22, 1843, she wrote Anne from Lexington, Kentucky: "I left Boston in September; visited en route the prisons on Long Island and in New York City, also those of New Jersey, and duly reached Philadelphia. There and at Harrisburg I was detained a fortnight. Proceeding to Baltimore, I visited prisons there, and so on as far as Pittsburgh west. Thence to Cincinnati, where I arrived the last of October.

"The first of November I came to Kent, and have been laboriously traveling through the counties, collecting facts and information ever since, except a week which I took in Tennessee. The Legislature being in session in Nashville, I desired to do something for the state prison. This effected, I crossed the country by a rapid journey to Louisville, traveling by stage two days and nights. I proceed tomorrow to the northeast counties, if well enough. I have engaged lodgings in Frankfort, Kentucky, for January and February, and shall probably go to the south prisons after the Legislature rises in this state."

She was becoming widely publicized as a reformer, had often been written and spoken of as "the American Mrs. Fry." Her friend, Lydia Maria Child, called her the "God-appointed missionary to the insane." She was constantly being approached by persons and groups in many states to investigate conditions, and her mails were swamped with requests from individuals, physicians, ministers concerned with social problems. One such letter came, replete with "thees" and "thous" from Charlotte Freedland, a Quaker, of Salem, New Jersey. She had read the memorials to the legislatures of Massachusetts and New York. She could not believe that there were such appalling cases in New Jersey. Yet in her town's poorhouse was a man who had been chained by his leg for more than twenty years, and the only warmth in his cell was from a small stove pipe passing through one corner. Could not Miss Dix come and investigate conditions in New Jersey?

Miss Dix could and would. In fact, she had already begun her crusade in New Jersey in her usual quiet unconventional way. One day in July, 1844, on her way to the Eastern Penitentiary in Pennsylvania, she arrived in New York on the boat at six in the morning. There were several hours before her train left. She decided to board it in New Jersey. Leaving her trunk in charge of the baggage master of the Philadelphia cars, she crossed on the ferry to Jersey City. She addressed the first respectable man she saw on the street.

"How are the poor of your city provided for?" she asked. He proved to be an alderman, and they talked together for about twenty minutes. He directed her to the old jail nearby, and she examined its exterior. Then she looked about for a further source of information. Seeing a stately mansion in the neighborhood, she mounted the steps and rang the bell. A servant appeared. It was now a quarter past seven.

"Please," she said with a confident smile, "say to the master and mistress of the house that there is a stranger to see them — that is, if this early hour finds them disengaged."

She was ushered into the parlor. Presently a gentleman and a lady entered. She told them simply that she was on a journey, that the interval between the arrival of her boat and departure of the cars allowed her to inquire concerning the institutions of the city and state, but being a stranger she had looked for knowledge where the exterior of the dwelling announced that the occupants might well be acquainted with the state of the county almshouses and prisons and the condition of the insane.

"Ah!" The man's face lighted. "Then you are Miss Dix!"

There followed an hour and a half of earnest conversation. The gentleman was both knowledgeable about conditions of the poor and anxious for her to pursue her investigations. They parted most cordially. As she was about to enter the train he came rushing up, laden with documents. He offered to give her letters to the governor and other persons of influence. In the train Dorothea became the recipient of the conductor's solicitous attention.

"Fine man, Mr. Gilson," he said, ushering her to a seat. "Best mayor this city ever had. Always fair and wanting to do good."

New Jersey, yes. But first more journeys to the west. Snatches from letters to Anne, to the Emersons, weave the intricate web of her travels.

"August. Lancaster from Philadelphia. Overseer of the poor in bad health and temper. Changed mood when he learned my name. Went to poor house, stayed four hours. He asked me to write for their paper. I objected, 'No one would know me.' 'You are mistaken. Every man and woman in Lancaster, if not in our state, knows who you are.' Had to write. . . . York the following morning. Visited jail. Through all sixteen counties I see the best minds, physicians, lawyers, judges. . . . Stage for Gettysburg, saw jail. . . . Chambersburg, saw jail. . . . Stage for Bedford, 13½ hours hard riding. Poor horse. Set off a little past midnight to cross mountains, reached top of Alleghenies at daylight. Wagon to Somerset . . . stage, three hours to Mt. Pleasant. Had to leave at once because it went only once a week. Dreadful night's journey. . . . Waynooburgh . . . Washington . . . stage for Wheeling . . . 6 a. m. to Carsville, Ohio. Saw almshouse and jail, horrible. Wrote four pages. . . . Stage, Columbus . . . midnight . . . prison, hospital for insane, very welcome. Next day almshouse and asylum for blind. . . . Wrote twelve pages for the Court. . . . Wheeling. . . . Thirty-four hours without stop except to change horses. Saw jail. Wrote for paper, tired. Took boat on the Ohio, sixty miles . . . boat to Pittsburgh, arrived ten p. m. Prisons, jails, almshouse . . . Meadville . . . Erie . . . to Warren, no road, would take more than fifty miles horseback, cannot attempt that, had to take long route through New York by Jamestown."

"How to get to Franklin?" she wrote Harriett Hare, her friend in Philadelphia. "A skiff for sixty-nine miles down the Allegheny or a wagon without springs over a road for which I have no terms sufficiently graphic? Wagon rejected, I proceeded to the banks, where I discovered an old waterman, astride upon a drift log half under water, chewing a cud and whittling away on a pine stick. Hair uncombed, face unshaved. Took myself at two the following morning to this precious vehicle and after 19 hours steady travel found myself with the U. S. mails in Franklin, 39 miles from Warren. Such roads by which I reached the interior country! Four carriages broke down. Why the horses did not is a wonder. The last carriage I hired in Indiana to convey me to Ebersburg had seen hard service. I suggested to my driver to proceed with more care over the rocks, but he graciously responded he 'knowed how to drive my horse and bein' as he had a woman aboard he'd been a-comin' slow as —' His eloquence was abridged by the creaking of the springs. Down one came crushed and broken. A dilemma. There seemed to be no alternative for me but to walk to Ebersburg, five long miles, or spend the night in the forest. The last bright beams of the sun touched the tops of the gigantic trees. The faint notes of the lingering birds were heard at longer intervals when an equestrian appeared, came nigh, and paused to consider our disaster, but he did more. He had a fine lead horse and said, 'If the lady will walk a quarter of a mile we may borrow a saddle, and she is welcome to either of my horses.'

"It was no time for demurs. I walked to the log hut, a saddle was borrowed, the steed suffered me to mount, and we entered the first town of Cambria County at dark. I alighted at the hotel and took leave, sending my saddle home and later getting my luggage from the dilapidated vehicle."

7

She finished her investigations in Pennsylvania on November 4 and left immediately for eight weeks of intensive travel in New Jersey, one of the many states which as yet had no insane asylum. Here was a challenge even harder than any yet faced. Not only must the power of public taxation be evoked, but people must be aroused to such a degree of concern that they would be willing, even *glad*, to be taxed.

In 1839 a survey had been made of the idiotic, epileptic, and insane of the state, but nothing had been done since. The survey had reported three hundred and five insane persons and two hundred idiots, a number exceeding the total population of the state prison. In her own thorough investigation Dorothea found as many — and more. In January, 1845, she completed her "Memorial Soliciting a State Hospital for the Insane." As in the other memorials she detailed the conditions of the mentally ill in jails, prisons, almshouses, many in as cruel and debased confinement as any she had found in other states.

She told of a judge she had found lying on a small bed in a bare basement room, his gray locks tangled about his pillow. As a jurist he had been distinguished for uprightness, clearness, impartiality. Now, his mind gone, a pauper, helpless, pitiably aware of his lost mentality, he had first been confined in jail and chained "for safety," then, his frenzied state abating, consigned to this bare cubicle in the poorhouse to wither away. She told of a madman chained, naked, except for a straitjacket laced to impede the motion of his arms, now raging like an imprisoned tiger, now soothed into quietness. "We try in vain," said the kind-hearted mistress, "to have him comfortable; we can neither keep him clothed nor warmed; the stove is of no use, and he destroys at once whatever is put in for bedding, thrusting it through the opening in the floor." Yet, if placed in a hospital, commented Dorothea, he could at least be made comfortable, and the lives and comfort of others would not be endangered.

In addition to these detailed observations she described at length the work of Pinel in France, Tuke in England, Jacobi in Germany, who had proved the efficacy of hospitals in coping with mental disease. She quoted the leading American asylum superintendents on the excellent possibilities of recovery for patients under proper medical and moral treatment: Doctors Isaac Ray of Maine, Chandler of New Hampshire, Rockwell of Vermont, Brigham of Columbus, Woodward of Worcester, Earle of Bloomingdale.

Just the preceding October thirteen of such superintendents had met with Dr. Kirkbride in Philadelphia and organized the Medical Superintendents of American Institutions for the Insane, a milestone in the history of American psychiatry. All thirteen were men of experience who looked on mental disorder as illness related to general medicine and not an inexplicable, and therefore terrifying, phenomenon. At the time the ratio of mentally ill to the population of seventeen million was estimated as one to 977. In the country there were some twenty mental hospitals of sorts, only three, Ohio, Kent, and Indiana, west of the Alleghenies.

"Shall New Jersey be last of 'the Thirteen Sisters'," Dorothea ended her memorial, "to respond to the claims of humanity, and to acknowledge the demands of justice?"

It was presented to the legislature in Trenton in January, 1845 by Senator Joseph S. Dodd, one of her strongest supporters, who moved that the session take measures to effect the recommended reforms. A joint committee was appointed to consider the subject. A month later the committee reported favorably and recommended immediate action. It did not hurt the cause that during the intervening month the Salem county almshouse had burned to the ground, its inmates all rescued, though several of the insane paupers had been chained in their cells. It was a narrow escape from tragedy. But, as expected, some legislators grew wary at the prospect of raised taxes.

Now Dorothea's work really began. Her technique had already become established. Eagerly she studied the list of representatives, trying to assess each one's humanitarian or self-seeking proclivities, his courage or servility to public opinion. She never entered the halls of legislation, nor approached legislators in their homes or the lobbies. Through the influence of friends a small room or corner was set aside for her, perhaps in the library. Here legislators sought her out or were induced to come by her friends. Always she was careful not to injure her cause by compromising the prevailing standards of feminine delicacy. Her only exception to this rule was to occasionally invite fifteen or twenty legislators to the parlor of her hotel or boardinghouse for informal conversation. From the time the memorial was presented until the final vote she worked indefatigably, writing newspaper articles, holding continual interviews, gently arguing, urging, challenging.

The days after the favorable report of the committee were most dangerous of all. Legislators were casting anxious eyes toward their constituents, assessing chances for reelection. New taxation was inevitably a "hot potato," likely to burn one's hands. Now Dorothea worked to exhaustion, usually until after midnight. She must generate both light and heat, instruct, educate, kindle courage, inspire. Night after night her hotel parlor was filled with up to twenty men involving her in three or four hours of steady conversation.

"You cannot imagine the labor of conversing and convincing," she wrote Harriett Hare. "Last evening a rough country member, who had announced in the House that the 'wants of the insane in New Jersey were all humbug'

*View of Trenton Hospital in the time of
Dorothea Dix, taken from a daguerreotype.*

and who came to overwhelm me with arguments, after listening an hour and a half with wonderful patience to my details and to principles of treatment, suddenly moved into the middle of the parlor, and thus delivered himself: 'Ma'am, I bid you good-night! I do not want, for my part, to hear anything more; the others can stay if they want to. I am convinced; you've conquered me out and out; I shall vote for the hospital.' "

But all reactions were not so encouraging. "I do believe," she read a newspaper account of one member's speech, "that if Miss Dix had been paid five or six hundred dollars, and escorted over the Delaware or to Philadelphia, or even a thousand dollars and taken to Washington city, and, if you choose, enshrined in the White House, it would have been money well laid out. Now, I should like the whys and wherefores for a building 487 feet long and 80 feet wide, for, maybe, twenty lunatics."

Far worse, however, for her peace of mind was the legislator to be found in almost every assembly who would call her punctiliously that "heaven-sent angel of mercy" and then proceed to insist that "it becomes us, gentlemen, to be borne away by no childlike sensibility, no generous enthusiasm, no over-zeal nor haste to accomplish an acknowledged good . . . therefore I am constrained to oppose this project. . . ." She preferred to be thought impressive enough to warrant her complete removal from the scene cheap at a thousand dollars!

She waited in tortured suspense in her hotel room when the bill was brought to a vote. Her hands trembled as she tore open a note from Joseph Dodd.

"Senate Chamber, N. J. I am happy to announce to you the passage unanimously of the bill for the New Jersey State Lunatic Asylum."

Victory! An end to the crusade here? Hardly! Suddenly she was faced with a glorious creative opportunity. Would she advise concerning the site and plans for the new hospital? *Would* she! Inspection of outmoded and inadequate buildings, consultations with superintendents, study of numerous books and pamphlets, all had prepared her for this challenge. She had a vision of exactly what such an institution might be — a beautiful long stone building with white columns, welcoming portico, majestic dome. The interior? Bright airy rooms, wide corridors, comfortable furnishings, no chains, no bars. The site? A high hill with a long view of fields, perhaps a river, a cool restful grove of trees. Surely in such a place disturbed minds could find peace, if not restoration. In the following months, though continuing her further travels, she returned often to Trenton to pore over plans, consult with architects, visit possible sites, see finally the sod turned, the walls rise, the finished structure which was the fulfillment of her dreams.

So much was Trenton asylum a part of her very flesh and blood that she would always think of it as her "first born child."

It came near being a twin. Her "Memorial to the Legislature of Pennsylvania" was written and submitted in Harrisburg in February, 1845, less than a month after the one in New Jersey. It was one of the longest and most exhaustive of the dozen memorials she was to complete within the next few years, running to nearly sixty pages in very fine print. She reported in detail her visits to the fifty-eight counties of the state, twenty-one of which had poorhouses, the other thirty-seven farming out their paupers and insane at "the lowest rate for which they are bidden." The number of insane and mentally defective in the state was "at least twenty-three hundred." More than a thousand of these were in county prisons and poorhouses, the rest supported at home or on private charity. There was no state hospital in Pennsylvania but several private ones, including the Friends Hospital at Frankfort, the Blockley Division of the Philadelphia Almshouse, and the Pine Street Unit of the Pennsylvania Hospital, all taxed to the limit of their capacity.

She approved wherever possible, commending many in-

stitutions for cleanliness, well-conducted farms, comfort
for inmates, but was caustically and devastatingly critical
of their weaknesses. She found the same shocking neglect
and tortured restraint as in other states, with slight vari-
ations: two nude women coiled in wooden packing boxes;
a man in a "tranquilizing chair," limbs tightly bound, legs,
body, arms, shoulders, head, all closely confined, a quantity of broken ice, melting, flowing over his person, which,
though in some degree protected by a stiff cape and
though it was a very hot day, was deadly cold. "How
long?" "Four days." "What, day and night?" "No, at night
we take him off and strap him upon the bed." "How long
will you keep him so?" "Till he is quiet." She begged the
legislators to travel with her up and down their state.

"Weigh the iron chains, and shackles, and balls, and
ring-bolts, and bars, and manacles; breathe the foul atmosphere of those cells and dens; examine the furniture of
these dreary abodes; some for a bed have the luxury of a
truss of straw; and some have the cheaper couch, which
the hard, rough plank supplies! Examine their apparel.
The air of heaven is their only vesture. . . ."

But her most devastating condemnation was of the
prison and jail system, which not only incarcerated the
mentally ill without remedial treatment, but herded together every type of criminal or law breaker without distinction of age, color, sex, or degree of conduct. Of one
jail in Allegheny County she was most sharply critical.

"If it had been the deliberate purpose of the citizens of
Allegheny County to establish a school for the inculcation
of vice, and obliteration of every virtue, I cannot conceive
that any means they could have devised would more certainly have secured these results than those I found in full
operation in the jail last August."

Of other institutions in or near Pittsburgh she was most
commendatory: the Orphans' Asylum, the almshouse, the
Western Penitentiary. But her denunciation of the jail
shocked and aroused the city. A public meeting was

called, a committee appointed, a recommendation sent to the legislature for immediate action. The memorial also aroused statewide support, and on April 14, 1845, the legislature voted to establish a hospital to be located at Harrisburg. Here also her services were solicited in the choice of site and plans for the building.

Wrote James Lesley on April 17: "To Mr. Haldeman as well as the other commissioners your wishes will be *law*. If I thought you would deem me a flatterer I would not tell you that at the close of a most enthusiastic encomium on your disinterested humanity and incomparable energy, he declared that no man nor woman other than yourself, from Maine to Louisiana, could have passed the bill under the discouraging circumstances with which you had to contend."

Before the year was out Dorothea was promoting a movement for a second state hospital in western Pennsylvania.

So strong were her convictions concerning conditions in the prisons she had seen and the divergent principles governing their administration that she determined to express herself in writing. During the year she had visited the prison at Wethersfield, Connecticut, three times; at Auburn and Sing Sing, New York, twice; those in Massachusetts and Maryland several times; at Philadelphia and Trenton more than twenty times. Previously she had visited others at Thomaston, Maine, in Vermont, Delaware, New Jersey. She was pleased with much of what she saw, but personal observations, consultations with wardens, interviews and correspondence with dozens of prisoners had given her invaluable information to share.

In September she returned to Boston to visit Anne and the Emersons and to discuss with Horace Mann and others her views concerning prison reform. Of the two systems of administration, the "separate" or Philadelphia system, which advocated the separation of prisoners both day and night, and the so-called "Auburn" system, where prisoners mingled during the day, Dorothea preferred the former. She had seen too many juveniles listening greedily to gray-headed, hardened criminals and absorbing lessons in crime techniques which would doubtless be put into practice on their release. There should be houses of refuge for juvenile offenders. She and Horace Mann were agreed that the purpose of imprisonment should be regeneration, and that moral and religious training should be a prime requisite. Wardens should be educated, men of high character, and not subject to political appointment or manipulation. She believed in mild forms of discipline, as at Sing Sing, definitely *no lashes*. She deplored the granting of unconditional and often hasty pardons. Let the periods of sentence be shortened, except for willful murder, but let them be served out. And the granting of pardons should be the prerogative of a special court, not of one elected official. Above all, the public should be educated in receiving the former prisoner once he had paid his price.

"You want to know why so many of us go to prison a second time?" wrote A. B., whom she had met in Cambridge prison, in a letter which might easily have been written more than a hundred years later. "We can't get work. The public gives us no encouragement to reform. They shun our company. Convicts would be reduced a half if proper steps were taken to assist them to get work."

Assembling all her facts, Dorothea wrote her *Remarks on Prisons and Prison Discipline* and sent it to the printer. She stressed humane treatment without relaxation of proper discipline: "The prisoner has a right in prison to comfortable clothing, wholesome food, pure air, and a free use of water, equally with a humane discipline and ample means of moral instruction. Government, securing these, may claim and expect in return diligence, subordination, and rigid compliance with the rules."

She stressed above all crime prevention. "It would be greatly more worthy of a rising nation, valuing itself on its rapid growth, political freedom and the diffusion of common school education, to expend more money, and extend a more vigilant care over the young, who, neglected in manners and morals, throng our cities and large towns, than to vaunt itself upon the exceeding excellence of its institutions."

8

"I have traveled over ten thousand miles in the last three years," Dorothea wrote Mrs. Rathbone early in 1845. "I have visited 18 penitentiaries, 100 county jails and houses of correction, more than 500 almshouses and other institutions, besides hospitals and houses of reform. I have been so happy to promote and secure the establishment of six hospitals for the insane, several county poorhouses, and several jails on a reformed plan."

The hospitals were Worcester, greatly enlarged; Butler in Providence, practically refounded; Trenton and Harrisburg, her own creations; Utica, doubled in size. Back in 1843 she had also memorialized the Provincial Parliament of Canada, resulting in a new hospital for the insane in western Canada.

Yet her travels were only beginning. While waiting for the bill to pass in New Jersey she had made a canvass of Kentucky and had been before the legislature in Tennessee. Seven days after the passage of the bill in New Jersey she was writing Anne from a steamer near Charleston, South Carolina.

"I designed to use the spring and summer chiefly in examining the jails and poorhouses of Indiana and Illinois, but learned the travel would be difficult, on account of mud and rains. This decided me to go down the Mississippi to examine the hospitals of New Orleans, and, returning, to see the state prison of Louisiana at Baton Rouge, of Mississippi at Jackson, of Arkansas at Little Rock, of Missouri at Jefferson City, and of Illinois at Alton.

Then I resolved to see the state institutions of Georgia, Alabama, and South Carolina. Though this has proved excessively fatiguing, I rejoice that I have carried out my purpose. . . . Do not keep my letters," she charged in a stern postscript. "I will continue to write only on this condition."

Anne gave her promise and of course intended to keep it — but not just yet. She took too much pleasure in rereading them again and again, difficult though they were to decipher. The small chest in which she treasured them grew fuller and fuller, fragrant with the bits of pressed flowers, herbs, evergreens which her friend loved to enclose. They would still be in existence, faded, yellowed, brittle, over a hundred years later.

It was Anne who sent Dorothea whatever wardrobe replacements she might need on a journey. Her demands were simple. She traveled with only one modest valise containing her plain gray dresses, changes of white collars and cuffs, one simple black dress for special occasions. On long trips she sent a small trunk ahead, but it was more likely to be filled with books and gifts for the households she intended to visit than clothes.

Anne scanned each letter anxiously for news of Dorothea's health. It was incredible that one who had been so many years an invalid could fulfill a grueling schedule, undergo difficulties both physical and mental which would have fazed the endurance of a Hercules. All her friends worried lest she succumb to sickness in some lonely place, and she often did. She had hemorrhages again and again. She was often prostrated with malarial fever, and not always in the homes of friends. "Her system became actually saturated with malaria," commented Dr. Nichols of the Bloomingdale Asylum. Yet, though her body might demand respite, her indomitable spirit never yielded. She was so completely dedicated to her cause that health had become of secondary importance.

"The weather has been severe and stormy," she once wrote from Canada, "but in proportion as my own discomfort has increased, my conviction of necessity to search into the wants of the friendless and afflicted has deepened. If I am cold, they too are cold; if I am weary, they are distressed; if I am alone, they are abandoned."

Not that she belittled the importance of health. That would have jeopardized the cause. But she had learned to economize her strength. She accepted no purely social engagements. She kept her journals, business affairs, and correspondence in perfect order and so avoided nervous tension. When she was forced to postpone travel because of a flood, washout, or other hindrance, she would take to her bed and store up sleep, sometimes almost around the clock, to make up for the all-night travel in jerking trains or rough wagons jolting over corduroy roads. She nourished her soul on daily prayer and communion with God, and on a keen delight in all the beauties of nature. If her body rebelled at the usual fare of corn bread, bacon and greens served at makeshift taverns, her soul was well nourished both on daily prayer and on her keen delight in the new botanical specimens she was forever finding.

True, travel was incredibly difficult, whether on land or water. Riverboats on the Ohio, Tennessee, Mississippi, and Missouri were manned by bold, often rowdy crews, who treated floods, rocks, sandbars with equal bravado, or drove the steam to bursting point the moment a rival steamboat came in sight. More than once Dorothea was sure the engines were going to explode. Progress was delayed by loose propellers, broken paddle wheels, hours of standstill on sandbars. The tiny suffocating cabins were infested with mosquitoes and flies and, occasionally, rats. The diet of salt pork, hominy, sorghum, rice, beans, black coffee was both monotonous and unhealthful. Sickness was prevalent. After her first experiences with the available medical remedies on steamers — quinine, laudanum, whiskey, turpentine — she supplied herself with medicine and salves, bandages, baskets of fresh fruit, as much for other ailing travelers as for herself.

While letters to friends were usually mere itineraries of her journeys, an occasional phrase or sentence cast a revealing light on such difficulties. "Cholera on board." . . . "Stuck fast on a mud-bar ten miles below Vicksburg." . . . "Up again from malarial fever, off for Jackson, Mississippi tonight."

The patrons were a motley crowd, ranging from northern traders and southern planters, often with their fashionably dressed wives, to flashy adventurers and gamblers. Though she was almost invariably the only single woman on board and an object of natural curiosity, she elicited only decorum and respect both on board the steamers and on visits to local institutions whenever there was a stopover of a half day for loading or unloading cargo.

"I feared," she wrote George Emerson, "when first I came to the western country that to travel here alone would certainly be to compromise my character as well as influence. I hesitated, for I think no woman who has a proper sense of self-respect will defy public opinion and established usage. But every place I am treated with respect, objects promptly and sharply advanced. I am met with the most flattering attention."

Difficulties on land were even more formidable. Railroads touched only the main points, and even they, with their dust, soot, hard seats, jolting motions, frequently over wooden tracks, were little better than stages and wagons. To reach the outlying towns and villages she traveled on the few lines of stagecoaches, hired carriages or lumber wagons, driven often by Negroes or poor whites rendered reckless by too generous dosages of whiskey. Roads, if they could be called such, varied with the seasons. In the spring the endless stretches of clay lands in the south and west became expanses of sticky mud into which wheels sank axle-deep. There were few bridges over creeks and rivers, and the fords were often swollen by rains. Roads which were not pure mud were of corduroy, so rough that the motion of the hard, iron-bound wheels pounded against the brain and set the teeth chattering. Not infrequently a wheel fell off or an axle broke, and they were delayed for hours.

After a few experiences of this kind and finding her drivers often ill-equipped for emergencies, she fell into the habit of carrying along a small bag of repair tools — hammer, wrench, nails, screws, a coil of rope, straps of stout leather, a can of axle grease. Then while the driver was repairing damages, often with her tools, she would sit in the carriage or on a stump by the roadside and read the latest book on mental ailments or the annual reports of hospital physicians, or scribble a few lines to Joseph or Anne or George Emerson.

"Jail to jail, prison to poorhouse, through almost trackless forests, over mountains, through swamps. Often the way lies through a wilderness, traced by slight cuts on trees, houses fourteen or twenty miles apart, if they can be called houses, single rooms of logs and a stone chimney. Four nights out of nine able to find such rest as I might in two chairs, wide chinks between logs. Cold. Far from well. Finally I discharged a horse, driver, and took the stage for eighty miles. . . ."

It was to Joseph that she wrote of another travel sequence involving several modes of transportation. "My plan for going through Tennessee was frustrated by a fall of rain. The coach in which I was to have left Nashville was replaced by a wagon without springs or seats. The stage broke down. I took a hired wagon for Louisville and a boat to Pittsburgh. . . . We had a narrow escape from loss of life and boat three nights since. The pilot at the wheel fell into a fit, and the boat went berserk, striking rocks and breaching the wheelhouse. A boy with the pilot was too terrified to give assistance. The mate dashed for the pilot house but could not enter, the pilot having fallen against the door. We were detained some hours to repair the damage."

October, 1845, found her journeying into the back country of Kentucky from Frankfort, using equally varied means of transportation: train, stage, carriage, lumber wagon. Occasionally she crossed over the state boundaries to inspect the prison at Jeffersonville, Indiana, or Cairo, Illinois. The continuous labor was taking its toll, not only in increasing weariness but in her appearance.

"How old may you be?" asked one country woman with ingenuous frankness. When Dorothea told her, the woman shook her head sadly. "Well, now, I should not think you was that old, but it looks like age is breakin' on you powerful fast and you've had a mighty heap of trouble."

In January, 1846, she submitted her "Memorial to the Legislature of Kentucky" soliciting an appropriation for the hospital for the insane at Lexington and urging the necessity of a new hospital in the Green River country. While commending the officials of the present hospital, she enumerated in great detail its building defects: too small and ill-equipped kitchen, lack of bathing rooms, insufficient water, defective laundry, no infirmary. She stressed the importance of adequate farm land not only for its therapeutic value in the treatment of patients but for the healthful and financial benefits of fruits and vegetables derived therefrom (the latter a potent argument for tax-minded legislators). She quoted Dr. Luther Bell and a dozen other superintendents on the importance of treating insanity in its earliest stages. "All experience shows that insanity seasonably treated is as certainly curable as a cold or fever. Recovery is the rule; permanent disease the exception."

The memorial was accompanied by a review of jails, prisons and almshouses in all the forty-four counties which she had visited. Her description of the state penitentiary at Frankfort included accurate dimensions of buildings, rooms, cells, yards; assessment of furnishings, ventilation, labor, punishments, diet, clothing, health, water, moral and religious instruction. Her comments on the forty-four jails were equally detailed, commendatory when possible, caustically critical when necessary.

"The county jails of our country, with few exceptions,

are seats of misery and schools of vice. . . . Franklin
County Jail is one of the best, if not the very best built
I have seen in the State. . . . The visitor finds two expen-
sive and massive man cages! I had supposed we had,
at this period of civilization, outlived the iron cage of
dungeons! . . . I have faith in the improvement of all these
prisons."

Again success! The Kentucky Legislature appropriated
funds for new wings at the hospital at Lexington and for a
new asylum in the Green River country.

Yet before the vote she was off again, this time for points
farther south. As often happened, friends prepared the
way for her. A letter from Mr. Butler, a member of the
Kentucky Legislature, to Dr. Mercer in New Orleans announced her coming.

"She is endowed with superior talents enlarged by liberal learning. She is allied to persons of the highest
influence and station, possessed of an independent fortune and all she is and all she has is with determined
benevolence dedicated to the cause of philanthropy."

From New Orleans she went to Mobile, then took outer
passage up the Alabama 260 miles to Montgomery, then to
Tuskegee, Columbus, Macon, and Milledgeville, Georgia,
investigating institutions all the way. In Georgia she secured an appropriation for a prison library and promised to
return next year. Augusta . . . Savannah . . . then by boat to
Charleston, where she made a survey of hospitals and jour-
neyed to the state hospital in Columbia. Back again
through Georgia and Alabama to New Orleans and up the
Mississippi and the Arkansas to Little Rock. As always on
these boat or stage trips, she visited jails and workhouses
while other passengers were taking their meals, cargoes
were being loaded and unloaded, or the horses were being
changed.

To her delight she found most of the southern prisons of
good construction, clean, ventilated, and well managed.
As for care of the insane, the same misconceptions con-

cerning the nature and treatment of insanity existed here as in the North. While many of the states recognized their responsibility and had established hospitals, all were overcrowded and understaffed. In the rural areas the deranged were usually confined at home or "farmed out" to the lowest bidder at the town's expense. However, the rate of insanity was less here than in the North, partly because of the large population of Negroes, who were far less prone to mental derangement than whites.

She spent the summer in states bordering the Mississippi and Ohio Rivers, visiting prisons and almshouses in Indiana, Illinois, Ohio, and Tennessee, spending her energies without stint. How could one take time to rest when so many were in need? One day in September she was visiting the hospital in Columbus after a strenuous survey of prisons and almshouses when all at once she collapsed. There followed weeks of fever with violent inflammation of the lungs. Sickness could not have come at a worse time. She was working on memorials to the legislatures of both Illinois and Tennessee. Delay might mean postponement of action by those states for a year. She had planned to go south again and make surveys of Alabama, Mississippi, and North Carolina. For the first time the spiritual uplift which she had found in times of illness deserted her. She was resentful, impatient. The fact that Dr. Awl, the skilled physician at the Columbus hospital, sternly prescribed complete rest without serious study or writing aggravated the frustration. She was no longer the gentle, timid invalid who had lain contentedly in the lap of Rathbone solicitude. At the end of eight long weeks she was moved to Cincinnati to the home of friends, Mr. and Mrs. Charles Stetson.

"I could not sit up for one hour at a time," she wrote Anne. "Now I sit up most of the day, can walk below stairs unassisted. I'm so changed and reduced that you could not recognize me." For once she yielded to discouragement and made confession in a poem:

My robe of life is travel worn
And dusty with the dusty way,
I have the marks of many a storm
And marks of many a toilsome day —
The morning shower, the damp night dews
Have lent their dark, discoloring hues.

Yet the letter ended on a cheerful note. "I do not regret having come. On the contrary I am thankful for having attempted all that I have done. Heaven has greatly blessed my labors, and I feel truly and more that a leading Providence defines my path in the dark valleys of the world."

The discouragement was short-lived. In December she was again on the road, and on January 16, 1847 her Memorial was presented to the Legislature of Illinois at Springfield, resulting in a bill passed in March creating a hospital for the insane at Jacksonville. Already she had carried her crusade into Indiana, Georgia, Missouri, Alabama, Virginia, South Carolina, North Carolina, Maryland, Ohio, Michigan, Arkansas. Between June, 1843 and August, 1847 she had traveled thirty thousand miles, from Canada to the Gulf of Mexico, west to the Mississippi and beyond. It became her habit to work from late autumn till spring in the south, then as the weather became hot, to turn north. She once made a list of the places she had visited in twenty months between 1845 and 1847. It began: "Boston, Worcester, Norwich, New York, Brooklyn, Flatbush, Bloomingdale, Newark, Trenton, Philadelphia, Salem, Harrisburg, Lancaster, Baltimore, Harper's Ferry, Cumberland, Nasontown, Brownsville, Pittsburgh, Wheeling, Marietta, Cincinnati . . ." For three long closely written pages the list continued, mentioning 411 cities and towns she had visited, some many times.

Providing suitable hospitals for the insane was the chief but by no means the sole outlet for her zeal. She was almost equally concerned with promoting the welfare of prisoners she was constantly encountering. A letter from the warden of Michigan State Prison highlighted one of the services she took great delight in rendering.

"Resolved that Miss D. L. Dix is entitled to the thanks of the Prison officers and the gratitude of the convicts for her liberal donation to the Prison library of upwards of 160 volumes of valuable books and several hundred tracts, together with several numbers of the Journal of the Prison Discipline Society."

A similar letter of thanks came from the penitentiary in Frankfort, to which she had sent books bought in Louisville. Seven large windows had been installed in the sleeping apartments, the letter continued, as she had suggested, and some of the cells were now tolerably comfortable. The governor had not acted on old man McGuire. It was often the undeserving who were pardoned. The Bible class now had forty members. The warden hoped that sometime he might be in a position to put into practice her views on prison discipline. The people needed to be aroused, as only she could do.

The bout of illness had taught Dorothea a lesson. In the summer of 1847 she went to Oakland for a rest with Mrs. Channing. It was good to be back in the familiar home again. The family of Dr. Joseph Hare of Philadelphia were nearby, adding to her enjoyment.

"I wish you and Sarah could spend a week on the island," she wrote her brother Joseph, who had been married two years before. He was planning to move into a house of his own and wanted to borrow some articles of furniture. Of course he could have some to use. There was a large mahogany table at the Channings' and some tea trays. At Mrs. Hilliard's on Pinckney Street there was a wash sink with two sets of ewers and basins.

While at Oakland she received a letter from Laura Bridgman, the deaf-blind mute whom Samuel Gridley Howe was teaching with such success. Written in neat slanting capitals, it spelled joyous release from a prison more grimly isolated than all of the hundreds Dorothea had visited.

"My dear Miss Dix. How is your health now. I wish you a verry happy morning. It is a great while since I saw you.

Miss Wight is my excellent teacher for almost nine years.
. . . I should like to have you come to see me verry much
this summer, and receive a long letter from you. I rejoice
that you are so willing to make sacrifices to do good to the
poor. . . ."

Dorothea was delighted. She felt again the small eager
hands exploring her features, creating an image which
must have endured all these years. The child actually remembered her! Dorothea had seen many deaf and dumb
persons, some blind as well, often confined indiscriminately with "idiots" and insane persons. On one trip to
Boston that summer she visited Dr. Howe's school, had a
joyous reunion with Laura, met his beautiful and brilliant
wife, who had been Julia Ward of New York, discussed
with Dr. Howe his crusade for the more enlightened treatment and training of idiots in Massachusetts. Dorothea
endorsed his plans with enthusiasm. She could hardly
wait to suggest its possibilities to other states.

She visited George Emerson and his family, welcomed
as usual with far more eager acceptance than in the homes
of most of her relatives. With only a few families did she
feel so at home — brother Joseph's, the Rathbones', the
Joseph Hares' of Philadelphia, Mrs. Torrey's, and of
course Anne's. Dear faithful Anne, who gave so much and
received so little! The letters Dorothea found time to write
her were hastily scribbled snatches, almost illegible. Yet
Anne's letters revealed only concern, affection, pride,
never reproach or jealousy.

"My dear Miss Dix . . . Our minister spoke of you in the
pulpit last Sunday, and my heart leaped!"

"You, my dear friend, have created for yourself a happiness which goes with you, is inseparable from your existence. You are the only person I know who is not in some
respects to be pitied."

"No matter how hurried and illegible your writing, it is
a pleasant study to find your words. . . . I wish the silk sack
were a robe of ermine. It would not be too good."

Visits with Anne meant rest, relaxation, self-indulgence, and there was no time for these. Boston was no longer a quiet haven for recuperation. It was a power house for stoking energies, acquiring information. There were consultations with Doctors Bell and Butler, always her mentors, interviews with Sumner and Mann and Howe, discussions of new plans with George Emerson, such as she was having now. And the plan she had just outlined was the boldest and most ambitious she had yet conceived.

"You see?" Excitement had turned the blue-gray eyes under the high strong brows a brilliant black. "Insanity is a national, as well as a state problem. It's just as much the responsibility of the whole nation as education and public improvements. All over the west I've heard them talking about these schemes for the transfer of public lands to states for these two purposes. Henry Clay of Kentucky and Thomas Benton, senator from Missouri, have been ardent promoters of such measures. Why should not such a grant be made for the benefit of the indigent insane of all states? Think what the proceeds from the sale of, say, five million acres of public lands can do if set apart for a perpetual fund for the care of the mentally ill!"

George Emerson's heavy eyebrows lifted in startled arcs. "Five million acres! My dear Miss Dix, do you realize what a territory — "

"I do," she returned calmly. "Yet it's a small amount compared with the more than 134 million acres which had already been granted for purposes of development by 1845, and even smaller compared with the thousand million acres still unassigned."

"But — " the scholarly hand sweeping up over forehead and balding head forced the eyebrows still higher — "have you considered the difficulties? It's no longer the states alone who are laying claim to these lands for education and improvements. Congress is being besieged by speculators, greedy adventurers, railroads, private development companies, all vying with each other for these fat, juicy plums, and all having powerful inducements to offer their senators and representatives in Washington."

"I know." Her dark eyes remained steady. "And why shouldn't I join this grasping horde and plead for the poor and helpless, so they won't be left out? Oh, I can foresee all the difficulties. I can offer no votes, no bribes, nothing but the opportunity of helping the unfortunate. But I am used to facing such obstacles."

George Emerson regarded the lifted head, the firm lips, the blazing eyes with mingled awe, admiration, and deep concern. He opened his mouth to protest, "But — your health!" then closed it again. The friends of Dorothea Dix had long since learned that it was useless to protest once she had made up her mind.

Sometimes, as now, George Emerson attempted to appraise this woman who at the age of forty had risen from chronic invalidism to superhuman feats of achievement. A fanatic? Yes, if fanaticism was utter selfless zeal and dedication to a cause; no, if it also embraced intolerance and bigotry. An eccentric? Doubtless she would be dubbed so a hundred years later. But was not human progress achieved largely through the creativity of eccentrics, those who dared to differ from the norm — Socrates, Augustine, Columbus, Copernicus, Jesus?

He well knew her faults, but, as her biographer Francis Tiffany was to comment shrewdly many years later, powers which had proved faults in a more restricted sphere had now become virtues. The persistency of will which had once been stubbornness was the unflinching compulsion which inspired such incredible acts of courage. The reticence which had defeated her yearning for affection and intimacy now enabled her to respect confidences, to defy tradition and convention with an armor of dignified aloofness. The consuming religious fervor which, without outlet, had been self-destructive, was the spiritual dynamic from which miracles were being made.

"More power to you," said George Emerson with devout humility. Of course there was no stopping her. One might as well try to halt the sun in its restless journey across the sky.

9

The land grant was a shining goal high above the horizon. But there were also lesser heights to climb.

Leaving Boston in the fall of 1847, she visited state prisons in Albany, on Blackwell's Island, in Trenton, in Philadelphia. In October she wrote Anne that she was sending her chestnuts from Washington's Mount Vernon, that she had no cough but her side was still painful. In November she was in Nashville, settled for the winter in a commodious apartment for which she paid, including fire, lights, candles, use of the drawing room, and board, $8.75 a week. Here she assembled her notes, the result of previous travels through the state, and wrote her "Memorial, To the Honorable, the General Assembly of the State of Tennessee." As usual, she prepared to work through prominent officials, first presenting letters of introduction to Governor Neill S. Brown. On December 14 the memorial was submitted to the legislature, and 4,000 copies were ordered printed.

"A hearing has been secured for you before both branches," she was told by a sympathetic legislator. "The session will be held at night in the Hall of the House."

"Oh, no!" she swiftly demurred, explaining that it was her custom to remain in the background, providing the information but depending on responsible officials for all public presentations.

"But you must! The meeting is all arranged, and the governor himself will present you to the body."

Dorothea continued to remonstrate. Except in prisons

and reform schools, she rarely spoke to more than a dozen persons at once. Her aversion to publicity was almost an obsession. Moreover, the spectacle of a woman addressing a public body, especially in this conservative South, might well jeopardize the whole crusade. But the legislator was insistent. She agreed with the utmost reluctance.

Certainly the experience was a novel one for the legislature of any state, and no doubt her appearance aroused initial prejudice. But it was soon dispelled. This was no bold female libertarian like the notorious Mary Wollstonecraft or Harriet Martineau or Fanny Wright, not a protagonist of that embryo movement soon to be known as Women's Rights. She was a modest, dignified, earnest advocate of a cause which some of their most respected members obviously approved. She presented facts forcibly and clearly, with gentle but persuasive intensity, and in a voice so rich, sweet, perfect in enunciation that it cast a spell over the most resistant listener. With succinct clarity she detailed the defects in the present state hospital: its construction, location, incapacity to accommodate a fourth of the state's ten to twelve hundred insane, epileptics, and idiots; its damp, cold, unventilated cells; its defective kitchen and laundry, lack of bathrooms, cisterns, wells, decent water, recreational and occupational facilities; its incredibly insufficient staff. She gave specific suggestions for a farm site and structure which would embody the most advanced ideas of science and urged the drafting of a measure establishing such an institution. Her appeal was practical rather than emotional. Only briefly in this memorial did she attempt to arouse sympathy by recounting harrowing details.

> Were I to recount the 100th part of the shocking scenes of sorrow, suffering, abuse, and degradation to which I have been witness — searched out in jails, in poorhouses, in pens and block-houses, in caves, in cages and cells, in dungeons and cellars; men and women in chains, frantic, bruised, lacerated, and debased, your souls would grow

sick at the horrid recital. Yet have all these been witnessed, and for successive years shocking facts have been patiently investigated. And why? In order to solicit and procure a remedy for such heart-rending troubles — the only remedy, the establishment of well constructed, curative hospitals.

Fortunately the Tennessee Legislature contained men of unusual ability and intelligence. One of her most loyal supporters was John Bell, who was later to become a powerful ally in pressing her legislation in Congress. She remained in Nashville several weeks, holding interviews, helping to frame a bill, despairing when it lost, hopeful when it was reconsidered, devoutly thankful when on February 5, 1848 it was approved, with $40,000 appropriated for the purchase of 100 acres of land and a building large enough to accommodate 250 patients. Subsequently the amount was raised to $75,000.

As usual after such a victory, she was showered with embarrassing and unwelcome honors. Twenty-five women of Nashville, "moved by admiration of her disinterested and persevering philanthropy so honorable to their sex" and "anxious of seeing in a permanent and pleasing form a countenance expressive at once of feminine delicacy and heroic sensibility and strength, compassion, and courage," begged that Miss Dix would sit for her likeness to Mr. Hall, a young American sculptor, "whose genius and skill in his beautiful art have been successfully exhibited in the busts of some of our distinguished citizens." Kindly but firmly Miss Dix declined. She wanted to live only in their memory and in the good which God might enable her to do. However, she could not prevent the legislature from passing a Resolution of Thanks or refuse its presentation, beautifully inscribed and framed.

Resolved, by this General Assembly of the State of Tennessee
That the thanks of this General Assembly and of the

People of Tennessee are due and are hereby most respectfully tendered to Miss D. L. Dix for her very valuable
efforts bestowed on a project to establish an institution for
the better security, comfort, and improvement of those
unfortunate classes of our community known as idiots and
lunatics and that her disinterested benevolence, sublime
charity, and unmixed philanthropy shall engage alike the
gratitude and admiration of our State.

Such tributes were frequent and unavoidable. A similar
resolution was unanimously adopted by the legislature of
Alabama in 1847. That same year the Society for the Moral
Improvement of Prisoners in the Netherlands sent her a
diploma of honorary membership. Her publications on
prisons in America, wrote John S. Mollet of Amsterdam,
had been very useful in helping to change the system in
his country. Even her sex, which she considered such a
liability, was the subject of one personal encomium.

"You as a woman have a great advantage over us," wrote
Dr. Francis Lieber, the eminent German publicist who
had been her friend in Boston and was now her ardent
supporter in South Carolina, "for with the firmness, courage, and strength of a male mind you unite the advantages
of a woman. Savarin, at the head of the French police, told
Napoleon, with reference to Madame de Cayler, that he
could not master the woman. This was in a bad cause; but
the same holds true in a good. You do not excite the same
opposition; no one can suspect you of ambitious party
views, and you can dare more because people do not dare
to refuse you many a thing they would not feel ashamed
of refusing to any one of our sex. Therefore take care of
yourself!''

In that year of 1848 the Women's Rights Movement was
just emerging as an organized force with its historic convention in Seneca Falls, New York, under the able stimulus of such giants as Lucretia Mott and Elizabeth Cady
Stanton. Dorothea Dix was never to become a part of it.
Though she felt keenly the injustices perpetrated on her

sex, she would have heartily disclaimed the title of feminist. She had no sympathy with extremism. She felt that women like Amelia Bloomer with their radical forms of dress hurt their cause, and to her the cause — her own CAUSE — was all-important. Like Elizabeth Blackwell, who in that same year of 1848 was doggedly pursuing the studies which would earn her the first medical degree ever awarded to a woman, she was too busy *living* the revolution in the role of womanhood to fight for it. To both, "women's rights" and "men's rights" were far less important than *human* rights. Of course women should be fighting for their God-given rights, but not just as women, as human beings, and for the sake of other less fortunate human beings.

Yet few women of the century would accomplish more for the cause of women's rights. In a day when a woman was soundly frowned upon for traveling alone, speaking in public, above all meddling in the man's world of officialdom and politics, she dared all these things without a hint of criticism. To be sure, the epithets of praise accorded her, especially in the more conservative South, were typical of the male cavalier — "gracious lady," "chosen daughter of the Republic," "angel of mercy," "apostle of humanity." But a hundred years later they would have become "noted reformer," "first compiler of case histories," "social worker par excellence."

10

By that spring of 1848 she had traveled 60,000 miles, visiting over 9,000 insane, epileptic, and idiotic persons, besides thousands in prisons and other detention houses. In state after state she had scaled a dozen and more lesser heights, obtaining legislation and appropriations for new hospitals, additions, innumerable improvements in asylums, jails, almshouses, orphanages, prisons. Now she was ready to scale an even bolder crest, the goal which would establish a perpetual fund for care of the indigent insane. For three years she had been gestating the idea, long before discussing it with George Emerson, formulating the memorial to present to Congress, studying political leaders in the various states who had national influence, appraising their characters with an astuteness which was the marvel of all her associates.

"How do you manage to get people to carry out your wishes?" William Rathbone once asked her.

She replied, "By going to people whose duty it is to set things right, assuming that they will do so without disturbance being made, and they generally do so."

Not always. Arriving in Washington, she painstakingly framed her memorial, then approached the man she had chosen to present it to Congress, Colonel Thomas H. Benton of Missouri, who had sponsored many other land bills. Both Senator Benton and his daughter, Jessie Benton Frémont, had become her personal friends. She had discussed the project with him, and he had seemed sympathetic. Now, however, he pleaded illness. In his weakened condition he could not do justice to her memorial as he would like to do. Surely she would understand. She did. She had encountered plenty of ardently sympathetic legislators who had suddenly changed their minds when pressured by some special interest group. Commiserating with him on his illness, she hoped he would soon be able to activate the interest he had often expressed in this worthy cause. Then she went to a person whose wholehearted support she knew was assured.

General John Adams Dix, formerly adjutant general and Secretary of State in New York and now senator, was an intimate friend. Dorothea had often visited with him and his wife Catherine. She had found him a strong supporter during her crusade in New York state. The relationship between them was more than casual friendship. Though they were not related, because of the coincidence of names so many people believed them to be that the senator had fallen into the habit of addressing her as "Sister." The affection between them fully substantiated this relationship. Indeed, there was a bond of mutual attraction and sympathy that at times seemed a bit more than fraternal.

"My dear Sister," he was to write her in less than a year's time, "I have burned your last two letters. If I had believed, as you said, that they were to be the last tokens of the true regard you entertain for me, I should have disobeyed your injunction and kept them. I will never give up your affection — never. Moreover, I shall exact from time to time (I will not be unreasonable) assurance that you are unchanged. . . . For some good purpose in the future it seems to have been ordained that the more than ordinary interest we felt in each other without avowing it should become mutually known. . . . Let us hope that in some future period, near or remote, some good purpose now concealed may become revealed to us in these unpremeditated developments of feeling — some course of mutual happiness in harmony with the fraternal affection which united our hearts — equally pure and less agitating than the past."

It was to this friend, a statesman of great culture, eloquence, and vigorous moral courage, that Dorothea entrusted the most important commission of her career, the presentation of her "Memorial to the Congress of the United States."

He fulfilled the duty with distinction, presenting the document to the Senate on June 27, 1848. He told of her achievements in alleviating the condition of the insane, many of which were known by his colleagues. Now she was asking for an appropriation of five million acres of public land to constitute a fund out of which this "too much neglected and most hopeless class" might be provided for. Among the thirty states according to the ratio of their population the total proceeds of this grant should be distributed. Surely this was a worthy and honorable request. A government which provided schools, homesteads, highways, railroads, canals, and other public improvements for the sane owed to its destitute and mentally defective at least shelter and humane treatment.

The Memorial was exhaustive, yet remarkably terse and trenchant. She noted the increase in insanity in advanced ratio to that of population, there being one insane person to every 800 in the country. She discussed the causes of insanity, noting its greater prevalence in countries and among groups possessing the greatest civil and religious liberty and thus subject to the greatest stress of competition, citing the statistics of numerous hospitals and superintendents as to the comparative ratio of ill health, intemperance, extravagant religious excitement, and other contributing factors. She summarized her own investigations of the past seven years, told of the "hundreds, nay, thousands" she had seen "bound with galling chains, bowed beneath fetters and heavy iron balls, attached to drag chains, lacerated with ropes, scourged with rods, and terrified beneath storms of profane execrations and cruel blows; now subjected to gibes and scorn and torturing tricks, now abandoned to the most loathsome necessities, or subject to the vilest and most outrageous violations."

Beginning with Maine, she went through state after state, twenty-six of them, documenting these generalities with specifics, all gleaned from her journals. It was the substance of her other memorials condensed into capsules of succinct detail, the horrors interspersed with incidents showing the benefits of humane treatment, the possibilities of cure.

> . . . insane man in a small damp room in the jail; greatly excited; had been confined many years; during his paroxysms, which were aggravated by every manner of neglect,

except want of food, he had torn out his eyes, lacerated his face, chest, and arms. . . . female confined in a garret, where, from the lowness of the roof and the restrained position, she grew double, and is now obliged to walk with her hands. . . . Under well-directed hospital care, recovery is the rule — incurable permanent insanity the exception.

Perhaps one incident not before chronicled was the most damning.

It was an intensely hot day when I visited F. He was confined in a roofed pen, which enclosed an area of about eight feet by eight. The interstices between the unhewn logs admitted the scorching rays of the sun then, as they would open way for the fierce winds and drenching rains and frosts of the later seasons. . . . no bench, no bed, no clothing. His food, which was of the coarsest kind, was pushed through spaces between the logs; "fed like the hogs and no better," said a stander-by. His feet had been frozen. Upon the shapeless stumps, aided by his arms, he could raise himself against the logs of the pen. In warm weather this wretched place was cleansed once a week or fortnight; not so in the colder seasons. "We have men called," said his sister, "and they go in and tie him with ropes, and throw him out on the ground, and throw water on him, and my husband cleans out the place." But the expedient to prevent his freezing in winter was the most strangely horrible. In the center of the pen was excavated a pit, six feet square and deep; the top was closed over securely; and into this ghastly place, entered through a trap door, was cast the maniac, there to exist till the returning warm weather induced his caretaker to withdraw him; there without heat, without light, without pure air, was left the pining, miserable maniac, whose piteous groans and frantic cries might move to pity the hardest heart.

And of course she quoted the greatest European and American physicians on the benefits of humane treatment, the possibilities of cure: Doctors Butler, Bell, Chandler,

Brigham, Kirkbride, Awl, Conolly of England, and many others.

"Should your sense of moral response seek support in precedents for guiding present action," she continued,

> I may be permitted to refer to the fact of liberal grants of common national property made, in the light of a wise discrimination, to various institutions of learning; also to advance in the new States common school education, and to aid two seminaries of instruction for the deaf and dumb. . . . But it is not for one section of the United States that I solicit benefits, while all beside are deprived of direct advantages. . . . I advocate the cause of the much suffering insane throughout the entire length and breadth of my country. I ask relief for the east and for the west, for the north and for the south. . . . I ask for the people that which is already the property of the people.

She was well known and respected by many legislators, and the memorial was accorded due attention. Five thousand copies were printed. She asked that a select committee be appointed to consider the bill — an unusual request — and was permitted to make suggestions as to its personnel. She chose prominent Democrats, the majority party: General Dix, Mr. Harnegan, Mr. Bell and Mr. Davis of Massachusetts, and Colonel Benton. This time she would not let him put her off with excuses. He was one of the most important men in the Senate. She herself had been sick, stricken with influenza, but as soon as she recovered she went to see him. He hemmed and hawed, finally agreeing that he would do everything for her that was "feasible under the circumstances."

It was not enough. "Sir," she corrected him firmly, "I have not come to ask any favor for myself, not the smallest. I ask for *yourself, your* state, *your* people. Sir, you are a Democrat and profess above all others to support the interests of the people, the multitude, the poor. This is your opportunity to show the country how far profession and practice correspond. Reject this measure, and you trample on the poor, you crush them. Sustain it, and their blessings shall echo around your pillow when the angel of the last hour comes to call you to the other life of action and progress."

He regarded her for a moment with something like awe. "My dear Miss Dix," he said at last, "I will do what I can."

"Then, sir," she replied, "the bill and the measure are safe."

But as days passed she was far from sure. True, on July 21 she was able to write her friend Harriett Hare, "You who understand me, you who always sympathize with my anxieties and rejoice in my successes, will be glad to know that my whole committee, even the impracticable Colonel Benton, concurred in my 5,000,000 acre bill, and it was read this morning in the Senate. . . ." But the letter ended, "I found last week my strength sinking under my anxieties. I, you know, am never sanguine, and feel confidence only when a bill passes into an act and is sealed by Governor or President."

She had reason to doubt. There was a movement in the northern states to curb Congress in its free distribution of western lands. The thousand million acres yet remaining, it was loudly asserted, should be retained to benefit future poor homesteaders, not parceled out to railroads, canals, improvement companies, and certainly not to greedy speculators. Dorothea knew that her bill was between two fires. These agrarian protests of the eastern states would deter Democratic politicians from voting away more land. On the other hand, the imperious demands of syndicates and land speculators would be loudly voiced against the issuance of more public grants. With grim patience she settled herself for a long and formidable struggle.

A special alcove in the Capitol library was set apart by congressional action for her use, and here she made herself available for interviews with members of Congress who might seek her out or who were brought there by her friends. A far cry, this quiet alcove, from the teeming corridors with the fierce competitive lobbying. Those who came could not fail to note the contrast between the clamoring vote-seekers and the calm, gentle-voiced yet powerfully appealing woman who asked nothing for herself but demanded and expected justice and mercy for the weak and helpless. They nodded, sympathized, agreed, then hedged when it came time to vote.

"Have great fears for the bill," Dorothea wrote Harriett Hare in July. "Whitney's bill, that was thought as good as passed, was laid on the table."

"Not a land bill has passed," she wrote in August.

Washington was a furnace in summer, but she seldom left and then only on a weekend to visit a jail or a prison in Baltimore or another neighboring city. Her days passed in unchanging routine: rising at 5:00, an hour for prayers, knitting in the dining room of Mrs. Johnson's quiet lodging house while some member of the family read from the morning papers, at her desk in the library from 10:00 to 3:00, writing until dinner at 4:30, writing until 8:00 when she returned to the parlor for tea.

"Now for the dissipations, the fashionable life you think I lead," she wrote Anne when the latter half jokingly inquired about her social engagements. "One day from twelve to four, since I have been in Washington, I have appropriated to returning calls, and left about fifty cards. Except for these I am still in arrears. These visits only have I paid, namely, dined at the President's, was one of the 300 friends at the mansion of the Secretary of the Navy, and one of the 200 at a select party given . . . to the heads of the departments, leading officers and families of the army and navy, and foreign ministers. So you see, I am not greatly dazzled by attractions of the gay life in Washington."

The ranks of her supporters grew steadily, and her hundreds of friends all over the nation fully expected her bill to pass speedily and receive the signature of President

Polk. The Association of Medical Superintendents, organized in 1844, had gone on record at every meeting supporting her work. But months passed, and the bill kept being deferred.

Very well, she had other irons in the fire of her constant fervor. Autumn found her again in North Carolina, continuing her survey. She spent three months inspecting thirty-nine jails and almshouses, much of the travel by carriage, which she found not only uncomfortable but hazardous.

"I have encountered nothing so dangerous in North Carolina as the river fords," she wrote Harriet Hare in November. "In times of drought and low water they are so bad, what must they be in high! Pilots are often to be had in the broad rivers, but even there they differ greatly. I crossed the Yadkin where it was three-quarters of a mile wide, rough bottom, rapid currents, water always to the bed of the carriage, sometimes flowing in. The horses rested twice on sand bars that rose above the water, but it was hard work for them. A few yards beyond the river, having just crossed a branch 200 yards wide, the axletree of my carriage broke, and away rolled one of the back wheels! I had but one feeling at the time, thankfulness that it was not in the river the accident had occurred!"

The condition of the mentally ill in the state was deplorable. There were more than a thousand insane, epileptic, and idiotic cases, many in jails and poorhouses, a few sent to hospitals in other states, most in private families. Six years before, Governor Morehead had recommended the establishment of three institutions, but no action had been taken. Nor was there prospect of it now. The Democrats, back in power after a long interval, were interested in nothing but a new railroad to the West. Already shadows of war were gathering, and "We'll need railroads, not lunatic asylums in case of war" was the prevailing sentiment. It was rumored that she was an abolitionist, though she had never made a statement to that effect.

"They say nothing can be done here," she wrote Mrs. Hare. "I reply, 'I know no such word in the vocabulary I adopt!' It is declared that no word will be uttered in opposition to my claims, but that the Democrats, having banded together as a party to vote for nothing that involves expense, will unite and silently vote down the bill. A motion was made to order lighting the lamps in the portico of the Capitol, and voted down by the Democrats. 'Ye love darkness because your deeds are evil!' said a Whig in great ire; and a voice from the gallery responded piously, 'For ye are of your father, the Devil!'

"The deep waters are yet to pass, but," she ended her letter,

> My heart is fixed, and fixed my eye,
> And I am girded for the race;
> The Lord is strong, and I rely
> On his assisting grace.

She was used to deep waters, whether in the Yadkin or in a hostile assembly. She found no legislator who dared support her bill — except one. In the Mansion House in Raleigh she met the Honorable James C. Dobbin, a member of the assembly, who was staying there with his wife Louisa. A few days after the assembly opened, Mrs. Dobbin fell ill. Dorothea, who had become her friend, spent every moment possible nursing her. Soon she was sitting up all night with the sick woman. One night as she sat beside her, reading the Bible aloud, Mrs. Dobbin murmured, "I fear I am sinking rapidly." Alarmed, Dorothea rushed out to summon the doctor and Mr. Dobbin. Returning, she found the woman so sick she could hardly speak but trying hard to say something. "What is it?" Dorothea leaned over her. "Tell me what you want."

"You — have been so — kind to me," Louisa Dobbin whispered, "a — stranger. I — wish to ask — husband to do something for you. What — shall I ask him?"

"Tell him," said Dorothea instantly, "to sponsor my hospital bill."

The memorial was completed. Though for the most part it was a summary of practical details, a chronicle of visits to institutions, examples of cures in other states and statements of superintendents — Dr. Bates of Maine, Dr. Stribling of Virginia, Dr. Allen of Kentucky, Dr. Kirkbride of Pennsylvania — in her introduction she ventured an appeal to the emotions.

"I come not to urge personal claims, nor to seek individual benefits. . . . I am the Hope of the poor crazed beings who pine in the cells, and stalls, and cages, and waste rooms of your poor-houses. I am the Revelation of hundreds of wailing, suffering creatures, hidden in your private dwellings, and in pens and cabins — shut out, cut off from all healing influences, from all mind-restoring cures."

Dorothea requested some of the leading Democrats, known to be opponents of any such measure, to come to the Mansion House.

"Gentlemen," she told them, "here is the document I have prepared for your assembly. I have written it under the exhaustion of three weeks' most fatiguing journeys and labors. I desire you, sir, to present it." She handed it to John W. Ellis, the leading proponent of the new railroad bill. "And you gentlemen," she continued, turning to the astonished delegation, "I expect you to sustain the motion which this gentleman will make."

Mr. Ellis introduced the bill. It was presented in both houses and referred to a joint committee of fourteen. On December 8 Ellis, as chairman of the committee, introduced a bill for $100,000 for a hospital for the insane, with a special order for December 21. Hot debate followed on the amount of the appropriation and how it was to be raised. The annual revenue of the state available was less than $200,000. Mr. Raynor, a Whig, offered an amendment levying a special tax on land and polls, but it was lost.

Meanwhile Dorothea had accompanied Mr. Dobbin to
Fayetteville with his wife's body. They returned to find
that the section of the bill relating to the appropriation had
been deleted. On December 23 Mr. Dobbin was back in
his seat clad in mourning, a black band circling his arm.
He moved a reconsideration of the bill. The request was
granted. He offered an amendment to the disputed section, providing a tax of one cent on every $100 worth of
land and two and one-half cents on every poll for four
years. Then he gave an eloquent plea for those like himself, smitten with affliction and bereavement and telling of
his promise to his dying wife. He was a powerful orator,
and the speech would become a tradition in the state's
annals. He had no idea of the effect he was producing until
he noted the stillness of the hall and the tears in the
speaker's eyes.

"Rejoice, rejoice with me!" Dorothea wrote Harriett
Hare. "Through toil, anxiety, and tribulation, my bill has
passed! 101 ayes, 10 nays. I am not well, though perfectly
happy. I leave North Carolina compensated a thousand-
fold for all labors by this great success."

She would have returned to Washington at once, but
they would not let her.

"No! You must help us select a site. You can't leave until
that is settled."

It always happened after the passage of a bill. She had
long since become an authority on the proper site for an
asylum: a good view, fresh water, not too far from the city
yet far enough to avoid smoke and noise. A good site was
found to the southwest, a beautiful hill overlooking a
broad valley where the new railroad ran, a grove of oak
trees surrounding it with shade and beauty.

"We shall name it Dix Hill," insisted James Dobbin.

No! Always she resisted any effort to enshrine her name
in any of her achievements.

"You will accept no money, no gifts from the legislature," Dobbin hastened to urge. "If not in your honor,

then isn't there someone dear to you whose memory we may perpetuate?"

Yes, she decided. Of course. Dr. Elijah Dix. Grandfather had so often told her of his dream of establishing a medical school in Boston, some institution which would help bring new life to people.

She let them name the new height of promise Dix Hill.

11

It was cold in Washington all through January 1849, but in her room were hyacinths from the garden. They were a warm bright spot in an otherwise chill and discouraging prospect. She was mourning with George Emerson and his wife the loss of their only son by suicide. Mrs. Emerson, alone in the house, had asked her son to come into the parlor to read to her. She had heard the sound of a gun. Her husband had returned to find their son shot through the head. Sometimes, thought Dorothea, she felt like a set of sensitive strings vibrating in sympathy with every human tragedy she encountered.

She was back in the same boardinghouse, the same quiet alcove in the Capitol library, pursuing the same rigid schedule of interviews, correspondence, writing for the newspapers, visiting prisons.

"Your friendly visit to the prison on Sunday last," wrote the warden of the Washington penitentiary on January 16, "with the address to the convicts, be well assured, has been highly appreciated. And the library you have selected for their use. It is pleasing to witness the scene on Sunday mornings, each convict wending his way to the librarian with a smile soliciting a fresh book. . . ."

But her precious land bill languished.

"I am neither sanguine nor discouraged," she wrote her

brother Joseph. "I think the bill may be deferred till next session. A new difficulty is to be combatted, the President having declared he will veto all and every land bill which does not make a provisional payment to the general government. . . . I fortunately am on good terms with Mrs. Polk and the President, knowing well all their family friends in Tennessee and North Carolina. The Vice President, Mr. Dallas, the intimate associate of my Philadelphia friends, is warmly in favor of the bill."

In March it was deferred, also her hopes. But she made other plans: March and April in Virginia, Maryland, and Tennessee, May in New Jersey and New York, June . . . With her friends the Hares in Philadelphia in June she became so ill that a doctor was summoned. To her relief he did not, like others, advise a long rest and cessation from labor. She could not, he said, and ought not to shrink from what seemed the necessary sacrifice of her life to her mission. Not that she would have heeded if he had advised otherwise. But his verdict silenced some of the concerned protests of friends and relatives.

They, as well as herself, must be sacrificed to the Cause. That year she wrote Anne Heath, "Few accidents of my life are so pleasant to meditate upon as our early friendship. Our affection must, will live when Time is no more." Yet a few months later, in September, when Dorothea had been in Boston a week without telling her, Anne wrote in gentle grief, "The fact is, you are independent of us all, and need no assistance or attendance. I am sorry you never need me and sorry to have it so clearly proved in the past week." But always forgiving, she urged, "Do make a winter dress here. Will you not need one?"

In November Dorothea went to Alabama. She arrived on a Friday after traveling from Baltimore for five entire days and three nights, stopping only once long enough to loosen her garments and bathe beyond a quick dip of hands and face. Saturday night she saw the governor and persuaded him to refer the subject of her bill and recommend it in his message. She obtained a similar promise from the president and speaker of the senate and house. Her memorial was presented, accepted, and 2,000 copies were ordered printed without a dissenting vote. While waiting for the legislature to take action, she prepared a memorial for the legislative assembly of the Province of Nova Scotia, where she had carried on an investigation in both 1844 and 1848. Then, just as a hard-won victory seemed possible in Alabama, the state capitol went up in flames . . . also, temporarily, her hopes. Not only was the legislature adjourned until the New Year, but its penchant for economy was magnified a hundredfold. To save time she moved on to perform duties in Louisiana and Mississippi. It took all her faith and courage to remain resolute.

She wrote Anne: "I have recollected amidst these perplexities that God requires no more to be accomplished than He gives time for performing, and I turn now more quietly to my work up the Hill Difficulty. The summit is cloud-capped, but I have passed amidst dark and rough ways before and shall not now give out."

But the climbing was hard. The first of January she was back in Montgomery, to find the state in no mood for increased appropriations. "I think," she wrote Mrs. Hare in near discouragement, "after this year I shall certainly not suffer myself to engage in any legislative affairs for a year."

Famous last words! The next three years were to be some of the most strenuous legislative battles of her life. The work in Alabama was not lost, however. Two years later an appropriation of $100,000 would be secured, and later $150,000 more. Opened to receive patients in 1860, the beautiful four-story hospital in Tuscaloosa, modeled after Dr. Kirkbride's plan, would be named in honor of Dr. Peter Bryce, who would act as its efficient superintendent until his death.

Mississippi was next. Her memorial was presented in

February, 1850, and her next letter to Mrs. Hare was jubilant. "Twenty-four majority in the Senate and eighty-one in the House, was something of a conquest over prejudice and the positive declaration and determination not to give a dime!" The same letter, written from a boat on the Mississippi and illustrated by a humorous sketch, highlighted some of the difficulties such travel encountered.

"We have on our boat both cholera and malignant scarlet fever. To add to our various incidents, a quantity of gunpowder was left in charge of a raw Irishman, who was directed, at a given time and place, to load the cannon and fire a salute. One hundred miles away from the point to be so honored, Pat, thinking the bore of the cannon as good a place of deposit for the powder as he could find, rammed it down. Then, discovering that the rain had wet the bore, he ran with alacrity to the furnace and returned with a burning stick, thrusting it in after the powder, 'to dry up the wather.' This it effected, but not this alone, for of course the powder exploded, and certain portions of Pat's arm and hand were sent in advance toward the distant city."

She neglected to add that it was she herself who cared for poor Pat and dressed his wounds.

The Mississippi legislature, the commission, prominent citizens insisted that the hospital be named for her, but once more she positively refused. As her biographer was to write long afterward, she "must be the incarnation of a purely disinterested idea appealing to universal humanity."

Even the suggestion by a Washington publisher that a short account of her labors be included in a work to be entitled *The Fact Book* aroused her unequivocal opposition. "My wish is to be known only through my works. I shall not be willing that any record, as proposed, be made of my late or present labors. If called for at all, it is well to defer it till the laborer ceases from work and has passed to that country where we believe suffering and trouble do not exist."

186

When in the following year Sarah Josepha Hale requested data for a book she was writing entitled *Lives and
Characters of Distinguished Women,* Dorothea was even
more unyielding. "I feel it right to say to you frankly that
nothing could be undertaken which would give me more
pain and serious annoyance, which would so trespass on
my personal rights and offend my perception of fitness and
propriety."

"I am not ambitious of nominal distinction," her letter
continued, "and notoriety is my special aversion. Reputation I prize above all present good and would not exchange it for fame nor transient popular applause."

Rarely, and then only to a dear friend like Mrs. Rathbone and with a humility which denied all credit to self,
did she acknowledge the magnitude of her achievements.
"Shall I not say to you, dear friend," she wrote in June,
1850, "that my uniform success and influence are evidence to my mind that I am called by Providence to the
vocation to which life, talents, and fortune have been surrendered these many years. I cannot say, 'Behold now,
this great Babylon which I have builded,' but 'Lo! O,
Lord, the work which Thou gavest thy servant, she does it,
and God in his benignity blesses and advances the cause
by the instrument He had fitted for the labor.' "

She returned to Washington to hear words of hot dissension on every lip — Slavery . . . Compromise . . . Secession . . . Statehood for California and New Mexico . . .
Underground railroad . . . Abolitionists. Could one hope to
add "Insane Poor," "Helpless Disabled" to the grim list?
One could and did. Opposition was but invigorating stimulus. This time she memorialized Congress not for
5,000,000 acres but for 12,225,000, of which ten million
should inure for benefit of the insane, the rest for the
blind, deaf, and dumb. James Pearce of Maryland introduced the memorial in the Senate and John Frémont of
California, son-in-law of the elusive Colonel Benton, in
the House. A committee was appointed, which reported
favorably. Again the Medical Superintendents for Amer-

ican Institutions for the Insane, at their annual meeting in Boston, passed a unanimous resolution of "unqualified sanction." The press and public sentiment endorsed the bill. Dorothea thankfully expected its early passage.

Once more she entered into the old routine, always beginning with an hour of devotions at four or five in the morning, never interrupted even in times of greatest stress. Indeed, those were the days she needed it most. By breakfast at eight she had finished her correspondence, which had now multiplied to serve the needs of twenty states. Details of new buildings, appointment of superintendents, even minor items regarding management, improvements, individual patients, were submitted to her for advice. By ten she was again in her quiet alcove. All that summer, through heat often mounting to ninety or a hundred degrees, she spent four or five hours each day explaining, reasoning, instructing, careful whatever the pain or weariness never to seem tired, impatient, or ill-humored.

The numbers of supporters were mounting. Colonel Benton now expressed approval. Horace Mann, who had been elected to the House in 1848 to fill the seat left vacant by John Quincy Adams, was always her faithful ally. The death of President Taylor in July and the succession of Millard Fillmore promised only added support for the cause, for the new President was not only an advocate of the bill but a personal friend. When she sent him a blueprint of the new hospital for the insane in Tennessee, he replied with far more than official courtesy. "Accept my thanks. . . . When I looked upon its turrets and recollected that this was the thirteenth monument you had caused to be erected of your philanthropy, I could not help thinking that wealth and power never reared such monuments to selfish pride as you have reared to the love of mankind."

She waited through the scorching summer days for the House, where the political dissension was greater, to take action. She was more hopeful of support in the Senate, unless, due to the pressure of business, it would again be deferred. The suspense was agonizing.

"None can tell what a mountain will be lifted from my breast if my bills pass," she wrote on August 29. "I shall feel almost as if I could say, 'Lord, let now thy servant depart in peace, for mine eyes have seen thy salvation!' "

Again President Fillmore manifested his concern. "I perceive," he wrote her again, "that you feel anxious and sad. I cannot wonder at it! I wonder your patience has held out so long and that you can speak with such equanimity. But yours is a goodness that never tires, a benevolence that never wearies, a confident hope that never seems to desert you. None but the most disinterested and self sacrificing can have such faith, or display such all-conquering perseverance."

If her patience was tried, few others were aware of it. Horace Mann commented after visiting her in the library that she filled all about her with a "divine magnetism." But a week later, on September 25, he wrote the Reverend S. J. May, his friend in Boston: "Poor Miss Dix, her bill has failed this morning in the House; or at least it has been referred to the Committee of the Whole on the State of the Union, from which it cannot be returned should the session continue for a year. I went to carry her the news, but she had not come up to the library today. Yesterday when her bill came up, men were starting up on all sides with their objections; but today the point under discussion is to pay an additional sum to the soldiers in the Mexican War, and almost all are in favor of it. . . . Christianity is 1900 years distant from them."

"Pray that my patience does not fail utterly," Dorothea wrote to Anne.

"Hope on, hope ever!" wrote the President two days later. Knowing that she was soon to leave the city, he hoped that she and her friend Professor Henry would take tea with him on Sunday evening. "Do come and see how a bachelor lives and it may induce you hereafter to take pity on some lonely gentleman and concentrate that affectionate tenderness upon one object that never circles in its embrace a suffering world."

The friendly correspondence she enjoyed with the President during subsequent weeks was balm for her disappointment, as she attended to pressing duties in New Jersey, Maryland, Pennsylvania. They exchanged letters every few days, continually discovering fresh areas of agreement. He believed with her that politicians as a class were ambitious and selfish. He was horrified by the number of insane persons she reported in prisons. She sent him a prayer book, and he begged her to accept a Bible as a slight token of his esteem.

The first Monday in December she was back in Washington at her little walnut desk in the alcove. This time prospects for the passage of her bill were even better. But delay followed delay. At last, on February 11, the bill came up in the Senate. She was so nervous, sitting in her alcove, waiting . . . waiting . . . that work was impossible. All she could manage was a running commentary to Anne.

"My dear Friend —My bill is up in the Senate, I await the result with great anxiety, but a calmness which astonishes myself. . . .

"A motion to lay on the Speaker's table is just lost, 32 to 14. It is said that this is the last vote. They are speaking on amendments. The danger is from debate. I dread Chase of Ohio. . . .

"Mr. Mason of Virginia sends me word the bill will pass. . . .

"A message from Mr. Pierce, who says the bill will, will pass. Ah, if it should fail now! . . .

"Mr. Shields just comes to say the bill will pass. You know not how terrible this suspense! I am perfectly calm, and as cold as ice.

"4 p.m. The bill has passed the Senate beautifully. A large majority, more than two to one! — thirty-six yeas to sixteen nays!"

Victory! But of course only partial. To become law, a bill had to pass both houses in the same session and be signed by the President. The latter was no problem, and the House had finally passed it in the last session. But — this one? Representatives, with their shorter term, were always more amenable to temporary pressures. The question of the bill's immediate consideration by the House was defeated by the "rigid enforcement of the rules." Twice the rules were suspended, and still action was delayed. Assuring her of their support in private, back with their colleagues representatives wavered, tacitly consenting to delay after delay.

Resolutely Dorothea conquered her impatience. Friends were her constant support. The pleasant association with the President continued with informal meetings at the White House. Dorothea became better acquainted with Mrs. Fillmore, now back in Washington after a long absence, and was able to recommend a dressmaker. The family of Professor Joseph Henry, an eminent scientist of the Smithsonian Institution, to whom Dorothea had sent many botanical specimens, had for years welcomed her into their home. Horace and Mary Mann, John Charles Frémont and his wife Jessie, Charles Sumner, who had been elected to the Senate in April — all were bulwarks of encouragement.

But the session closed without action being taken. Once more the bill had failed.

12

She went south on a tour of prisons and hospitals, but this time she did not travel alone. Fredrika Bremer, the noted Swedish novelist who was visiting the United States and who had accompanied her on several short trips, was her companion. Dorothea had met Miss Bremer the preceding year, and the two had formed a rewarding friendship. Fredrika was fascinated by the beautiful patrician woman whose passions were all directed toward the alleviation of others' suffering. She once expressed her admiration in a letter to her niece in Sweden.

"She is one of the most beautiful proofs of that which a woman, without any other aid than her own free will and character, without any other power than that of her purpose and its uprightness, and her ability to bring these forward, can effect in society. . . . I love the place she occupies in humanity, love her figure sitting in the recess of the window in the Capitol, where amid the fiery feuds, she silently spins her web for the unfortunate, a quiet center for the threads of Christian love which draws across the ceaseless contests, undisturbed by them, a divine spinner she is for the House of God."

They came to enjoy a feeling of unusual kinship. Miss Bremer herself was recovering from overwork and mental stress and was drawn to this woman who was devoting her life to such victims. Moreover, like Dorothea at an earlier time, she was seeking for some avenue of greater service in her career.

"What influenced you?" she asked once when the two were enjoying a brief holiday in a friend's villa overlooking the Chesapeake. "What made you want to become a public protector and advocate of the unfortunate?"

Dorothea considered, then replied slowly, "It was no remarkable occurrence nor change in my inner or outer life. It was merely an act of simple obedience to the voice of God." She told of her illness and depression and longing for some noble purpose to fill the vacuum of her life, of her visit to the East Cambridge jail. "I saw the path marked out for me, and it, and what I have done in it have, as it were, been done by themselves."

Miss Bremer, deeply impressed, wrote later, "Washington lay behind me, with its political quarrels, its bitter strife of state against state, man against man. . . . And here was a small human life which by an act of simple obedience had gone forth out of its privacy . . . fraught with blessing for neglected beings throughout every state in the union, like that little river before us, had poured itself into that glorious creek and in that united with the world's ocean."

On one matter, however, they were in sharp disagreement. Already Dorothea was looking beyond the bounds of America and longing to carry her crusade across that same ocean. Why not Sweden? She suggested the possibility to the Swedish singer, Jenny Lind, who was on a concert tour of the States. No, replied the artist with decision, no good could be accomplished there by a foreigner. Dorothea wrote Miss Bremer about the same possibility, and the author's answer was even more bluntly negative.

"Sweden lacks neither will nor means. What is wanted there is energy and impulse of will; and *that* a foreigner unknown in the country, and herself not knowing its language and forms of government, could not give. . . . It would be easier for you to climb to the Chinese wall than to work any good *personally* for the unfortunate insane in Sweden." But her work in America, be assured, would spread to all countries, including Sweden.

The episode was but a brief hiatus in their friendship. Now, on the trip south, through North and South Carolina, Georgia, visiting prisons and hospitals all along the way, Miss Bremer marveled at Dorothea's energy, her selfless concern for the sick and helpless — yes, and her cheerful acceptance of the most distressing discomforts and accommodations! Going down the Savannah River there was no fresh water, and they had to drink muddy river water. After they changed boats at Pulaski mice ran across their faces as they tried to sleep. Cockroaches got into their baggage. Dorothea got out of bed, lighted a candle, and moved their baggage to a safer place. Whenever the boat tied up at a wharf to load or unload, she was first to cross the plank, off on foot or in a two-wheeled cart to visit the local poorhouse, prison, or hospital. There was no one to compare with her, thought Fredrika Bremer, not even Mrs. Fry.

"Should I not kiss her hand?" she wrote. "I did and do it again in spirit, with thanks for that which she is and that which she does."

Surely it was no coincidence that soon Fredrika Bremer was to turn her great literary talent to objectives of social reform!

The periods in 1851when Congress was not in session Dorothea filled to the brim with these other activities. In the summer she made hurried trips to New England and Canada and during the Christmas holidays visited southern hospitals and prisons. She sent an exhaustive report to the Bloomingdale Hospital, complaining about its overcrowding, insufficient heat, lack of bathrooms and sinks in the lodges, lack of a night watchman, the difficult service of food, lack of a supervisor, defective ventilation, and gave two plans for improvement. Contrasted with her letters to friends, so hastily written and often illegible, the ten pages of neat, careful writing were a model of penmanship. She listed the functions of a physician in such an institution, the duties of its matron and steward, emphasized the need for employment of patients. She outlined in great detail the proper procedures for the whole household for a single day. The superintendent, Dr. John H. Nichols, was a close friend and regular correspondent, and he agreed heartily with all her comments.

She had long been concerned with the crowded condition of the hospitals in Maryland, and in February, 1852, she submitted a memorial to the state legislature. A state hospital was needed capable of caring for 250 patients, the maximum number recommended for a first-class curative institution. There was much opposition from wealthy landowners, but again the combination of gentle persuasion and iron will, plus the support of the Baltimore *Sun* and such humanitarians as Moses Sheppard and Dr. R. S. Stewart of Baltimore, prevailed. An appropriation was made to enlarge the facilities of the Maryland hospital and a committee appointed to purchase a new site. In December R. S. Stewart wrote her that stone would be hauled before winter and that the beautiful site at Spring Cove near Catonsville pleased him more and more.

Back in Washington Dorothea once more took up the burden of legislative pressure. On February 11, 1852, the *Morning Post* reported:

> Miss Dix, the good Samaritan, the blessing of the Lord upon her head! has got her ten million acre insane bill before the Senate again. The gallant General Shields introduced it, and four other gallant men put upon the select committee with him to consider and report on it, among whom is Mr. Hamlin of Maine. The bill will become a law this time, because it is the only chance the old states will ever have of getting a slice of the public domain. They must take it in company with the insane, and for the insane, and it is well they should, for they were insane enough once to defeat the distribution of the proceeds of this treasure.

Now, in addition to the request for 12,225,000 acres Dorothea asked for $100,000 for a hospital for relief of the army and navy insane in the District of Columbia. Heretofore patients from the District had been sent to other hospitals at government expense. Now these other institutions were overcrowded. The need was obvious. Again friends rallied. Mary Mann was with her husband in Washington. Lucretia Mott, the Women's Rights leader, was there. President Fillmore had been wondering what became of that "angel of mercy" and had been constantly hoping to see her cheerful face.

"It is strange to me," he wrote her in March, "how you find time to accomplish everything and especially everything good. But so it is. You are my mentor — my good genius — not any evil genius like that which haunted the footsteps of the noble Brutus, but my friendly, charitable, confiding guide like the Mentor of Ulysses. Mrs. Fillmore joins me in the request that you will favor us with your company at a private family dinner on Saturday at 4.30 p.m. I expect no one else."

This was election year, and Dorothea feared the coming of a new, less sympathetic President. With two bills now to promote, she felt driven as by a pitiless scourge, expending all her energies in the familiar treadmill of persuasion. Still she found time for other service, like writing an eight-page letter to the boys in the Illinois Institute for the Education of Deaf Mutes.

"You cannot speak audibly, you cannot hear . . . but, oh, my young friends, you can see!" And with all her fine discernment and love of nature she described for them some of the wonders open to their gaze. She had not forgotten the sign-name they gave her when she visited, "Smile of the Eyes."

That summer during a congressional recess she made another trip to Nova Scotia, where for years she had been pressing for the building of an asylum. This time she was fortified with a letter from the dour but brilliant Daniel Webster, now secretary of state to Mr. Livingston, the United States consul at Halifax. "She visits Nova Scotia in pursuance of the benevolent objects to which she has devoted her life. I would be personally gratified with any attention you can bestow." Once more she infused courage into the Honorable Hugh Bell, tireless but often despondent advocate of the cause. "I fear," he had written her recently, "that even the thunders of Demosthenes would scarce disturb our apathy and insensibility respecting such subjects," "Yet," he wrote again, "with you by my side (like Minerva, in the shape of Mentor, by the side of Telemachus) even *I* would become courageous." But success was not to come yet.

The bill for the Washington hospital passed in August, with $100,000 appropriated. Now, with this project joyfully attained, she could devote herself completely to the land bill. At last the House voted 98 to 54 in its favor, but in the Senate it was the same old story of delay.

"What should we do?" she asked Horace Mann, for once almost in despair. He tried to be encouraging, was sure the bill would pass in the next session. But — should she press for it *now*? With the approach of a presidential election interest in humanitarian projects was already subsiding. After much indecision she postponed further action for the present and turned to other projects.

But she was soon back in Washington, summoned by another crisis. An ideal site had been chosen for the new government asylum, a commanding hill at the junction of two broad rivers, the Potomac and East Branch. All the features which Dorothea approved: a superb view, gentle slopes to effect perfect drainage, surrounding woods and fields! But the estate was the prized possession of Mr. Thomas Blagden, and he was reluctant to sell. Moreover, the amount appropriated by Congress for the site was only $25,000, and Blagden would not think of parting with the property for less than forty.

"There is nothing more to be done!" exclaimed Dr. John Nichols, who, since resigning the superintendency of Bloomingdale, had devoted his entire energy to the passing of this bill. "And it's the finest site for a hospital in the world."

Dorothea regarded him calmly. "We must see what can be done." She requested an interview with Mr. Blagden, went and reasoned with him. Of course the land was precious to him and his family, but they were only one household. Could he not sacrifice for the good of thousands of his suffering fellow-creatures? The melodious voice, the lustrous, compassionate eyes, the impassioned concern were irresistible. Yet she left him in obvious agony and indecision. That night he wrote her a letter.

"Dear Madam — Since seeing you today, I have had no other opinion (and Mrs. Blagden also) than that I must not stand between you and the beloved farm, regarding you, as I do, as the instrument in the hands of God to secure this very spot for the unfortunates whose best earthly friend you are, and believing sincerely that the Almighty's blessing will not rest on, nor abide with, those who may place obstacles in your way."

Yet when Dr. Nichols brought Blagden the papers to sign the next day, he found him walking the floor, weeping. "I don't want to part with it! I don't want to. It's dear to me and my family. But I won't break my word to Miss Dix — I won't break my word!"

"What an ideal site for an asylum!" People would exclaim over the stately buildings crowning the impressive elevation. First St. Elizabeth Hospital, later the Government Hospital for the Insane, a hundred years later it would house 7,500 patients and become internationally known for its distinguished achievements in psychology and psychiatry, its skills in training social workers and chaplains. A fitting memorial to one man's sacrifice and one woman's single-minded, almost ruthless, dedication!

13

"I am glad you are alive and not in your bed," wrote George Hilliard, Dorothea's lawyer friend in Boston, "but why you are not dead and why you are able to be about is a marvel to me. I believe if you were cut in two with a pair of shears, you would unite and go on as before." Or, better yet, Dorothea amended, remain in two parts, so she could be in more than one place at once!

"So glad you were not injured in that collision of cars in your late journey to Washington from Harrisburg," wrote

Mrs. Torrey that same month of February, 1853. "The cold and wet feet and exposure in the night so bad for you! But at least your life was spared. And what a fine New Year's gift from the Legislature of Pennsylvania!"

"I saw Miss Dix this morning," Horace Mann wrote his wife Mary later that month from Washington. "She is an angel. She has got two or three hundred dollars out of the government for a library in the District. She has induced Mr. Corcoran to give a bit of land, fifteen thousand for a building and ten thousand for a library to be called the 'Apprentices Library' here. . . . Isn't she a woman's rights woman worth having, going in for their rights in the right way?"

Her friends were constantly urging her to rest, reminding her that she had already accomplished enough for one lifetime. In the twelve years since her visit to the East Cambridge jail in 1841 she had promoted and secured the enlargement of three hospitals: Worcester, Massachusetts; Providence, Rhode Island; Utica, New York. She had helped to establish thirteen, one in each of the following states: New Jersey, Pennsylvania, Indiana, Illinois, Kentucky, Missouri, Tennessee, Mississippi, Louisiana, Alabama, North Carolina, and Maryland, plus the government hospital in Washington. Enough? How could it be when the needs were still so great, when every mail brought an urgent plea for help? "We can do nothing without you," was the constant cry. Her personality was the determining factor. At her presence enthusiasm waxed, appropriations were forthcoming. When she left interest waned. Once a bill was passed, the demand for her services was increased. She must help select a site and decide on the type of buildings, inspect the plans. Then she must advise with commissioners on the choice of personnel, not only superintendents and physicians, but assistants, stewards, attendants, nurses. Mental health was a whole new medical field, and the success of each enterprise depended on these choices. Many of the persons she selected or recommended would become national, even worldwide, authorities on insanity.

But first of all priorities was her precious land bill. This was not the year to press for its passage. A new President, Franklin Pierce, was in the White House. A new Congress was assembling, unpredictable. She needed time for assessment, reassembling of necessary leadership. Meanwhile there were other projects.

In April the Honorable Hugh Bell, chairman of the Board of Works in Halifax, wrote that at last the legislature had appropriated twenty thousand pounds for a hospital and placed the building of it in his hands. "You always said it would be done. I confess I had given up during my life. But on such subjects I believe the word 'impossible' is not in your vocabulary. . . . You see how much I need your aid. May I expect it?"

He certainly could. In June she was in Nova Scotia helping in the choice of a site, appealing to the governor and council for more funds (the amount appropriated was only half of what was needed), assuring them that if they could raise two thousand pounds she would secure a gift from England for another fifteen hundred, appealing to the Rathbones for help in raising it. Then she went on to St. John's, Newfoundland, where her friend Henry H. Stabb had been aiding her efforts to establish a hospital — not an "asylum," she had corrected in one of his letters. She preferred "Hospital for Mental Disease."

Journeys in these northern waters were always precarious. On previous trips she had encountered perilous experiences. Fortunately she had a pleasant passage from Sydney, Cape Breton, to St. John's. But soon after her arrival she awoke one night to the sound of roaring winds, thundering seas, booming guns, the crashing of giant waves against the seven hundred foot high cliffs which rose nearly perpendicularly from the water's edge. For days the surf raged, pounded, hurling spume, driftwood, wreckage sky high. Many families had fishermen on the

Grand Banks or traders plying the coastal waters. Faces were gray. Bells tolled. Tragedy was on every lip.

"Worst storm of the century. . . all hell's devils let loose . . . God have mercy on our men and boys! . . . Heaven help the poor souls caught near Sable Island!"

"Sable Island?" Dorothea inquired of Henry Stabb.

"They call it the 'Graveyard of Ships,'" he replied.

It was an island, she learned, some four hundred miles to the south, desolate, harborless, with sunken bars reaching long tentacles far out into the Atlantic. There was no lighthouse, for the shifting sands would support no stone structure. Shrouded in mists and fogs, beset by thundering waves in a storm, it was a veritable death trap for ships of all kinds. Since 1583, when it had first brought recorded tragedy to a ship in the fleet of Sir Humphrey Gilbert, it had passed through notorious phases, first as a convict colony, then, as commerce increased, as the abode of piratical wreckers. Then in 1802, after the wreck of the British transport *Princess Amelia*, the provincial legislature had established a relief station, and buildings for a life-saving crew had been erected. Still, between 1830 and 1848, according to official records, sixteen full-rigged ships, fourteen brigs, and thirteen schooners had been wrecked, and only God knew how many more. The island was strewn with whitened skeletons.

Back in Halifax Dorothea could not forget that night of fury. The storm had left appalling wrecks all along the coast. Sable Island had taken its usual toll. Concerned by the loss of life, she began making inquiries. What kind of life-saving apparatus did they have on the island? Was it sufficient? Were there modern lifeboats? How many? If equipment was efficient and adequate, then why so many lives lost? She could find no answers. Very well. There was obvious need for further investigation. It was not the first time her aroused concern had been challenged by a dearth of facts. She would go to Sable Island herself and find them.

Hugh Bell tried to dissuade her. It was a risky trip even in fair weather, and she had seen what a storm could be like. Besides, didn't she have enough to do without taking on the problems of a provincial government, admirals and captains, the rich merchants of eastern coastal cities? He might have been talking to the same winds which had so aroused her anxiety. She went to Sable Island.

It was a calm day when she made the crossing, but the approach to the island, even on the north sheltered side, through a thick fog, was torturous. A vessel must remain at a considerable distance offshore, ready for the first sign of an unfavorable wind, to put out to sea. She hired one of the little native ponies and for several days rode intrepidly about the island, seeing with her own eyes the shifting dunes, the bleaching bones of ships. She investigated the surfboats, the station buildings, the life-saving apparatus, and found all inadequate. However, she was able to see it in action, for while she was there a wreck actually occurred. A fine new vessel, the *Guide*, bound with a cargo of flour for Labrador, went ashore on the south side, lost in the dense fog.

Dorothea rode to the beach on horseback. She was there when the last lifeboat came in. Her visits to the station had made her well acquainted with the crew, and, relieved to have completed their mission in safety, they were happily communicative. Yes, all the ship's crew had been saved, all, that is, except one. The captain had become a raving maniac and had refused to leave. A kind-hearted man, his sailors said, but the loss of his ship had overwhelmed him. Mad as a hatter! A good thing, probably, for him to go down with his ship. Better to die than be put in a cage the rest of his life!

"No! You must go back!" Dorothea pleaded with the sailors. "Get him — please! Bind him if necessary for his safety, but bring him back."

What! Go back there, risk their lives again in that peasoup death trap, just for a loony! But, like others who had encountered the compulsion of that soft voice, those compelling eyes, they obeyed. The captain was brought to shore bound hand and foot. To the amazement of both sailors and lifeboat crew, as well as other onlookers, Dorothea went to him, loosed the bonds, took him by the arm, and led him to a boathouse built for the shipwrecked. There she spoke kindly and stayed with him until he was sufficiently restored to thank the sailors for saving his life.

"Have no fear," she assured the amazed crew. "Rest and nourishing food will soon restore his reason."

Strange, she thought, that the two concerns presently consuming her energies should be so curiously linked!

She returned to Halifax and finished her business in planning for the new hospital. Some days later Hugh Bell called at the Admiralty House to leave his card for the visiting Earl of Elsmere.

"Where is Miss Dix?" asked the admiral, cordially shaking his hand.

"She left for home yesterday," replied Hugh Bell. "She has been to Sable Island and back."

The Admiral's eyes opened wide. "She's a gallant woman!"

Back in Boston on August 20, Dorothea lost no time. She sent a letter to Captain Robert W. Forbes, who was chairman of the Humane Society of Boston and an expert on nautical matters. Would the captain oblige Miss Dix by calling at the residence of Charles Hayward, Esq., at the earliest hour of his convenience, on Wednesday, August 21? The captain could and did. She detailed to him the deficiencies of the life-saving equipment at Sable Island: no mortar for throwing a line across a wrecked vessel, no cars or breeches buoys, boats outmoded, clumsy and unsafe, and far too few of them. Captain Forbes heartily endorsed her plan to solicit funds from merchant friends in eastern cities to purchase and equip some modern lifeboats. On September 16 he was writing in his journal:

"Trying experiments with life-preservers and boat. I went into the river with a neighbor to show Miss Dix how to capsize and how to right a boat. We invited her to throw herself over and permit us to save her, but, as she had no change of clothes, she declined."

Soon Dorothea had collected enough money to construct four lifeboats, one financed wholly by Boston merchants, one by others in Philadelphia, two by New York contributors. By November 25 the boats were completed, and three of them, constructed by Francis of New York, were placed on exhibit in Wall Street. Dorothea wanted to send the four to Halifax by the first sailing vessel, but at Captain Forbes's advice, not to "put all the eggs in one basket," the *Victoria*, the gift of Boston merchants, was sent by a Cunard steamer. The other three boats sailed on the brig *Eleanora* November 27, together with two boat wagons, one life car, the mortar with ammunition, coils of manila rope, and other accessories. Already Dorothea had forwarded a library of several hundred volumes, the joint gift of friends and liberal Boston booksellers. A letter to Sir George Seymour, K. C. B., urged also the building of a lighthouse.

"Too many eggs in one basket?" The warning proved all too true. The brig *Eleanora*, carrying the three boats, which she had named *The Grace Darling*, *The Reliance*, and *The Samaritan*, was driven ashore in January about nine miles from Yarmouth and was a total wreck. One boat was lost, set adrift, one badly broken, the other, still in the ship's hold, uncertain. It was a sad disappointment, but Dorothea was used to such frustrations. She gave directions for the two broken boats, together with the one picked up at sea, to be brought back to New York for repairs and for the fourth, *The Victoria*, to remain in Halifax until the whole fleet could be assembled. It would be the following October before the outfit would land on Sable Island. And in the months before that time Dorothea was fighting the most dramatic battle of her life.

14

With the opening of Congress that winter of 1853 to 1854, the time seemed auspicious at last for the passing of her land bill. Excited protests over the indiscriminate disposal of public lands had died down. President Pierce's policies of compromise and reconciliation had effected a positive, if brief, detente in the conflicting interests of North and South. A host of prominent leaders — doctors, superintendents, educators, politicians — favored her proposal. Her reputation was at an all time high. Newspapers all over the country were lauding her achievements. Seated at her old desk in the library in Washington, she held audience like a queen as one after another congressman eagerly pledged his support and went forth to gain other adherents.

She went to call on the President, who received her graciously. A handsome man, slender, graceful, smooth-shaven, he possessed also the impeccable manners of a southern gentleman. The engaging and conciliatory approach with which he had attempted to appease all conflicting segments of the country — slaveholders, abolitionists, expansionists, strict Constitutionalists, industrialists, cotton growers — became evident as he listened carefully to Dorothea's earnest presentation. He nodded his aristocratic head with its becoming wealth of waving hair, agreed that the bill was an interesting solution to the problem and he was heartily in favor of its objective. Dorothea felt the interview had been satisfactory, and yet . . . She must have hinted at a slight uneasiness in one of her letters to Millard Fillmore, now mourning the recent death of his wife and living with his daughter in his old home in Buffalo, for he wrote on December 20, 1853:

"I was much interested in your call on the President. His language seemed to leave you in great doubt, how far you might rely on him for your land bill. My inference is that he is really and truly sympathetic with the object but he has not fully satisfied himself that as President he can constitutionally approve the measure. Think of this as the matter progresses and see if I am not right. If I am, he will seek to avoid the veto, by having his friends defeat the measure in Congress. God grant that this may not be the case."

Her memorial was again presented, and 5,000 copies were printed. A bill was introduced which would distribute 10,000,000 acres of public land among the states, 100,000 to be given each of them initially and the remainder to be distributed among them on a compound ratio to the geographical areas and their representation in the House. This would create an endowment certain to provide for all exigencies of the future. Never had there been such interest and support. Horace Mann was no longer in Congress, having left to become president of Antioch College, but Charles Sumner was a bulwark of energy. Dorothea drove herself mercilessly, indifferent to fatigue or the recurrent bouts with pain and weakness. Hopeful, yet warily on guard against failure, she studied the record and character of each doubtful congressman, concentrating all her efforts on the most obstinate. Confidence surged then waned to new lows. In February Fillmore wrote that he was sorry to see her write so despairingly about her bill. He himself was not without apprehension, fearing that the Nebraska bill would open again the bitter fountains of slavery agitation. All his letters these days were edged in black.

But on March 9 came the first victory. Dorothea wrote jubilantly to Anne, "Yours this morning received just when I was putting pen to paper to tell you that my bill has passed the Senate by more than two-thirds majority, 25 to 12. Congratulations flow in. I, in my heart, think the very opponents are glad, and, as I rejoice quietly and silently, I feel that it is 'the Lord who has made my mountain to stand strong.' " She was full of exultant scripture. "My cup runneth over." . . . "I have lifted up my eyes." . . . "The Lord doth build up Jerusalem."

A letter from Edward Everett was typical. "It is often the fate of public men who pursue moderate counsels to fall below the tone of one party, too often of both. It will be my consolation, in the dark days of civil discord which I fear are impending, and which, advanced in years as I am, I may yet live to see, that I have done and said nothing to inflame the angry feelings against each other of the opposite sections of the Union. . . . Allow me to congratulate you on the passage of your bill through the Senate."

Now all that remained was action by the House. It came, the bill passing by a fair majority.

Victory at last! Even in her terrible fatigue she was walking on air, mounting up with exultation to the highest heavens. The long struggle was over at last. She could vision the blessings now assured for the future — sufficient income to every state, with the steadily increasing value of this vast amount of land, buildings everywhere needed, doctors and equipment sufficient to minister to all the diseased minds, farms, libraries, gardens, teachers, chaplains — everything she had agonized and labored for these thirteen long years!

Felicitations poured in from friends, physicians, congressmen, strangers.

Dr. Kirkbride, with whom she had planned so many hospitals: "A thousand congratulations on the success of your noble, disinterested and persevering efforts! There is some virtue yet in Congress, and a large hope for the Republic!"

Dr. Francis Lieber, her old friend in Columbia, South Carolina: "Te deum Laudamus! How do you feel? Like a general after a victory? Oh, no! much better. Like people after a shipwreck? You are saving thousands, and not by one act, but by planting institutions, and institutions of love. And when man does that, he comes nearest to his God of love and mercy. Deus tibi lux! F. L."

Anne Heath: "No more need of those long exhausting journeys . . . no more explorations of the depths of human misery . . . no more long and weary wrestling." Now could she not come back to New England and retire, or at least take a long rest?

She could not believe the rumor when it came, that President Pierce was considering vetoing the bill, that he was questioning the constitutionality of grants for humanitarian purposes outside the District of Columbia! It was impossible. The President had personally expressed to her his interest in the measure. The action had been taken by a Congress dominated in both houses by his own party. Twice in four years the bill had passed both the House and the Senate. It was the clear will of the people. At first she refused to believe the rumor.

But there was no disregarding it. She began to receive indignant, commiserating letters. If Franklin Pierce vetoed the bill, wrote Dr. Kirkbride, he deserved to see the ghosts of the insane hovering around his bed at night for the rest of his life. Even Anne, as far away as Boston, had heard the rumor. "I shall not believe the telegraphic report until I hear from you." On April 28 Dorothea wrote her that the veto had not happened yet, but she was expecting it any day. "Poor weak man!" Even in her numbed discouragement she tried to be compassionate. "It will be a bad day's work for him. How he is to get out of the fetters this will put upon his freedom, I cannot misgive."

But of course, she assured herself as well as Anne, the bill was not lost even if it was vetoed. It had easily passed both houses with a two-thirds vote. She had been so busy and concerned that she had not taken time to attend to her spring clothes, and the weather in Washington was becoming unbearably hot. Perhaps Anne would see if her last year's spring bonnet was worth whitening, pressing, and, if so, line it with light green silk? With silk tulle trimming around the face, and a green ribbon or bit of lace, it would be presentable. If she had to remain in Washington into the summer . . .

She had expected it, yes, but when the veto actually came, it was no less stunning a blow. The President's statement that he had "been compelled to resist the deep sympathies of his own heart in favor of the humane purposes sought to be accomplished" was an empty euphemism. Congress, he went on, had power to make provisions of an eleemosynary character within the limits of the District of Columbia and nowhere else. While insisting on the right of Congress to grant lands on a lavish scale for schools, colleges, railroads, and other features of internal improvement, he condemned all efforts of Congress to provide for the indigent disabled of any sort as transcending its power.

"If Congress have power," he continued, "to make provision for the indigent insane without the limits of this district, it has the same power to provide for the indigent who are not insane, and thus to transfer to the federal government the charge of all the poor in all the states."

There was hot rebuttal to this argument. Was the fact that a power may be abused reason why it should not exist? Because Congress had the right to declare war against Spain, should that power be taken away because it might declare war against England, France, or Germany?

Said the Honorable Albert G. Brown, Senator from Mississippi, "To my mind, this is the first land bill ever brought forward in the true spirit of the deeds of cession. It is the first bill that ever proposed to divide the lands among the States having in them a common interest, share and share alike. . . . Unless it shall be shown that it is unconstitutional to endow a lunatic asylum per se, it will follow that if you can give to a college in Alabama from the common fund, you may give to an asylum in Delaware from the same fund." The remainder of the Senator's statement was equally caustic and, at times, bitingly sarcastic.

William Darlington of Pennsylvania wrote, "My sympathies have been so long and so fervently enlisted in behalf of your great philanthropic enterprise, now so cruelly thwarted by the Executive, that I find it difficult to express my sentiments in reference to that procedure in terms of moderation. I have lost all patience with those narrow-souled caviling demagogues who everlastingly plead the Constitution against every generous measure and recklessly trample it under feet whenever it stands in the way of their selfish purposes and foregone conclusions. . . . But what has more especially excited my disgust and contempt in this connection is the course taken by the servile partisan press. During the years of your untiring efforts to get the recently vetoed bill through the two houses of Congress, the manufacturers of public opinion (so called) seized every occasion to ingratiate themselves with the humane portion of the community by lauding the objects of Miss Dix's bill. . . . Had the bill been permitted to become a law, no doubt it would have been pronounced and claimed by the despicable echoes of the presidential will and pleasure as one of the noblest acts of his administration."

Senator Solomon Foot of Virginia opposed the President on his claim of unconstitutionality. There were on record a hundred acts in the last fifty years where grants had been made for education, fifty for internal improvements, twenty-five for state and county seats, and others to individuals and corporations. "Congress shall have power," he quoted, "to dispose of and make all needful rules and regulations respecting the territory and other property belonging to the United States."

"Millions for speculation and monopoly," he exclaimed in one speech before the Senate, "not one dollar for benevolence and humanity is the practical maxim which rules in the high places of power in our day."

But Dorothea's friends did not hold out much hope.

Many former supporters were now siding with the President. The debate in the Senate was long and bitter. It began in May and continued through June and into July, waxing hotter as the temperature steadily mounted. Dorothea, wearied to the bone, wilting in the long skirts and petticoats and neck ruffles which fashion dictated, throat hoarse both from constant interviewing and from the dry winds which turned Washington summers into a welter of thick brown dust, waited in an agony of suspense.

"The debates are sustained by my friends with great spirit and ability," she wrote Anne on May 18, "and in this controversy I am waging with the President thus far I hold all the advantage. The last vote closing the debates, on my side 34, that of the administration 13, but I cannot bribe or threaten. I cannot control, so a final vote on the question may not give me two-thirds. I would certainly not exchange either mental, moral, or social state with the President. Poor man!"

On July 6 the vote was taken. Twenty-one yeas, twenty-six nays. With grim foreboding she studied the list of yeas and nays. Who had been for, who against? The number of absences was appalling. Foot, Fish, Houston, Morton, even Edward Everett from her own state! Sumner had been present, had voted to overrule. Others she had depended on had at the last minute deserted.

It was over. The shock, the pain, the bitterness, the sorrow, even the regret, were all past. She felt drained of emotion. Letters besieged her. Of condolence. She scarcely had the energy to read, much less answer them. Of requests. Hospitals she must visit, plans of buildings in process of erection, doctors faced with problems about which she, and she only, could give advice. She had no advice to give. She was bereft of desire, of ambition, of compulsion to act. She knew she must get away. But where? Boston, Newport? No. Farther, much farther, where there would be no solicitations of friends, no demands of relatives. Europe? In February Senator Dix and his wife had invited her to go there with them, but of course she could not think at that time of leaving Washington. She had long wanted to visit hospitals and asylums on the continent, inspired by the exciting reports of American associates who had gone there to study: Dr. Isaac Ray in 1846, Dr. Pliny Earle, always her faithful correspondent, in 1837 and again in 1852. Wonderful research was being done in Prussia, Austria, and other German states. It had been her dream to see the cottage asylums at Gheel and the nursing school of Pastor Fliedner at Kaiserswerth. But now she felt no urge for study, for travel, for — anything.

Only once before in her life had she felt so completely empty of desire, when her health had utterly failed and she had realized she would never teach again. What had she done then? Suddenly came stirrings of memory. Greenbank! A place of utter peace and loveliness, a garden breathing perfumes through open windows, green lawns gently soft and yielding as velvet, sloping to a quiet lake. Best of all, friendship that was unquestioning, undemanding. The Rathbones had long been begging her to come again. Yes. She would go to England.

Five

American Invader

Rest is not quitting the active career;
Rest is the fitting of self to its sphere.

1

"WHAT —? I don't understand." Dorothea regarded the paper handed to her with puzzled astonishment. It was a receipt for payment of her passage on the Steamship *Arctic*.

"I was instructed not to take your money," said the clerk in the office of the American Steam Packet Company. "Mr. E. K. Collins, the chief owner of the line, directed me to request your acceptance of the passage."

"Oh!" For once Dorothea gave vent to deep emotion. "How very generous of him!" She indulged in a rare outburst of confession. "Do you know, this will make it possible for me to carry out a plan which I have had much at heart."

The plan, her friends learned later, was to insure her life for $4,000 for the benefit of her "first born child," the hospital at Trenton. This money would take care of the first year's premium.

It was by no means the first time she had been given free transportation by interested individuals and companies. In 1848 the Adams and Company Express Office had accorded her free use of their line whenever it might serve her philanthropic purposes, agreeing to send all her packages free. Considering the hundreds of books and other commodities she was continually sending to prisons, asylums, hospitals all over the country, this was no small contribution. Her friend John Adams Dix, President of the Chicago and Rock Island Railroad, had sent her a pass in one of his letters. And there had been other such gratuities. But she never failed to be surprised and gratified at this manifestation of interest in her work.

On board the *Arctic* she found that Mr. Collins had provided other features for her comfort, ordering that no one else should occupy her stateroom, a virtual gift of two passages instead of one. Learning that he was on board the ship before its sailing, she went to thank him, but in her weakness she could find no words. Tears were close to the surface. Understanding, he took both her hands in his.

"The nation, Madam, owes you a debt of gratitude which it can never repay, and of which I, as an individual, am only too happy to be thus privileged to show my own sense of obligation."

Rest! It was all she needed, wanted. The grueling months in Washington, the bitter disappointment, had left her prostrated. Yet her definition of "rest" was by no means empty and purposeless inactivity. It was a discipline as necessary and purposeful as labor, well defined by one of her favorite poems by John S. Dwight, which she had copied dozens of times and sent to friends, and which began:

> Rest is not quitting the active career;
> Rest is the fitting of self to its sphere;
> 'Tis loving and serving the highest and best;
> 'Tis onward, still onward, and that is True Best.

She quoted it to Anne in a letter written on September 11, 1854, sometime after the *Arctic* sailed.

"Thus far, by the good providence of God, we are safely on our voyage. I am now free from seasickness, and but for the roughness I could easily employ myself pretty constantly. I pass the time with such measure of listlessness as affords but few results that will tell for others' good. However, I give you an example of my success. I had observed on Sunday several parties betting on the steamer's run. I waited till the bets were decided, and then asked the winner for the winnings, which I put in the Captain's care for 'The Home for the Children of Indigent Sailors' in New York. Tonight I am going to ask each passenger for a donation for the same object as our thank offering for preservation thus far on our voyage. I shall, I think, get above $150, or perhaps but $100." A thank offering which would prove far more significant to the indulgent passengers in days to come, when they should learn that on its return trip the *Arctic* had gone down with all on board!

She had no plans, certainly not for travel. In the same letter she wrote Anne: "I have not the slightest interest in going into France, or even Italy. In contrast with the aim of my accustomed pursuits, it seems the most trivial waste of time. I should like to have some person take my place who would fancy it, if I could receive in exchange a good amount of working strength."

Greenbank again! It was coming back to the only real home she had ever known. She might never have been away. The same loving and concerned friends, the same restfulness and beauty, the same stimulating conversation. Of course the years had brought changes. The children were all married, Mary to the Reverend John Hamilton Thom, Bessy to John Paget. William Rathbone, now in his late sixties, had retired from business and from the mayoralty, surviving a period of bitter opposition when he and his party had thrown the Corporation schools open to all religious denominations and sects. Always in the vanguard of reform movements, he had never been one to court popularity at the cost of principle.

It was Dorothea who had changed most. Certainly she was no longer the shy, uncertain recluse of her first visit, whom young William Rathbone would later recall as "at this period an invalid, a very gentle and poetical and sentimental young lady, and in the then state of her health, without any appearance of mental energy or great power of character." She had acquired not only complete poise and confidence but a noteworthy reputation.

People of distinction clamored to meet her. The Baroness Anne Isabella Byron, a friend of the Boston Tuckermans, wrote that she simply must meet Miss Dix. Perhaps she would not care to visit London during the epidemic, but she might think Brighton worth seeing. Dr. Daniel Hack Tuke, son of the Dr. Samuel whom Dorothea had met on her previous trip, came from his York Retreat, eager to consult with her on her work for the insane. A year before, in 1853, he had received his M.D. from Heidelberg, then had visited a number of European asylums before returning to York to become visiting physician at the York Retreat, founded by his great-grandfather. She must come to York and examine the retreat. Yes, and he would be glad to show her other institutions in England where great progress was being made in areas of mental health. But she would discover also that there were vast deficiencies in the British Isles, especially in Scotland.

Rest? Yes, but not idleness. Not long after her arrival at Greenbank she was writing Anne, "I am still here with dear friends, much occupied with charitable institutions and the meetings of the British Scientific Association. All this tires me sadly, but I shall take things easier in a week. It is my purpose to go to Scotland to see the hospitals in ten days." *Take things easier!* Anne must have echoed in despair.

A week later Anthony Ashley Cooper, the Earl of Shaftesbury, was writing, "I have just received a letter from my friend Mr. Hills who states that you desire of obtaining facilities to inspect our varied lunatic asylums. It will give me great pleasure to render it."

Not yet! the Rathbones protested. Let Scotland wait! First why not see some of the beauties of the British Isles, perhaps Ireland? Doubtless they knew that Scotland would present too much challenge, that in quiet, peaceful Ireland the asylums and workhouses might be more efficiently regulated. Reluctantly she agreed, and for four weeks she toured Ireland, visiting friends of the Rathbones, presenting letters of introduction, sightseeing, and, of course, inspecting almost every hospital and workhouse and asylum in the island. For once she yielded to pure enjoyment. She loved the clear air, the little cottages, the country lanes, the people. Even the hospitals and workhouses presented few problems, though they did not compare with the best in America.

She visited the new prison and the Island Hospital at Dublin, then went to Galway, stopping to see all the hospitals on the way. She was excited by a visit to the castle at Parsontown, where Lord Ross invited her to look through his telescope, and, as she wrote Mrs. Rathbone, she was "swinging in mid-air, sixty feet from the ground at two in the morning . . . on a massive gallery, looking through the most magnificent telescope in the world." From there she went deep into the county of Wicklow, spent a day seeing the Institute for Deaf Mutes and the botanical gardens in Dublin, then went on to Belfast.

It was well that she had this respite, for, returning to Greenbank, she was once more plunged into awareness of human misery. The news of the *Arctic's* wreck came with a profound shock. The war in the Crimea with its violence and plague cast its shadow into the sunny tranquility of the Rathbones' home, for many of their friends had relatives in the army, and they were personally acquainted with Florence Nightingale.

"If I could only meet her!" yearned Dorothea. But as

yet she had no desire or plan for travel on the Continent.

"Few traveling parties would suit my tastes or habits," she wrote Anne in November, "And I as little would suit theirs. In fact, the institutions of England *do* interest me, both literary, scientific, and humane, and in becoming familiar with them I shall acquire much to remember with pleasure and advantage."

The news was not all of tragedy or loss. In October Hugh Bell wrote that at last her three lifeboats had reached Sable Island, and, strange coincidence, the very day after the arrival of the *Reliance* there had been a frightful shipwreck.

"A large American ship from Antwerp, with upwards of one hundred and sixty passengers, men, women, and children, was cast upon one of the sandbanks off the northeast end of the island, and lurched so that the sea beat into her and rendered all chance of escape hopeless. The sea was so heavy and the weather so boisterous that none of the island's boats could live in it. To reach the wreck from the station was over twenty miles; your wagon thus came into use. Your *Reliance* rode over the waves like a duck, and with her and two of your smaller boats the whole of the passengers were safely landed."

Later Hugh Bell sent her a letter from W. D. McKenna, superintendent of the Relief Station at Sable Island, describing in graphic language the heroic efforts of his men, struggling with "tremendous seas, strong currents, and high winds." "The Francis metallic lifeboat *Reliance* has done what no other boat could do that I have ever seen." Other letters came, of congratulation, of gratitude, even in one case of envy, from an Englishwoman, Anna Gurney, who, living on a dangerous coast, had procured apparatus for saving the lives of seamen.

"I can only tell you, I have been on the lookout these thirty years, and tolerably sharp, too, I hope, and never got so much as a pussy-cat to my own share of a wreck, though I have had plenty to do with crews and dogs and cats, too.

But I never had really the joy of being the instrument of deliverance, as you may truly feel yourself."

But surely the letter which Dorothea most treasured was one of simple gratitude from a Lucy S. Adams in Castine, Maine, whose son had been one of the crew rescued from the ship *Arcadia*.

Dorothea accepted all this excess of praise and gratitude with grains of salt. It was the gallantry of the lifeboat crew, of course, which had been as responsible for the miracle of salvation as her lifeboat. A few months later, when passing Trafalgar Square in London, she saw a sign, "Humane Society for Saving Life." Stopping her cab, she went in, asked for the secretary, made some inquiries, and proposed her ten brave men on Sable Island as suitable recipients for the honor of the society's medals. Learning that the Royal Humane Society gave medals to seamen in all the British dependencies and that their rooms were on the Surrey side of the Thames, at the south end of London, she immediately drove there and, after exploring long passages and corridors, found the office of the secretary and stated her wishes.

"Oh, yes," he said, "I know you very well, Madam. We shall be most happy to comply with your request if you will forward the names."

The result was that some months later still she was able to forward to Captain McKenna the gold medal of the corporation for himself and the silver medal for each of his crew, with her personal gratitude and congratulations.

Though the Sable Island episode had been but a tangent, a short detour off the highroad of major concern, all her life she would continue an unflagging interest in lifesaving stations along the Atlantic coast, sending them libraries, supplying new information and equipment. Liverpool was the ideal place for further research. In fact, soon after receiving news of the arrival of her lifeboats, she was recording in her Journal, "I have been trying lifeboats and visiting ship-yards, listening to lectures on the variation of

the compass, also much interested in a project for supporting lighthouses in loose soils by screws that work down
deep in the sands."

2

But November found her back on the highroad. She accepted Dr. Hack Tuke's invitation to visit the York Retreat
and of course was delighted with its every feature. Situated about a mile from York, in the midst of a fertile and
smiling countryside, it was more like a large farm than a
hospital. The comfortable buildings, surrounded by a
great walled garden, had no bars, no grilles at the windows.
It was a Quaker world, with "moral treatment" substituted
for physical restraint, an appeal to responsibility instead of
fear of punishment. Great emphasis was placed on a
concept of "family," a community as much as possible like
that of the community of Quakers. Religion was its
dominating feature. The theories and methods of Dr.
Samuel Tuke, Dr. Hack's father, had become guiding
principles for many of the more progressive American
institutions, including the Hartford Retreat.

Then, provided with the letter from the Earl of Shaftesbury authorizing her to visit all the 188 asylums of England, she ventured into other areas. But usually she kept
the letter in her pocket, finding it far more satisfactory to
make her own way. There had been great improvement in
the last twenty years, due to the "Society for Improving
the Condition of the Insane," headed by Shaftesbury,
who, with Drs. Conolly, Hill, and Charlesworth, had
worked ceaselessly to make life more tolerable for the
mentally ill. New laws had been passed. In most of the
institutions she visited she found little to criticize and was
able to learn much.

"But in Scotland —" As she consulted with Dr. Hack Tuke and others, the unfinished phrase kept rearing its head like a vague and nameless serpent. She asked no questions. Facts, she had long since learned, were better obtained first hand.

To allay her friends' worries, her first trip to Scotland was as a tourist. Letters from the Rathbones and others brought insistent invitations which resulted in lifelong friends. One, Annie McDiurmid, wrote after her visit, "Missed you so much after you left. Your friends the jackdaws have been very importunate at breakfast time, and even the sparrows have been quarreling over their morsels most disgracefully. Your precious botanical specimens went to Liverpool. . . . You would think it foolish, my dear Miss Dix, if I told you how much I loved you."

The Starks in Glasgow, to whom Mr. Rathbone had written of her coming, regretted that they had no room for her, but they secured a lodging for her in the George Hotel and invited friends to dine with her. Helen Hay Carnegy of Trinity, near Edinburgh, deplored the severe winter weather when Miss Dix made her first visit. These social contacts were all pleasant, but friendly visits and sightseeing trips were like Nero's fiddling. Content to explore castles, be lunched and dined, even to collect more rare specimens of flora, where fires of misery might be burning? She was soon visiting all the public institutions at Dumfries, Marston, Glasgow, Perth, Dundee, Aberdeen, and Edinburgh, as well as thirteen private asylums. To her dismay but not surprise she found the same evils rampant as in her investigations throughout America.

Thirty years later Dr. Hack Tuke was to record in his *History of the Insane in the British Isles* that "judging from the records of the past . . . no country ever exceeded Scotland in the grossness of its superstition and the unhappy consequences which flowed from it." The prevalent belief in witchcraft, as in its heyday in New England, had inevitably led to inhumane treatment of the insane.

True, vast improvements had been made. In 1813 East House had been opened under wise and enlightened management. In 1839, after years of agitation first instigated by Elizabeth Fry and her brother J. J. Gurney the Dumfries Asylum had been established and was now a progressive institution under the direction of Dr. W. A. F. Browne. The county was justly famed for its excellent chartered asylums, established by philanthropic endowments and supported by high-class patients.

But there had been no attempt at legislation for the indigent insane until 1848. Then a bill to regulate existing private institutions and establish asylums for "pauper lunatics" was designed but withdrawn on protests of its expense. Some private institutions took in pauper patients paid for by their parishes. Many were housed in poorhouses and prisons. In spite of a bill passed in 1815 providing for the licensing and inspection of asylums, enforcement was lax. Though Dorothea found all the public institutions in the seven principal cities "good, very good," she was shocked by conditions in the thirteen private institutions she visited. Patients were shivering with cold. Licenses had been granted without proper qualifications. The law, she found, was singularly defective, allowing, without consent of the proprietors, no admission to these places, except in the person of the Sheriff of Mid-Lothian. Visits of medical men, only semi-annually, were unproductive of criticisms, due to their pecuniary interests. The proprietors had things all their own way.

When she tried to inspect the asylum at Musselburgh, six miles from Edinburgh, she was refused entrance. She appealed to the Sheriff, the sole authority. He trifled, jested, prevaricated. "The sheriff is a bad man," she wrote Anne, "wholly despotic and he ridicules the entire idea of reform." But she was able to see enough of the asylum's management to assure herself that it was another "Bedlam."

"The sooner I address myself to this work of humanity," she was writing in February, "the sooner will my conscience cease to suggest effort, or rebuke inaction."

The Rathbones and other English friends were shocked at her decision. She needed rest, not more intense labor. She must have a case of nerves, making her so restless! But — most serious objection of all — she was a stranger, a visitor. People would think her an interfering busybody!

Some would, no doubt. Some had before, where she had been a "stranger and a visitor" in most states in America. Some did now, chiefly Dr. W. A. F. Browne, an Edinburgh official who dubbed her "the American Invader." But she pursued her usual course, going to the people responsible for the situation and assuming that they would want to set evil conditions right. Most of them did.

On February 20, 1855, she was writing Mrs. Rathbone, "I am fairly in for reform of the establishments at Musselburgh and have consented under advice and request of Mr. Comb [*sic*], Sir Robert Arbuthnot, Lord Irving (Senior Judge), the Lord Provost, Dr. Lincoln, and others, to delay another week. I fear the next move connected with this may be to London, but possibly not. Lord Teignmouth and Sir Walter Trevelyan are numbered with my allies. Your excellent friend Dr. Traill is earnest in this business."

During consultation with some of these aroused citizens it was decided that the best plan was to demand of the Home Secretary in London, Sir George Grey, a Commission of Investigation. But — who was to go? One of the party was an invalid. Others had urgent professional business. "You, Miss Dix!" was the general outcry. "Why can't you go?" It became clear that, if she wanted the thing done, and done at once, which she certainly did, she must go.

At least one Edinburgh official, Lord Moncrieff, the Lord Advocate of Scotland, was not anxious to have the reports of "the American Invader" carried to London. While staying in the home of Dr. Coombe, the phrenologist, Dorothea heard via the grapevine that he planned to anticipate her arrival. She looked into her purse, counted the time, considered her health, which had not been good for some days, and consulted her conscience. It was eloquent as to her duty. She took her carpet bag, wrapped herself in warm traveling garments, called a cab, and at a quarter past nine that night was in the express train for London, four hundred miles away, a twelve-hour trip. Before leaving, she had telegraphed to Lord Shaftesbury, asking for an interview at three the next afternoon and naming King's Cross Station as her arrival point. She did not sleep but spent the night comfortably. An accident at nine in the morning detained the train and made her an hour and a half late.

She had never been in London before and knew not a single location, but as she stepped from the royal mail carriage, a gentleman approached, asked if she was Miss Dix, and announced a message from Lord Shaftesbury, confirming her appointment. She looked at her watch. No time to dress for presentation! Taking a cab, she asked the distance to Kensington, which she had learned was the residence of the Duke of Argyle. In the cab she exchanged her traveling cloak for a velvet one, folded about her a cashmere shawl, and hoped she looked fairly presentable.

She was at Argyle Lodge when the clock struck twelve. A servant answered the bell. She sent in her card. Admitted to the library, where the Duke and Duchess were entertaining two guests, she asked his Grace to arrange an appointment for her with the home secretary. It was done. His Grace would call for her at Whitehall Place at three and a half, to go to Downing Street.

Fortunately at half past two Lord Shaftesbury had the board in session at Whitehall Place. The matter was discussed, and it was decided that no time must be lost in contacting the usually tardy home secretary. The Duke arrived and reported that Sir George Grey had been summoned to a council at Buckingham Palace.

"You shall see him yourself," he promised Dorothea, "but I shall now meet him at the palace and will state what you have said."

Four p. m. Nothing to do until the next morning, so she sent for a cab and drove to her banker's, Mr. Morgan's, at 38 Gloucester Square, asked for a basin of water, a cup of tea, and bed, which were all promptly secured. In the evening she received a note from the duke. Sir George doubted his authority to order a commission without consulting the Lord Advocate. This was not at all to her liking. The Lord Advocate was too bound by social and political interests. In the morning she drove again to Argyle Lodge. The Duke promised to see Sir George again. Meanwhile she saw Lord Shaftesbury and discussed some matters concerning English hospitals.

More waiting! The next day the duke wrote her that the home secretary had written to the Lord Advocate. Determined to see Sir George herself, she drove to Downing Street, sent up her card, and was ushered into the reception room in some state. His Lordship was courteous. He doubted his power to issue warrants without the concurrence of the Lord Advocate, who might be in London by Monday. He thanked her for her efforts, and she congratulated him on his early attention and unprecedented alacrity, and proceeded to see Sir James Clark, the Queen's physician. He entered cordially into her plans. More waiting!

Monday. No Lord Advocate. Tuesday. Wednesday. Misjudging the efficiency of "the American Invader," he had proceeded with his usual business, packed his trunk, and departed for London at his leisure. He arrived on Thursday, only to discover to his discomfiture that his protests were too late. The home secretary's mind was made up. So was the Lord Chancellor's. His concurrence was expected and grudgingly accorded. The commission of reform for all Scotland, he informed Dorothea on Friday, should at once be formed.

But the grueling labor was taking a painful toll. Already weakened by her tour of institutions and the trip to London, with all its nervous tensions, Dorothea suffered a severe chill during a hurried trip to Westminster Abbey and Saint Paul's, which left her with distressing symptoms. A pain in her arm was so intense that for four days she wore it in a sling. Sir James Clark, the Queen's physician, treated her but obviously did not consider her seriously ill, since one antidote prescribed for her suffering was a large dinner party. She longed for the pure bracing air and quiet restfulness of Greenbank, but negotiations were in the most sensitive stages, and she could not leave.

"I have been looking for lodgings," she wrote Mrs. Rathbone soon after her arrival in March. "Saw some in Hanover Square at six and seven guineas a week. The sole need I have now is for rest, and that I cannot take, for you would not have me abandon the poor insane in Scotland. I am in Sir James Clark's care . . . very painful . . . do not think it neuralgia and doubt if it is inflammatory rheumatism. No prescription has relieved me. I go tonight to the House of Lords with the Duke of Argyle."

She took a room at 18 Gloucester Square and was finally able to write, "Today I have all business closed. I have two Commissions, one of inquiry, one of investigation in Mid-Lothian. This assures, first, reports into the conditions of all the insane in Scotland; next, the *entire* modification of the Lunacy laws, the *abrogation* of all *private* establishments, the establishment of two or three new general hospitals, etc. My odd time I have spent chiefly in securing the interest and votes of Parliament for the Bill to be introduced, and now I go back to Edinburgh tomorrow to report this to all parties interested and to rest if I need it, which is more than probable."

Back in Scotland she discovered that the Lord Advocate was attempting to frustrate her plans by not abolishing the board of commissioners but merely changing its members. Very well. She would not be outdone in diplomacy. Proceeding directly to Dalkeith Palace, she urged his Grace the Duke to address the home secretary demanding fulfillment of her first claim, which had been promised. Sir George Grey replied that all Miss Dix desired should be done. Still there was no time to rest. She spent several weeks journeying to inspect workhouses and private houses for the relief of the demented in order to have reports ready for the commissions which were shortly to come on duty. In one she found that the proprietor had flogged a patient so unmercifully that his teeth had to be drawn, yet had been suffered to hold his place for months after, without fine or punishment. In some houses, it seemed, one of the methods of controlling patients was strapping them into a shower bath and pouring over them from a high point two washing tubs of water. Worse torture than chains or straitjackets! Massachusetts had scarcely done worse. But she left Edinburgh having added some of the chief citizens, including the powerful Duke of Buccleuch, to her allies in favor of reform.

Rest? One might call it that, a few days in Wallington, near Newcastle, as the guest of Sir Walter-Calverley Trevelyan and his lady. Though distressed by a region where there were no middle classes and the rich controlled the poor, she yielded to the luxury of a vast house with thirty huge bedrooms, leisurely meals, walks and drives, conversation and music, and, best of all, communion with an ardent fellow naturalist. Her sleep was undisturbed by the ghost of a woman in white who for two hundred years had supposedly been haunting the gallery adjoining her apartment.

But she could not really rest until the Scotland issues were resolved. Fortunately the new commissions worked swiftly. By May 14 Dr. James Coxe, one of the members, was writing, "We came home yesterday from a hurried *raid* upon Perth and Dundee, and start tomorrow for Glasgow. We have seen enough already to convince us that there is ample field for work before us which cannot fail to bring a glorious harvest. Hitherto, we have scarcely scraped the ground."

Dr. David Skaye, of the Royal Edinburgh Asylum for the Insane, bombarded her with letters. He was amazed at her power to impress influential people. The work, he insisted, could not be completed without her help.

The "harvest" would take two years for fruition, but it would be "glorious" indeed. The commission report substantiated all of Dorothea's findings. A legislative measure was introduced in Parliament. In spite of the resistance of town councils, county meetings, parochial boards, and the existing large asylums, reform was finally effected. But it would be six years before Sir James Clark could write her, "The treatment of the pauper insane is now more carefully attended to than in any other part of Great Britain, I may say."

It was Dr. Hack Tuke who would give the final encomium to her achievement. "I think you might say to the Scotch, 'You are my joy and my crown,' for they have gone on wonderfully since the 'American Invader' aroused them from their lethargy."

3

The cold of Northumberland had proved even more debilitating than the fogs of Edinburgh, and Dorothea turned south for a milder climate. She was settled in a hotel in London, trying at last to rest and recuperate, when Dr. Hack Tuke insisted that she come to York. She yielded thankfully, not so much because the York Retreat offered an ideal opportunity for regaining health, but because she had long been anxious to investigate conditions in its environs. She consented to rest no more than a day, then started out bravely with a reluctant Dr. Tuke to visit the fourteen public and private institutions for the insane in the immediate vicinity. Over thirty years later Dr. Tuke would recall that as they drove to one place in a hired vehicle Miss Dix remonstrated with the driver over his inhumane treatment of his horse.

"So," he thought with amused appreciation, "her sympathies are not restricted to the insane nor to human beings!"

But she was more ill than she realized, and at last she was obliged to succumb. For weeks she lay incapacitated in a cheerful, quiet apartment, ministered to by the skilled Dr. Tuke and his medical associates. In the next apartment, close to death, lay the aged Samuel Tuke, even in his helplessness shedding a blessing throughout the haven of healing by his sheer presence. Only to Dr. Buttolph, superintendent of the Trenton Asylum and long her personal physician, of her friends in America, did Dorothea confess the seriousness of her illness.

"Counting the time since I left the steamer," she wrote, "I find that rather more than half the period I have been either really too ill or too languid to do anything. The irritation of the mucous membrane of the stomach has of late affected me more seriously, and the inaction of the heart has left me feeble."

But the letter dwelt only briefly on her health. It soon turned excitedly to a happening which had opened wide new doors of possibility.

Soon after her arrival Dr. Tuke came into her room with some pamphlets.

"Do you read French?" he inquired. At her nod he continued, "Here is an interesting report from Dr. Van Leuven, of Jersey."

Jersey! What a coincidence! In Dr. Simpson's house in Edinburgh she had met a woman from the south of England who had asked if she had ever visited the islands of Jersey and Guernsey in the British Channel. When Dorothea replied in the negative, the woman and her uncle had detailed some of the great abuses to which the insane there were subject and had begged her to go there. Now she read the reports with mounting excitement. Apparently the movement on behalf of the insane in Jersey was confined to the employment of this young Dutch physician to visit and report on hospitals abroad. If there were evils to be corrected —! "Do write to the doctor for more information," she told Dr. Tuke that evening.

The return letter came promptly. There was indeed a great impending evil. A Mr. Isaac Pothecary of Grove Place near Southampton, well known for its inhuman treatment of lunatics, was planning to establish an asylum in Jersey, since he could not continue in England, where the commissioners were so severe, the laws so stringent, and the formalities for the reception of patients so embarrassing. To escape or avoid all this nonsense in England, he had written Van Leuven, he intended to transport not less than twenty private patients to Jersey, where even no license was required. He wanted Van Leuven to look for some fit place. "I would then," he continued, "have you visit my asylums twice a week, and be well paid."

The young Dutch physician was in a quandary. The man was coming with his patients next week. He could not stop him. Should he refuse to assist? He certainly did not want the money, but if he withdrew entirely he would leave the poor patients at the mercy of their *owner* and of some of the mercenary doctors in Jersey.

"So the matter stands," he ended, "in an island whose government does not care one bit for its own pauper insane, and much less for those imported from England. Could Miss Dix persuade the English government to admit *no* asylums in Jersey or Guernsey, but under the same laws as exist in England? . . . If Miss Dix will come to Jersey, I will give her a hearty welcome, that she may counterbalance the odious *Insanity Trade* now begun."

Coincidence? No, Dorothea instantly decided. A leading of Providence, another call from God. Of course she would go to Jersey.

"So I wait a little now," she wrote in that same letter to Dr. Buttolph, "till returning strength comes to assist the weakened *instrument* of the Divine Will. . . . There, my friend, this must help me get well soon!"

Not nearly soon enough to suit her. For four weeks she was unable to leave the house. Not until the first of June did she venture, still weak and ailing, into the garden. Seated there in the Bath chair which had once belonged to Lindley Murray, the well known *Grammar* author, she read the series of articles by which Dr. Van Leuven had tried to rouse public sentiment in Jersey, planned what measures she must take to prevent these miscreants, frightened away by England's increasingly rigid laws, like rats scuttling from a falling house, from taking their vile business elsewhere. The rigid laws must be extended, of course, to cover the whole United Kingdom. She pictured the freedom she would bring to those poor souls whose only crime was sickness.

"I shall see their chains off," she wrote Anne with exuberance. "I shall take them into the green fields, and show them the lovely little flowers and the blue sky."

Patience! She had never learned its lessons. Perhaps the most healing balm to her restless spirit was a letter written by William Rathbone during these frustrating days.

"My dear Friend: Not being inclined to sleep, I have thought that a quiet hour before breakfast could not be better employed than in saying, God bless my valued and loved friend and speed her successfully in her progress. . . . He has tried you in the success of what you have undertaken beyond what I have ever known, or, as far as my recollection serves me, have ever read of any other person, male or female — far beyond that of Howard, Father Mathew, Mrs. Chisholm, or Mrs. Fry. I speak now of the entirety of the success as much as of the extent, and it has not turned your head or as I believe, led you to forget the source from which your strength has been derived.

"In the most tender love, therefore, to a faithful and self-sacrificing minister to His designs, may He fit the burden to your strength, and not try you too far by allowing you to carry the *World* before you. That your head has not already been, as we say, turned by the magnitude and vast extent of your success, is, as much as the many other parts of your character, the subject of my respectful admiration."

Dr. Van Leuven's letters were less soothing. He described the wretched conditions of the insane in their cells in the general hospital, twenty-five males and five females, with no physician, exercise, occupations, amusements. He had found a suitable site for an asylum, Crown's property, good water, elevated, splendid view. Mr. Pothecary had already settled in Jersey and imported a few rich lunatics. The Jersey climate was at its best, days fine and warm. If she preferred arriving alone, she would do best to take a cab at the pier and drive to 8 Queensroad.

"But I would like to meet you. On your arrival if you see a fair-haired, blue-eyed, flush-faced, rather long-nosed Dutchman coming down the plank and staring round for his unknown friend, you may freely address him and ask, 'Are you not Dr. Van Leuven?' He will tell you, 'Yes, I am, and how do you do, Miss Dix?' "

It was mid-July before she felt able to go. She left London on a Friday in the evening, was delayed off Guernsey by fogs, just escaped the sunken rocks, and landed on Saturday at 5 p. m. Sunday she rested. Monday she drove with Dr. Van Leuven to the hospital, finding the insane in a "horrid state, naked, filthy, and attended by persons of ill character committed to this establishment for vice too gross to admit of their being at large." Then she went to call on the governor. He was not at home, but she left a note with Sir George Grey's letter requesting an appointment. He reacted promptly. She came to this mission not as an "American invader" but as an accepted emissary from the home secretary, one who had already achieved success with Parliament. He hastened to invite her for a conference the following morning. Meanwhile Dorothea inspected the site which Dr. Van Leuven had discovered, Les Moraines, the property of an insane woman who had died without heirs and which had reverted to the Crown.

The governor received her evidence respectfully and promised to take up the matter. Though he approved her plan for the hospital, she still had to fight her way with three dozen members of the states, twelve rectors, twelve yeomen, twelve chief constables. She went with the attorney general to inspect Mr. Pothecary's residence. Thursday she drove into the country, further surveying farms and seeing the scattered insane.

"Today I can only be brief," she wrote Mrs. Rathbone from 8 Queen's Terrace, St. Helliers. "I am very much occupied. First I have gotten Mr. Pothecary under the custody of the High Constable of Jersey, by order of the Governor and counsel of the Attorney General. So *that* business is well settled and the laws will protect the patients he has so far boldly transported. I have seen them. Next, I have got a farm for the hospital that I hope shall be, and the hospital I will call 'La Maison de l'Esperance.' I shall stay in Jersey so long as will settle the question of hospital."

By July 18 she was writing Dr. Buttolph asking for hints, plans, and specifications for a building for a hundred patients *without cost* and by return steamer. "I must push these people, or the building will not be finished till next century." A few days later she was back at Greenbank.

"How did it go?" asked young William Rathbone, he who twenty years before had kept her sick room bedecked with flowers.

"Oh! Perfectly satisfactorily," she replied calmly.

When he pressed further, she gave more details. "I just went to the governor, explained the whole matter to him, and he called together the governing body of the Channel Islands, who have a distinct constitutional system of government apart from that of the United Kingdom. I laid the matter before them, and they were very much shocked but were anxious that I should not make a stir about it, for they are very jealous of having their peculiar constitution interfered with, and said they were willing to do right if I would just tell them what it was."

"And you did." The words were more statement than question.

"Of course. I told them there was no other cure but to build a lunatic asylum costing ten or twelve thousand pounds, and before I left the island they passed a unanimous vote authorizing the expenditure. This Mr. Pothecary was stopped in his nefarious plans and when I left he was in jail for some breach of their island laws. You see, it was all very simple."

Simple! Knowing the conservatism and stubborn frugality of such rectors, yeomen, and constables, William shook his head in wordless wonder. This the shy, fragile creature to whom he had brought sympathy and flowers, childishly, blushingly grateful for loving acceptance?

News of her achievements was bringing congratulatory messages not only from dignitaries in the British Isles but from America and the Continent. Some of her own countrymen, then abroad, were stirred to patriotic pride.

"Pray remember me to Miss Dix," wrote Mrs. E. H. Walsh, wife of the American ambassador to France, to a friend in England. "If with you, tell her that I kiss the hem of her garment, and bless God that our country has produced such a noble heart. She will see the honorable mention of her services by the Earl of Shaftesbury in Parliament, and Mr. Walsh is about to add his testimony to her immense worth, in his correspondence. He regrets very much not having made the acquaintance of Miss Dix. He is right. Such a woman is to be worshiped if anything human could be worshiped."

The annual convention of the Association of Superintendents of American Insane Asylums, held in that summer, 1855, sent a resolution requesting her to give an account of her new investigations at their next meeting.

"We all miss you from the country," the statement continued, "and especially do those of us miss the great benefits of your personal encouragement and cooperation, who are the immediate masters of those 'many mansions' of beneficence, which owe their existence under Providence to the extraordinary success of your appeals to humanity in prosperity in favor of humanity in adversity."

William studied her narrowly for some evidence of natural pride, if not smugness. He knew she had been showered with similar encomiums by great public bodies — at least twenty state legislatures, the Congress of the United States, Parliament. Satisfaction might well have turned into arrogance, confidence into a passion for power. Not, however, in Dorothea Dix. Of course she was aware of the peculiar endowments which made her achievements possible. But, like her name "Dorothea," they were "gifts of God," not self-acquired virtues — if they could be called virtues. So keen was her discernment of character that she could recognize in herself qualities contributory to her success which some might term faults — a rigid inflexibility, a tendency to dictatorship controlled only by the stern necessity for infinite tact, a reserve which inevitably erected a barrier in the most intimate friendships. Satisfaction she could feel, yes, and thankfulness. But never pride.

"People here seem to think I have done a great work," she had written Anne after the appointment of the Scottish Commission. "Perhaps I have. I know it is certainly very satisfying and I feel right about it at heart, and a thousand times happier than if I had wasted my time doing nothing for the good of others."

She had not intended to visit the Continent, but later in the summer the Rathbones, then in Switzerland, begged her to join them. She must get away and turn a deaf ear to all these loud calls of the suffering and renew her strength. Yes, and she should secure a capable woman to travel with her as maid, to save her fatigue and prevent her feeling desolate when alone. A maid! Desolate! She had never felt desolate in her life when alone, and they should see some of the places where she had traveled! It was the maid who would have felt desolate! Moreover, she would be only in the way, with nothing to do. But she agreed that she must "go beyond the reach of the sound of the many afflicted ones, till I have gathered up force to renew — should it please God that I work longer, the work whereunto I am called."

The holiday in Switzerland was a mountaintop experience, high as the magnificent peaks which invigorated her body and exalted her spirit. Rising as usual at dawn, she steeped herself in scenes of ever-changing, glorious beauty. Her letters home abounded in descriptions of "snow-clad peaks, mantled with their regal robes of pasture and forest, as a sublime cathedral anthem to God." For a while she did indeed turn a deaf ear to the cries of suffering and yield herself to that second deep passion of her being, love of nature. She reveled in studying glaciers, geological formations, in collecting new specimens of plants, many of which she had described graphically in her *Garland of Flora* but had never seen. She took a trip to Mont Blanc, made a journey of ten days, four of them by carriage and six in the saddle, through mountain passes. In walking she seemed to lose all strength, yet she could drive for ten hours and ride for six or eight without much fatigue.

Even here she could not avoid suffering. Mrs. Rathbone became desperately ill, and Dorothea, the supposed invalid, became the nurse. For sixty hours she did not once leave her patient. Then a nephew of Mr. Rathbone, with them on the trip, was seized with partial paralysis, and she had two patients to attend. But, as usual, the needs of others provided a reservoir of strength. All finally went to Paris, to remain until the invalids recuperated.

4

When Anne had suggested nearly a year ago that she might like to visit the prisons of Italy, Dorothea had scoffed at the idea. "What should I gain," she had replied, "or what would others gain, by my passage through those dreary dungeons and under the Piombini? Where I do visit prisons, it is where I have before me a rational object and a clear purpose."

Now suddenly she had just that and, best of all, the strength to do it. Not only prisons, and not just Italy, but all hospitals, asylums, almshouses; France, Germany, Greece, Russia, Norway, Holland, perhaps even as far east as Turkey. So near the heritage of Pinel, the colony at Gheel, the model hospitals of Vienna, and not discover what other nations were accomplishing in areas of mental illness? Perhaps she could even stray from duty long enough to fulfill a lifelong dream and visit Palestine!

"But not alone," her friends protested. "You don't even know the languages!"

"No," she admitted. "Just a little rudimentary French. But I will manage."

In September she was making her headquarters in Paris, taking trips into various cities of France to inspect institutions at Yonne, Orleans, Blois, Tours, Mettray, Nantes. At Rouen she visited hospitals for the aged and an establishment for juvenile offenders five miles away, at Quilly. Soon she was in possession of a full Police and Magisterial Sanction under seal, giving her entry into all the prisons and hospitals of Paris. Though her old friends the Emersons were there from Boston, she found little time for sightseeing. However, she did manage to attend the Exposition.

In November she was still residing at the Hotel de Lille et d'Albien, Rue St. Honoré and making the rounds of the city's charitable institutions, hoping to finish in two weeks. The weather was dull, the days short, and need for rest made the work slow, but she pursued it thoroughly, not two weeks but well into January. For the most part she found the city's charitable institutions, liberally supported by government, excellent in both structure and administration. Nonrestraint prevailed. Philippe Pinel would have been well pleased with the progress made since his revolutionary reform.

She wrote glowingly to Dr. Buttolph about her visits to Pinel's La Bicêtre and La Salpêtrière, the farms which supplied all their needs, the plays in which patients often participated both as performers and as audience, the gymnastic exercises, the devoted teachers. However, she noted two radical defects: a want of ventilation, which explained the amazing mortality in many of the charitable institutions, and the experimental methods of treatment by the interns, who were resident students. She found in France marked forms of paralytic affection. Could it be the effect of water in lead pipes?

The second week in January, 1856, she left Marseilles for Italy. In Naples, where she spent thirteen days, she applied for leave to visit the asylums through the American minister, but permission to do so was sent her only when they knew from her passport that she was leaving Naples the next morning.

"But," she was to tell young William Rathbone on her return to England, "I saw everything notwithstanding."

"How?" Already nonplussed, young William was prepared for anything.

"As I always have done," she replied. "If I have not distinct permission to visit an asylum, I go there, and if my entrance is objected to, ask to see the director or manager. I talk the matter over with him, and he almost always ends by becoming interested in the subject. And when they see

I am not a troubler of the peace but really interested in the matter and know something about it, it always ends in their showing me the whole thing. And this is what happened in Naples."

Apparently even language was no barrier to understanding, marveled William.

She regretted that she had little time in Naples, Florence, and Rome to see the works of art, ancient and modern, but saw a good deal in odd moments. A new hospital was badly needed in Florence. However, it was in Rome that she found the greatest challenge. After seeing the hospital in Rome, she wrote Mrs. Rathbone, she regarded all other institutions in the country with comparative favor. Six thousand priests, three thousand nuns, and a spiritual sovereignty joined with the temporal powers had not assured for the miserable insane a decent, much less an intelligent, care. "I could not bear to know this, see this, and do nothing." But what to do? See the pope, of course. A delicate task indeed for a Protestant and a woman! How approach the supreme pontiff, tell him that in the light of modern knowledge his insane asylum was a disgrace and a scandal, without offending or insulting him, and, more important, win his favor and cooperation? It must be no perfunctory interview, with ceremonial bows and kneelings, but an actual face to face encounter.

"The appeal to the Pope involved care, patience, time, and negotiation," she was to write afterward. Simple words for an incredibly bold, not to say audacious, enterprise.

Fortunately she had made the acquaintance of Cardinal Antonelli, a humane and intellectual man in spite of his somewhat unsavory moral reputation. Notwithstanding her rigid puritanical standards, Dorothea would suffer no criticism of his conduct to the end of her days. He agreed with her heartily on the need for reform and arranged for her an interview with the pontiff.

She donned her best black silk, its severity relieved by

snowy ruffles at the neck, and adjusted her plain neat bonnet. The rich brown hair rimming its white silk lining was scarcely touched with gray, and the face beneath was almost as smoothly youthful as in young womanhood. Only a slight flush along the high cheekbones and a heightened brilliance in the wide-spaced eyes betrayed her emotion, and these were more from excitement than from nervousness. Shawl draping her shoulders, head high above the long, slender neck, she went calmly forth to challenge the "Anointed Vicar of Christ on Earth."

She found Pope Pius IX graciousness and benignity personified. Happily he spoke English well, so the interview was not complicated by an interpreter. He listened intently to her recitals of the evils she had observed and professed shock at the details. He would make a personal examination immediately, he promised, and gave her a future appointment to discuss the subject. She came away hopeful, yet she had learned to take all such promises with a grain of salt. Red tape was doubtless as plentiful in the Vatican as in American legislatures and Congress. However, the second interview was even more satisfactory. The pope had driven unannounced to the insane asylum and inspected the wards himself. Distressed by the conditions, he warmly thanked her, a woman, a Protestant, a foreigner, for apprising him of these conditions.

"And did thee really kneel and kiss his hand?" a Quaker friend inquired later.

"I most certainly did," replied Dorothea. "I revered him for his saintliness."

The surprise that others of her Protestant friends evidenced at this respect accorded to a *woman* was, she well knew, a confession of ignorance. For the Catholic church had long been ahead of Protestantism in opening careers of distinguished service to exceptional women. There had been Catherine of Siena, Saint Theresa, and many others. Yet the pope had certainly been gracious far beyond her expectation.

So far, so good. Yet, as always, she would never be satisfied until the promises had been fulfilled. A church could be as cumbersomely bureaucratic as a government. Her fourteen days in Rome completed, she held herself in readiness to return whenever needed. Great was her relief, later, to find that a physician had been sent to France to study methods there and that a tract of land near the Villa Borghese had been purchased. Later still she was assured by an American friend, Dr. Joseph Bancroft, that steps had been taken by the pope toward the erection of a new asylum on the most approved plan.

Genoa . . . Naples . . . Turin. "The General Hospitals here, as in Italy at large, are very good, but that in this city for the insane is so bad that I feel quite heartsick. I drove to the hospital in the country — very bad. Then I drove to the hospital within the walls, made an appointment with the chief doctor for tomorrow. . . . I shall appeal in writing to the King."

Milan . . . Florence. . . . "My plans appear to be about as stable as spring breezes." . . . "I get daily news from Constantinople which moves my sympathy for the poor insane of Turkey." . . . "You need not be much surprised to hear of me in Constantinople."

Venice . . . Trieste . . . Ancona . . . Molfetta . . . Brindisi . . . Corfu . . .

"I find traveling *alone* perfectly easy," she wrote Dr. Buttolph while her steamer was lying at anchor in the harbor of the Island of Corfu. "I get into all the hospitals and prisons I have time to see or strength to explore. I take no refusals, and yet I speak neither Italian, German, Greek, or Slavonic. I have no letter of introduction and know no persons en route. I found at Trieste a very bad hospital for the insane. Fortunately a physician attached to the suite of the Archduke Maximilian has promised the intervention of government at Trieste and assured me that all the institutions of Austria shall be open to my visits if I come to Vienna."

As soon as the boat landed on Corfu she went on shore, took a cab and drove to the Greek institutions. *"Saw all!"* she wrote Mrs. Rathbone. Cephalonia, Zante, Patras, Missolonghi, Mycenae, Corinth, Piraeus . . . She came to Greece by the Isthmus, in order to land at the Ionian Islands to visit the hospitals. It was dark on April 1, 1856, when she reached Athens, and she left at noon the next day for Piraeus to resume her sea journey. No time to visit the Acropolis and the Parthenon, though she had dreamed for years of their beauties! From a distance she saw Mount Parnassus looking as white as Mont Blanc. She had hoped after crossing the isthmus to visit Corinth, but the captain would not consent to her leaving the protection of the powerful guard of one hundred soldiers which surrounded the transport carriages. A fierce band of robbers had attacked the carriage twenty days earlier and gotten away with all the luggage and money, so in each vehicle there sat an armed soldier and at the side, in close file, rode a bodyguard.

While she waited in Piraeus for a ship from the Peloponnesus, a French steamer brought the glad news that peace had been declared in the Crimea. Immediately Dorothea transmitted her joy to Mrs. Rathbone. "We give devout thanks that the hours of warfare are ended, but how long it must be before the wounds on social and domestic happiness are healed or forgotten! . . . I feel that Miss Nightingale will have a great work still in the East. God bless her efforts!"

Florence Nightingale! Dorothea was almost as anxious to meet this kindred pioneer in human healing as to tread the stony streets of Jerusalem and the green paths of Galilee. The hospital at Scutari where Miss Nightingale and her nurses had been ministering to soldiers was one of her most urgent goals. It was on a ship from Piraeus to Constantinople that she finally decided she must relinquish all hope of visiting the Holy Land. She felt like the would-be disciple called on to sell his pearl of great price. All her life she had dreamed of this opportunity. In her morning devotions she had followed the footsteps of the beloved Master, picturing the little lanes, the lake blue as sapphire, the hills where He had gone to pray, and hoping . . . It was April now. The stony hills would be clothed in green and the lilies of the field would be in bloom. But she knew that she could not afford the additional expense and visit all the places she felt called to go. She must confine herself to regions which had hospitals, or the lack of them, where she might render service. The decision was all the harder because one of her companions on this steamship was an Austrian doctor on his way to Jerusalem to execute the will of a Viennese lady who had given 50,000 florins to establish a school for poor children in the Holy City.

"We are only twelve days from Jerusalem," he reminded her when he prepared to leave the ship. Resolutely she turned from the temptation.

As usual, she went ashore at each landing, finding her way to the hospitals by noting the positions of flagstaffs before landing. Syros . . . Tenos . . . Samos . . . At Smyrna she found a good English hospital for sailors, also one for the Dutch and Greeks. Mytilene . . . Gallipoli . . . Marmara . . . Though peace had presumably been declared she saw signs of military preparation all along the coast. War, she thought, as she neared the fighting areas, one of the breeding grounds for mental illness!

At last Constantinople. A bright spring sun turned the hundreds of onion-shaped domes into a frieze of pure gold. The hospitals of the city could wait. First Scutari and the inimitable Miss Nightingale! Taking a boat, she was rowed to a landing at Galata, where she toiled through streets that seemed designed as public drains, the hem of her long full skirt soon bedraggled with mud and slime. Presently she stepped into a caique with two rowers.

"Hospital, Scutari!" she said in English. They nodded. In half an hour she was landed at the wharf of upper Scutari. She paid and discharged the boatmen, then, meeting an English sailor, inquired the way to the nurses' quarters. No, she was told, Miss Nightingale was away, had been for a month at Balaklava on the Crimea, where there was much sickness among the British and French troops. Dorothea was bitterly disappointed. She toured the chief hospital, which was in excellent order, a far cry from the filth and blood and stench which had greeted the "Lady with the Lamp" and her gallant female pioneers. There was another large hospital, but by now Dorothea's feet in their delicate lady's boots were too painful for further travel. Had she but known it, she was being given a preview of a situation which in less than five years would be taxing her own skill and ingenuity to the limit. A meeting with the woman who had created this cleanliness and order out of an Augean stable of war's filth and misery would have been of inestimable value.

Now — Constantinople. Not her ancient mosques, her delicate icons, her palaces, her oriental treasures, but her hospitals, asylums, prisons. Dorothea was the guest of Dr. Cyrus Hamlin, president of Robert College, who was not only a gracious host but a means of entrance into the city's most exclusive institutions. To her delight and surprise she found a remarkably well directed psychopathic hospital in the Turkish quarter. Instead of the dungeons, chains, brutal treatment she had been told to expect, there were excellent order, good ventilation and cleanliness, careful diet, and intelligent doctors. The director, a native Turk, had been educated in Paris and was using all the best new methods of treatment.

"The insane of Constantinople," she wrote Mrs. Rathbone after visiting this institution, "are in *far better condition* than those of Rome or Trieste. . . . The hospital was founded by Solyman the Magnificent, and the provisions for the comfort and pleasure of the patients, including music, quite astonished me. I had substantially little to suggest, and nothing to urge!"

Not so in some other institutions. She visited all the

prisons and hospitals of the great city — Armenian, Greek, Catholic Armenian, English, as well as Turkish. Dr. Hamlin obtained permission for her to visit the great Greek hospital of Ballocli, also the major Armenian hospital. In both she found departments for the insane, but was not at all pleased with the management. The English prison called forth her severest criticism. Dr. Hayland, who had its medical care, was not pleased with her intrusion. The Turkish debtors' prison she found nauseous for filth and want of ventilation. But the Turkish insane hospital made up for all the disappointments.

Dr. Hamlin wrote of her visit, "Miss Dix made the impression at Constantinople of a person of culture, judgment, self-possession, absolute fearlessness in the path of duty, and yet a woman of refinement and true Christian philanthropy. . . She was equally worthy with Elizabeth Fry to be called the 'female Howard.' "

She traveled on, through the Bosphorus, up the shore along the Black Sea to Varna and Sulina, hoping all the time to meet Florence Nightingale on her way back to Constantinople. When the *S. S. Franz Joseph* started up the Danube bound for Pesth, she gave up hope. In fact, Miss Nightingale would not leave Balaklava until near the end of June, when peace was at last implemented and her work nearly finished. They were never to meet, either in the East or in England, these two women who did more to alleviate the miseries of sick human beings than any others in their century.

"I find traveling here alone *no more difficult* than I should in any part of America," Dorothea wrote Anne on May 9 as the steamer made a landing in Assora, Hungary. "My usual experience attends me. People are civil and obliging, who are treated civilly. . . . I am the sole representative of England and America on the boat. There are, besides, people of many tribes, and persons of far distant English possessions, affording a singular association of oriental costumes and occidental attire. As for speech,

Babel is not illy illustrated. You will wonder that I give so meagre descriptions of persons and places, but if one is busy in examining, while pausing for a few days or hours in a city, there is little time for putting on paper in an interesting manner details worth sending so far."

Fortunately there was no need to return to Rome. The pope had listened to her pleas and appointed a good director, and this augured well for the fulfillment of his promises. She spent an extended period in Vienna, where she was impressed with the revolutionary changes made by Maximilian Jacobi and other physicians. She promoted plans for a much needed hospital in Dalmatia, on the east coast of the Adriatic. The friendships made in Pesth and Vienna would continue for a lifetime.

She went on to other countries. In July she was in Stockholm, Sweden. She visited Russia, Norway, Denmark, Holland, parts of Germany, Belgium, and, again, France.

"I have been greatly blessed in all my travels," she wrote on August 1, having arrived in London. "In Russia I saw much to approve and appreciate. As for the hospitals in St. Petersburg and Moscow, I really had nothing to ask. Every comfort and all needed care were possessed, and much recreation secured. Very little restraint was used."

She had seen the best and worst of Eruope's mental institutions, had consulted intimately with her most famous authorities. Farewells were difficult. She was besieged with letters and testimonials.

"I am inclined to envy you," wrote Dr. Hack Tuke from York in mid-September just before she sailed, "the feelings which you must have in the retrospect of what you have been enabled to do since you set foot on British land."

And from Hanwell Dr. John Conolly, aged peer of Pinel in the history of the treatment of insanity, wrote, "Your words of approbation, dear Miss Dix, are very precious to me; for I honor you and your great labors for the benefit of your fellow creatures in many ways. . . . I trust that there are regions where, after this world, all will be more congenial to such spirits, and to those who sympathize with you, and share your good and noble aspirations."

It was *this* world which most concerned Dorothea. Already any good she had been able to do in Europe was left behind. She could hardly wait to get back to America to put some of her new knowledge and experience in practice.

⚜ Six ⚜

Interim

I have had great cares, greater fatigues, countless blessings unmeasured, preserving mercies, and am joined to all occasions for thanksgiving.

1

LUMBERING RAILROAD CARS trailing smoke and sparks, loose-jointed wagons fording swollen streams, river boats with near-bursting boilers, stages beset by bandits . . . all these Dorothea could face without a nervous quiver. Not so an ocean liner! "I do not actually fear the sea," she wrote Anne before sailing from Liverpool on the *Baltic* September 16, 1856, "but I never for an hour forget the vicinity of the presence of danger, and in the event of accident the almost certain loss of life." Remembrance of the ill-fated *Arctic* made the prospect even more disquieting. But this time the passage was smooth and sunny. When they came within fifty miles of shore and the land birds flew low, sometimes picking food from their hands, she could write gratefully, "I have been brought home safely for some good purpose."

But what? She was bombarded with suggestions, invitations, requests, demands. She should write a book about her travels and new discoveries. She must come to visit Anne, brother Joseph, the Hares in Philadelphia, the Burnaps in Baltimore, the Henrys in Washington, the Torreys and Emersons in Boston. The Buttolphs in Trenton had a new baby that she must come and see. But most urgent were the requests for assistance. "We need another hospital." . . . "must have your aid in choosing a proper site." . . . "We cannot possibly raise the funds without your help!" . . . "I am having problems with my board of directors and need your advice." . . . "Could you help us find the right superintendent?"

Some decisions were easy. There would be no book. She had made important discoveries, yes, but they must be put into action, not words. Friends also must wait. The hard decisions were related to the requests and demands. Which were imperative? What matters could be handled by correspondence? Which institutions could be combined in a single trip? Were there any areas where she might not be made welcome?

For she found the country in political turmoil. In Washington strife between the slave and free states was mounting in harsh crescendos. Kansas, open to "squatter sovereignty," had erupted in blood. In May Charles Sumner, having delivered a speech condemning the proslavery leaders in Kansas and their southern abettors, had been attacked bodily on the Senate floor and nearly killed. Repeal of the Missouri Compromise had lost Franklin Pierce the support of the North, and he was not renominated. A new party calling itself Republican, its platform based on the sole issue of resistance to the extension of slavery, nominated John C. Frémont for President, and the South warned that the election of a "Black Republican" would mean the dissolution of the Union.

Dorothea's old friend Millard Fillmore, who was still a frequent correspondent, was persuaded to run as presidential candidate of the "Know-Nothing" or American Party. Originally a movement opposed to the flood of immigration of the forties, it had become a rallying ground for many northern Democrats disgusted with the policies of Pierce and his proslavery Secretary of War, Jefferson Davis, and was dedicated to preserving the Union at all costs. Dorothea did not approve of her friend's participation in the American party, founded on principles of secrecy and religious intolerance, and she told him so.

"I will only say now," he wrote her after his defeat in the November election, "that if you understand the whole subject, and after a deliberate consideration of it have come to the conclusion that it is wrong, I should distrust and doubt the propriety of my position. For I regard you — as I ever have — as my Mentor, more likely to be right from that intuitive knowledge peculiar to the elevated mind of one intelligent and refined female than man is, with all his boasted powers of reasoning."

A hundred years later the belated discovery of such missives exchanged between the two would be extravagantly headlined as "love letters." Though expressive of mutual affection and admiration, they were never that. There was now a second Mrs. Fillmore, and the friendly correspondence continued unabated. If, as some of her friends suspected, Dorothea might have filled that role had she so desired, she would no more have considered the possibility than a dedicated nun would have thought of renouncing her vows.

She plunged into the round of visits, inspections, consultations, fund-raising campaigns, as if she had never been away. On December 26, 1856, she was writing from New York: "I arrived safely and without accident on Monday night. Tuesday I spent at Ward's, Randall's, and Blackwell's Islands, Wednesday up the Hudson to Sing Sing prison, on Thursday (today) High Bridge, to juvenile asylums and reformatories; tomorrow to Bloomingdale; Saturday, hospitals in the city, and Saturday evening to Trenton. Thus you see the progress of my doings. I now think I shall go to Philadelphia on Tuesday, on Wednesday make the purchases for the hospital at Harrisburg, on Thursday go to Harrisburg, a day's journey, see the patients Friday; return to Philadelphia Saturday, spend Sunday at the hospital; Monday, almshouses; Tuesday, Trenton; Wednesday set out for Buffalo, Geneva, Canandaigua, etc., to explain anew the miseries of their almshouses, so if you do not hear from me, please do not consider yourself forgotten or even unbeloved."

But less than a week later she was in Toronto, called there suddenly by an urgent summons that she could not resist, and finding there such neglect, ignorance, and mismanagement that it stirred her sensitive nature to the depths.

Never had she been so busy. In 1857 the Hospital for the Insane of the Army and Navy was completed in Washington, one of her most cherished projects. The site so sacrificially yielded by the Blagdens was truly the best setting in the world. In the room on the third floor set aside for her by Dr. Nichols, its superintendent, she could look over the broad sweep of the Potomac into the heart of Washington. It would always be waiting for her just as she had left it, as much her home as the room in the tower at Trenton. But she was seldom in either one. With sectional strife mounting and the country heading for almost certain explosion, she felt driven to activity, especially in the South, where the presence of a "Northern invader" might at any time become unwelcome.

Always work came first. In November it kept her from attending Dr. Nichols's wedding to his "dear, beautiful and accomplished Miss Ellen." The more hospitals she founded, the more problems were presented. To each, like her "first born" in Trenton, she had given birth. Now she must help to bring up the lusty growing child. Often there were dissensions among the members of a hospital staff, or, far more insidious, complaints of deranged minds which, though totally unfounded, could whip the imagination of a gullible public into flame and threaten the careers of even such dedicated specialists as a Bell, a Woodward, a Ray, a Nichols, or a Kirkbride. Again and again Dorothea was appealed to in such emergencies. Her clear mind and unbiased judgment often enabled her to get to the crux of a problem and fearlessly aid in its solution, whether it meant elucidation of facts to a board or committee, discharge of an incompetent staff member, or defense of persons unjustly accused. Often she herself was harshly maligned in the process, but such criticism left her unperturbed.

"My dear Annie," she wrote once to her anxious friend, "do not take too much to heart that which people say in Worcester, it is as the weight of a feather to me. I am *right*, what harm can these do me? The Lord is the strength of my life, whom shall I fear?"

Probably no one in the country, except possibly the President, had such power of controlling personnel. Committees, often high government officials, were constantly appealing to her for suggestions for appointments. Even from Scotland, where the new laws were just going into effect, she received letters urging her to recommend various parties to official places. This she firmly declined to do. And at home no man ever helped his cause by personal solicitation. All recommendations she made must be kept in inviolate confidence.

"I understand I owe my appointment to your strong recommendation," said one superintendent, and was about to express his gratitude when she interrupted sharply, "You should never have been told. It was an unpardonable breach of confidence."

In July of 1857 she was in the vicinity of Pittsburgh, where she had already assisted in procuring funds from the legislature for the building of a new mental hospital separate from the Western Pennsylvania Hospital, which since 1855 had been admitting mental patients from a district comprised of twenty-one counties in the western part of the state. The managers of the proposed institution were planning to locate it in Pittsburgh proper. No, she insisted, that was no place for a mental hospital. She found a magnificent site about eight miles from the city "both salubrious and cheerful, joined with outlooks of rare beauty associated with some elements of grandeur." It was a farm comprising some 106 acres with large frontage on the Ohio River. Her powers of persuasion were effective, for not only was this tract purchased the following year, but an adjoining farm of 177 acres would soon be added for auxiliary buildings. The new institution, she hoped, would have the features of the celebrated Rauhe Haus near Hamburg.

"Snow two feet deep," she was writing Mrs. Rathbone from Oneida, New York, the following January, "thermometer 27 below zero, gas burners easily lighted by the spark transmitted by the finger."

The next July, 1858, she was writing Anne from Nashville. "I do not know whether you have followed my devious journey, but if you will look on the map for Philadelphia, Baltimore, Washington, Chesapeake Bay, Norfolk, Williamsburg, York, Hampton, Portsmouth, Raleigh, No. Carolina, Weldon, Petersburg, Richmond, Charlottesville, Trenton, Rockbridge, Central Virginia, Salem, Abington, Bristol, Virginia, Dalton, Georgia, Chattanooga and Nashville you will follow my devious course."

That year of 1858 saw the passage of her bill in Maryland, the successful climax of many years' work. Her friend, George Washington Burnap, the Unitarian minister in Baltimore, and his wife Nancy, who had been ardent supporters through the years, were as happy over the achievement as she was. Though these years of the late fifties marked progress and heightening interest in her mission to the insane, Dorothea was alarmed and disillusioned at the state of the country. President Buchanan, she felt, though starting his administration under favorable auspices, had committed the most ill-considered acts.

The country seemed to be hurtling toward tragic disunity. Yet alarm gave way finally to resignation.

"I am coming to look with much composure on the public affairs of the world," she wrote Mrs. Rathbone, "having ceased to look for peace, repose, political tranquility, and harmony among the nations. I will not permit myself to be distressed at what I cannot help to an end. Some honest patriots I may live to see command the issues of government, but it is not probable."

Her friends were shocked when she determined in the spring of 1859 to go to Texas, that far outpost of primitive civilization. Of course she was not dissuaded. True, travel was incredibly difficult. How, she wondered, could the poor, the sick, the insane endure transportation such distances and over such roads! To her amazement she was received, not as a stranger to be politely tolerated, but as a beloved friend. She almost wept at the constant heart-warm welcome, the confidence and cordial good will which greeted her at every turn. She was astonished that her wishes in regard to institutions, her opinions touching organization, were considered authoritative.

"You are a moral autocrat," a gentleman in the state service told her. "You speak, and your word is law."

"Oh, you are no stranger," she was often greeted. "We have known you for years and years."

One day she was taking dinner at a small public house on a wide, lonely prairie. The master stood, with the stage waybill in his hand, reading it and eyeing her. Because I'm the only lady passenger, she thought. When she drew out her purse to pay, he said quickly, "No, no, by George! I don't take money from you. Why, I never thought I should see you, and now here you are in my house! You have done good to everybody for years and years. Make sure now there's a home for you in every house in Texas. Here, wife, this is Miss Dix! Shake hands and call the children."

It was only one of many such incidents in the state. She

must be careful, she thought, in the demands she made for hospitals, for her every word seemed to be unquestioned!

Travel in the great state was long and tedious. From Houston by rail eight miles to Hempstead, all the way surrounded by kind and attentive travelers. Stagecoach for Austin, costing $13.50, six horses for a day and two nights, stopping only long enough to change horses and give the passengers "time to lighten the coach." On the first night out the driver undertook a descent and ascent without the usual precautions. Down they rushed into the black abyss across three yards of muddy bottom and water, ending up against some broken logs intended to mend the road. The racing leaders broke off every trace short and, clearing the logs, shot off across the prairie, leaving the passengers in a ditch four miles from the last change in the midst of sizzling rain. At last someone went back to fetch the leaders left at the last stop.

"We mought get off," calculated the driver, "by six in the morning."

Some passengers rolled up in blankets on the logs, some remained in the coach, some went walking. The driver deposited himself on top of the stage and slept. " 'Tis an ill wind . . ." thought Dorothea, recalling the old saying with appreciative humor. The driver had already been on the road a night and two days without sleep, his colleagues having been indisposed by reason of late gambling.

"No serious accident marked my journey," was Dorothea's terse comment.

Such narrow escapes were frequent. The gift of one hundred dollars for a new lifeboat for Sable Island reminded her that she had almost needed one herself the preceding month in the Gulf of Mexico, when the captain for twenty-four hours had not once left his station on deck, and the boat had barely escaped foundering.

In spite of the steady westward march of railroads, their comforts had not improved. True, the new invention of the "sleeping car" was just appearing, but one look at it was enough for Dorothea. "Nothing could induce me to occupy one of them," she wrote Anne. "They are quite detestable."

Later, however, she did make one night's experiment, between Pittsburgh and Cincinnati, which would suffice for the rest of her life. "I cannot suppose," she commented, "that persons of decent habits, especially ladies, will occupy them, unless some essential changes are made in their arrangements and regulations."

Physical discomforts were often the least of the evils of travel. The foibles of fellow passengers were far more irritating than sitting bolt upright on a hard seat for several days and nights, wiping dust and cinders out of reddened eyes. Occasionally she was forced to speak her mind, as when three young ladies, all dressed in the height of fashion, came on the train. Fashion at that period dictated the "wasp waist," which she especially abhorred. Almost as bad, she felt, to so fetter the vital organs as to imprison the insane in cages! When the three began making loud sounds of ridicule about a fourth young woman a few seats away whose generous bulk was obviously unconfined, Dorthea began to seethe.

"Better be dead than so out of fashion!" proclaimed one of the three.

Dorothea could restrain herself no longer. "My dear," she interposed, her rich voice carrying to every point in the carriage, "if you continue to lace as tightly as you do now, you will not long have the privilege of choice. You will be *both* dead and out of fashion."

2

The following months found her in Louisiana, in Minnesota, in Wisconsin, in Pennsylvania. That winter she asked for more than a third of a million dollars from various state legislatures. As a result of the support of men like Thomas Bakewell and John Harper, Dixmont Hospital was established near Pittsburgh, the only institution which she ever permitted to bear the family name, and this, she insisted, was not in her honor but in memory of her Grandfather, like the site of the other hospital at Dix Hill. Construction of the majestic new buildings was begun about May 1, 1859, and on July 19 the cornerstone was laid with appropriate ceremonies, as the annals of the hospital recorded, "in the presence of a large concourse of friends of the institution from various parts of the state. It was a source of great regret to the assembly that the philanthropic engagements of Miss Dorothea L. Dix in other parts of the Union prevented her attendance at the interesting occasion of commencing an institution which has been favored with so large a measure of her counsel, sympathy, and assistance. The hospital site was named Dixmont because the managers desired to honor Miss Dix for her 'exertions for its existence.' "

Absence from such an event was typical of Dorothea's techniques of operation. It was the sowing of the seed, the harrowing, the weeding, that were important. Let others reap the triumphant harvest. She would not be present, either, on November 11, 1862 when the new hospital was finally opened and a special train of cars transferred the entire household of 113 patients, attendants, and other employees from the Western Pennsylvania Hospital to the sumptuous new buildings. But she would visit it many times, taking great satisfaction in its two spacious wings, its central chapel where religious services were held each Sunday afternoon, its gaslights, hot-air heat, abundance of water and excellent ventilation; in its opportunities for employment, facilities for recreation and cultural education, including games, a revolving stereoscope, a billiard table, oil and water paintings, magic lantern slides, a Chickering piano, and several marble statues; most of all in the employment of the most modern methods, stressing the necessity of early treatment for the best chances of recovery.

She was also pressing these days for special training for feeble-minded children, so that they need not be helpless burdens on society but become useful citizens, a need which had greatly impressed her in Europe. She favored their being taught trades but strongly opposed their labor being exploited for profit. Persevering efforts obtained an appropriation of $20,000 for the erection of new buildings at the Pennsylvania Training School at Media.

In the summer of 1860, when North and South were rushing toward collision, she was in the Middle West. Writing at a side table in a telegraph office in Prairie du Chien, Wisconsin, and waiting for a boat to La Crosse, from there to push up the Mississippi to St. Paul, Fort Snelling, and St. Anthony, she described in glowing language the "wonderful country of vast prairies, wide, deep, ocean-reaching rivers, and lakes that deceive you into the idea that you are where the Atlantic rushes in." She was favorably impressed with the industrious Germans and Norwegians, intent on wresting new life from the virgin soil, here where there was room enough for all. Among the brutal and disorderly few, however, she found an alarming degree of insanity, often incurable, so there was work to be done. It was good to be far from the threatening war clouds in the East.

But in November she was back in South Carolina, hotbed of dissension and threats of secession. She arrived just after the election of November 6, in which a raw, ungainly Republican from Illinois was elected on a platform calling for no further extension of slavery. Four days later the state legislature called a convention to consider secession. The state was seething with emotion. Could she possibly arouse interest in a bill for funds now pending before the state legislature asking for $60,000 for support of the asylum, $5,000 for repairs, $10,000 for back debts, and

Dixmont Hospital for the Insane.

$80,000 for a new extension? If not, the labor of long years would be lost.

"I made a rapid journey hither by railroad from Jackson, Mississippi," she wrote Mrs. Rathbone on November 9, "traveling without stopping a half hour three days and nights, and arriving to find all hospital business not at a standstill merely but looking very unpromising. I had no time to lose and at once saw the Senate and House Committees, reasoned, explained, persuaded, urged, till I secured a unanimous report from these parties to their respective bodies in favor of extension by new wings, etc. of the state hospital."

On December 19, just one day before the convention passed its Ordinance of Secession, she was able to write, "My Bill has passed both Senate and House by an almost unanimous vote. Providence seems leading me on, and He, by whose mercy I am preserved, blessed all my labors for the afflicted." It was a happy climax to other successes of the same season, including an appropriation for a new hospital at Knoxville, Tennessee.

But back in Washington for Christmas she could feel little triumph, no rejoicing. "We illustrate a national contagious frenzy; it is downright madness," she wrote Anne in despair. "The seat of government that was is all but a city of the dead, not literally a shrouded corpse, but dead in action — intellectual force of resources." Yet she hoped the worst had passed, and at the end of her sad description of a dead and bankrupt capital she added the postscript, "Be of good cheer, for sadness cannot heal the national wounds."

3

The country might be ablaze, but there were still unfortunate sufferers to be rescued from fires of mental anguish. In the next three months, while the nation tottered under the leadership of a weak, lame-duck President and state after state seceded, Dorothea went calmly about her work, in Harrisburg, in Trenton, in Philadelphia. In February 1861, she was writing Anne from Illinois, the home state of the new President, whose inauguration the South so feared and dreaded.

"I thank God, dear Annie, I have such full uses for time now, for the state of our beloved country, otherwise, would crush my heart and life. I was never so unhappy but once before, and that grief was more selfish perhaps, viz, when the 12,225,000 acre Bill was killed by a poor, base man in power."

It was while she was on one of these trips that she learned through some source which she would never be willing to disclose of an extensive, well-organized conspiracy to prevent Abraham Lincoln from being inaugurated President of the United States. Instantly all her keen faculties were alerted. She must take steps to counteract the fanatic but extremely dangerous plot. The action she took may well have saved, not only the life of the new President, but, as events would develop under his leadership, the very existence of the Union.

One Saturday afternoon Mr. Samuel Felton, president of the Philadelphia and Baltimore Railroad, was sitting in his office when a woman asked to see him.

"Miss Dix? Of course. I have known her for years. Send her in."

"I have an important communication to make to you personally," said Dorothea.

He listened attentively while the well known philanthropist talked to him lucidly and in full detail about the plan she had unwittingly discovered. As he already knew, the South was in deadly fear of what the new President might do, and rumors had reached his ears of various schemes which might be employed to prevent his inauguration. Now, Miss Dix informed him, there was an extensive, fully organized conspiracy through the South to seize Washington, with its archives and records, and then declare the Southern Confederacy de facto the Government of the United States. At the same time they were to cut off all means of communication between Washington and the North, East, and West, thus preventing the transportation of troops to wrest the capital from the insurgents. Mr. Lincoln's inauguration was thus to be prevented, or his life was to fall a sacrifice.

"In fact," Miss Dix told him with calm clarity, "troops are even now drilling on the line of your own road, the Washington and Annapolis line, and other lines of railroad. The men drilled are to obey the commands of their leaders, and the leaders are all united in the plan to capture Washington."

Mr. Felton listened with amazement and respect. This woman, he knew, was no alarmist. She also had powerful friends among the Southerners. When she spoke, one listened. "I shall get to work at once," he promised tersely.

Detectives were hired. They succeeded in enlisting in the squads secretly drilling along the lines of railroads from Harrisburg and Philadelphia to Baltimore and Washington. The conspiracy was confirmed. It was the intention of the conspirators to assassinate Lincoln on his way to the Capital for inauguration. Samuel Felton was an equally bold and clever conspirator. On a historic night several weeks later Lincoln was smuggled safely into Washington. The peril was averted.

A few months later Samuel Felton wrote Dorothea Dix, "I wish your consent to my making known to several parties the fact that you were the first to give the alarm of danger threatened on Washington early last winter. . . . The information you gave me led to most impressive results which thus far have been credited to parties who had nothing to do with them. May I use your name to put this matter right when the proper time comes? It must become a matter of history which should be founded on facts and not fiction."

Dorothea gave a pointblank refusal. She had merely been doing her duty in serving her country, and she wanted no credit. That duty performed, she was again on the road. She was called by telegraph to save a bill in Springfield. She went to Jefferson City, then to St. Louis to help there with legislation.

"All my bills have passed," she wrote Anne in March. "My winter has been successful. I have had great cares, greater fatigues, countless blessings unmeasured, preserving mercies, and am joined to all occasions for thanksgiving — well, and still able to work very satisfactorily. . . . God spare our distressed country!"

Little did she realize that within a month's time she would be launched on an utterly new and equally onerous career.

⚭ Seven ⚭
Superintendent of Nurses

This is not the work I would have my life judged by!

1

THE WAR CLOUDS erupted into violent storm. With the firing of Fort Sumter on April 12, 1861, all hopes of compromise with the new "Confederacy" ended. War was inevitable. On Monday, April 15, President Lincoln called on the governors of the loyal states for 75,000 volunteers from their militias to serve for three months. None of the southern states which had not seceded obeyed the call, but the response from those north of the Mason and Dixon line was instant and vehement. On Tuesday the militia of Massachusetts began to muster. On Wednesday, the day Virginia seceded, the Sixth Massachusetts Regiment was on its way to Washington. On Friday it arrived in Baltimore.

Here a mob was roaming the streets. Colonel Jones, in command of the regiment, knew that the troops must cross the city from one station to another but assumed they would cross on foot. However, it was the custom to move the whole train between stations. He was about to order the regiment out of the train when his car and five others moved swiftly away. A crowd was watching. As the cars moved they were bombarded with bricks and stones. Windows were broken and some soldiers wounded. A gun blazed. The crowd coalesced into a mob. Tracks were torn up in front of the train. The soldiers had to leave the cars and proceed on foot, fighting their way across the city for a mile and a half. Four soldiers were killed as well as some of their assailants. It was the first bloodshed of the Civil War.

News of the massacre burned across the telegraph wires within minutes. Dorothea was with the Buttolphs in Trenton, resting from her arduous western trip, when wild rumors began to circulate. The streets of Baltimore were strewn with dead and wounded, flowing with blood!

"I must go," she decided immediately. "If they don't need help in Baltimore, they will in Washington. The wounded will be pouring in. There is my next port of duty."

Friends knew from previous experience that it was useless to dissuade her. Marion Buttolph helped her pack a few things, promised to send her trunk later. A carriage was ordered, and she was on her way.

She arrived in Baltimore three hours after the riot. Excitement was still rife, mobs milling about the streets, but she learned that the wounded were being cared for in hospitals, and there was no need there for her services. Somehow she managed to make her way by carriage through the thronged thoroughfares and boarded a train for the Capital in the late afternoon. It was the last train to leave for Washington, for directly afterward southern sympathizers tore up the tracks, leaving the city without rail connection with the North. Even now it was a harassing and dangerous journey, for mobs kept hurling ties across the tracks in an attempt to delay the train. But she had encountered far worse hazards in travel. Desperately tired, clothes soiled and disarranged by the crowds she had pushed through, she still sat calmly upright, chin firmly raised above the slender neck, eyes ablaze with determination.

She found the capital aflame with excitement, the streets alive with rumbling wagons, frightened civilians, marching soldiers. Rumors of early attack were rife. There were four to five thousand men under arms in the city. Hotels were crowded to suffocation. Even the White House had been turned into a barracks. She went at once to the War Department building and was admitted to the office of Surgeon R. C. Wood, who because of the fatal illness of Surgeon-General Thomas Lawson, was the Acting Surgeon-General.

Dorothea offered her services. "I propose," she said, "to organize under the official auspices of the War Department, an Army Nursing Corps made up of women volunteers. I am sure many will be glad to enlist, in fact will insist on doing so. They should not be prevented, but it is imperative that their services should be subject to regulation. I hope you will permit me to serve in this capacity."

Her reputation not only as social benefactor but as hospital founder and organizer was of nationwide knowledge. The harassed officer accepted her offer gratefully and without question.

"We have been much impressed, with the conditions surrounding us," recorded one of the President's secretaries, "by the arrival this evening of Miss Dix who comes to offer herself and an army of nurses gratuitously for hospital service."

The dreaded attack did not come. Again it was Samuel Felton who helped avert disaster. Since the secession element in Baltimore had succeeded in shutting off all rail communication with the North by pulling up tracks and burning the railroad bridge between Baltimore and Philadelphia, to save Washington troops must be rushed in by water, via the Susquehanna River and Chesapeake Bay to Annapolis, then twenty miles to Washington. Mr. Felton seized steamboats on the river, collected them on the north shore, provisioned and coaled them, and had them ready to start the next day when the second contingent of Massachusetts troops arrived under General Butler. For the second time Washington was saved.

On April 23 Dorothea Dix's services were officially accepted by Secretary of War Simon Cameron, but not until June 10 would she be granted her commission as "Superintendent of United States Army Nurses," the first appointment of its kind ever made. The magnitude of such a responsibility, so hurriedly bestowed, was uncomprehended by neither conveyors nor recipient. It was expected by all parties that the rebellion would be only temporary, sure to be over within three months. For a woman of near sixty, inclined to malaria, weakened by overwork and by lifelong pulmonary infection, especially one who was a confirmed perfectionist, to attempt the herculean task that was soon thrust on her shoulders required grim courage, if not audacity. Three months? It would be four years before she could lay the appalling burden down — years of back-breaking labor, of opposition and intrigue bordering at times on persecution, of criticism, resentment, even ridicule, of only moderate satisfaction in having done her best to serve country and humanity.

But on the morning after her arrival she awoke ablaze with eagerness and confidence, certain that once more she had heard the divine call. She was Queen Esther, summoned to the kingdom for just such a time as this. She was Florence Nightingale setting out to bring healing and order to the bloody chaos of Crimea. Her first task was to discover the facilities of the military hospitals and the extent of their staffs. Their deficiencies were appalling. In peace time the Medical Department had consisted of thirty surgeons and eighty-three assistants. Three of the

Be it known to all whom it may concern, That the free services of Miss D. L. Dix are accepted by the War Department; and that she will give, at all times, all necessary aid in organizing Military Hospitals, for the care of all sick or wounded soldiers; aiding the Chief Surgeons by supplying nurses and substantial means for the comfort and relief of the suffering; also that she is fully authorized to receive, control, and disburse special supplies bestowed by individuals or associations for the comfort of their friends or the citizen soldiers from all parts of the United States, as also under sanction of the Acting Surgeon General, to draw from the Army Stores.

Given under the seal of the War Department this twenty third day of April, in the year of our Lord one thousand eight hundred and sixty one, and of the Independence of the United States the eighty fifth.

Simon Cameron
Secretary of War

surgeons and twenty-one assistants would resign to join
the Confederates. Organized to care for about 10,000, the
department was now responsible for 85,000! The largest
military hospital, at Fort Leavenworth, Kansas, had only
forty beds. Lesser facilities were almost nonexistent. It
was expected by the War Department that each detach-
ment of citizens in uniform would bring its own medical
officers and provide its own equipment. It was planned,
however, to create a few general hospitals in Washington
and vicinity to care for cases with which the regimental
facilities could not cope. These were to be the concern of
Miss Dix and her staff of volunteer nurses, and their organi-
nization was to be largely her responsibility. Acting Surgeon-General Wood, harassed to distraction, was soon
sending her multiple requests. On the very day of her
official appointment came an urgent appeal:

"Dear Madam: I called to see you yesterday and also
spoke to Mr. Cameron. A very large quantity of medical
supplies has been ordered from New York and will ulti-
mately come through. We are deficient in lint and bandages. I would most respectfully suggest that you institute
preliminary measures for these important items of surgical
necessity." The next day he asked her to arrange for 500
hospital shirts to be made "long and of common cotton
material."

Already she was working furiously. Washington was
glutted with new soldiers constantly streaming in, sometimes arriving after thirty-six hours in cattle cars, half-
starved and groggy, then required to stand on the streets
for long hours in hot sun or rain while officers rushed
about trying to find them food and living quarters. Sickness
was prevalent, epidemics in constant danger of erupting.
She visited the buildings set apart for temporary hospitals,
saw that they were stocked with all available furnishings,
organized local women to staff them, rented a house to
store the medical supplies being sent from New York,
despatched circulars all over the country listing her

requirements for women nurses and making urgent demands for supplies.

But action long preceded the arrival of such requests. The women of the North were already in feverish activity. Sewing machines were whirring. Women were organizing into "Soldiers' Aid Societies" by the dozens, the hundreds, the numbers to reach 10,000 before many months had passed. By April 15 groups had formed in Charlestown, Massachusetts, and Bridgeport, Connecticut. Soon came units in Boston, Lowell, Concord, Philadelphia, Cleveland. In New York prominent women met at the Infirmary for Women and Children, where Dr. Elizabeth Blackwell and her sister Dr. Emily had already established the first nurses' training school in the country, and soon the Women's Central Relief Association of New York was formed. One of its charter members was the wife of General John Dix, Dorothea's old friend. Others were Mrs. Hamilton Fish, Mrs. William Cullen Bryant, Mrs. S. F. B. Morse, Mrs. Peter Cooper, and Miss Louisa Lee Schuyler. Though the army looked askance at these grass roots organizations, Dorothea was glad to make use of them as sources of lint, bandages, and hospital garments. But as to their rushing in nurses, her response was adamant.

"They should by no means come on now," she wrote Louisa Lee Schuyler on April 29. "If a conflict ensues let the leading surgeons of New York direct and decide the course which should be adopted. . . . No young ladies should be sent at all, but some who can give their services and time and meet part of their expense or the whole, who will associate themselves by two to be ready for duty at any hour of day or night — those who are sober, earnest, self-sacrificing, and self-sustained; who can bear the presence of suffering and exercise entire self-control, of speech and manner; who can be calm, gentle, quiet, active, and steadfast in duty, also who are willing to take and execute the directions of the surgeons of the divisions in which they are stationed." It sounded like a character description of the ideal woman in *Proverbs*!

Supplies, as well as nursing applications, poured in. When Dorothea made a request of the Boston women for the five hundred shirts on Thursday, they were ready to send on Friday. From cities all over the North came hospital garments, bandages, bushel on bushel of lint (used for packing wounds and made by unraveling coarse material or scraping it with a sharp knife blade). A pile of shirts came from Bunker Hill. Havelocks (duck caps to protect soldiers from sunstroke) arrived by the thousands. Most had to be destroyed because the soldiers refused to wear them. To her receiving station also, at Dr. Wood's request, came special articles of diet: eggs, jellies, milk, chickens, canned goods. This service of collection and distribution was all in addition to the establishment of medical centers throughout the city and its vicinity.

Hotels, clubs, warehouses, and other public buildings were converted into hospitals. One after the other was opened: the East Street Infirmary, the Union Hotel in Georgetown, the C Street Infirmary. When Dr. Howe visited the latter about the middle of May, he commented on its quiet and efficient management, adding, "The ladies of Washington visit the infirmary frequently, and Miss Dix, who is the terror of all mere formalists, idlers, and evildoers, goes there, as she goes everywhere, to prevent and remedy abuses and shortcomings."

Dorothea's first temporary quarters at 500 12th Street between E and F soon became inadequate, and at her own expense she hired another house on H Street, large enough to store supplies received and to accommodate new nurses and women with no other place to go. For in spite of her warnings women came without applications or permissions: mothers, sisters, daughters, girl friends anxious to be near their men in the camps; members of the organizations checking to see that their supplies reached the proper channels; would-be nurses with no other qualifications than a desire to help, or, worse yet, a thirst for adventure. Already there were women attached to the various regiments, wives of officers who insisted on traveling with them, matrons who performed menial tasks such as washing and cooking, the usual camp followers of dubious morals, and, oddly enough, a surprising number of women, like the redoubtable Emma Edmonds, going to war masquerading as men. Dorothea was determined that her nurses should be above reproach. Professional careers, including nursing, were in an infant and delicate stage. Witness Elizabeth Blackwell's long struggle to become a doctor! Their repute must not be jeopardized. She must create a set of requirements for admission to her Army Nursing Corps which would keep out all undesirable women, as well as prohibit all unregulated nursing activities by the "matrons" or so-called "daughters" who accompanied the regiments and, if sickness occurred, were not above taking over the nursing of their soldiers.

Dorothea was unalterably opposed to such "nurses." Since she was responsible for all army nursing, their doubtful character or inefficiency might well damage the reputation of her own nursing corps. She determined immediately to fight the presence of all such women in the regiments, whether relatives, matrons, or "daughters," and on May 29 she issued a firm statement:

"All persons are respectfully and earnestly requested not to send to army headquarters, or moving stations, women of any age in search of employment, unless the need is announced by either letter or advertisement, there being no provision made by the government for such persons. There are many who are anxious to join their friends, who believe they will readily find remunerative employments. They arrive without means either of support or defraying return expenses, and so far from meeting fathers, brothers, or husbands may learn that their regiments are on the march to distant stations. The expense for providing for these ill-counselled but well-intentioned and helpless persons in Washington falls inconveniently on individuals who are not willing to witness needless exposure or suffering." Usually on herself, she might have added, for often her house was filled with such transients.

Even more important, she set up a list of requirements for admission to the Army Nursing Corps which would keep out all undesirable women, sending out a press release published in newspapers throughout the North, which, together with an appeal for volunteers, stated her unequivocal requirements. They included the same qualities stressed in her letter to Louisa Lee Schuyler. Then followed more specific demands

"No woman under thirty need apply to serve in government hospitals. All nurses are required to be plain looking women. Their dresses must be brown or black, with no bows, no curls, no jewelry, and no hoop-skirts."

They were sensible stipulations in the main. Dorothea's experience in scores of insane hospitals, her thorough inspection of the military hospital at Scutari involving a study of Florence Nightingale's methods, her familiarity with the work of the British Sanitary Commission, had schooled her to the necessity of good health, maturity, dedication, and high moral character in hospital nurses, especially in such rough and taxing situations as the new army camps. But the minor stipulations as to dress and age aroused instant and loud protest in female aspirants burning with patriotism yet under thirty or feeling undressed if bereft of curls, jewels, and hoop skirts. Especially hoop-skirts! In the months that followed one such aspirant, Mary Holland, later to become a well-known writer, found this an almost prohibitive restriction. But finally the yearn for service triumphed. As she was to record later, she decided, "Well if I can't walk without it, I will crawl; for I must go, and I will do the best I can."

"I am in possession of one of your circulars," she wrote, "and will comply with all your requirements. I am plain looking enough to suit you and old enough. I have no near relatives in the war. I have never had a husband and I am not looking for one. Will you take me?"

Dorothea's reply was quick and to the point. "Report at once to my house, corner of 14th Street and New York Avenue, Washington."

As the war progressed, she was known to let her keen judgment of character and her innate sense of humor triumph over this puritanical rigidity of norms. Once an applicant came for her interview in the popular female cycling garb of the day: baggy trousers buttoned over the tops of boots, a full skirt reaching a little below the knees, and a short, tight-sleeved jacket. Dorothea examined the young woman's credentials, then rose to her full height and, without saying a word, looked her up and down several times from head to foot until she flushed and seemed visibly to shrink in size. Then the superintendent suddenly smiled.

"That dress you wear is abominable," she said abruptly, "and I am unwilling for any of my nurses to dress in this manner. But you come highly recommended, and I know something of your work. I certainly had no idea you would let yourself be seen in such a costume. However, you are accepted."

The age restriction proved even more unfortunate, for it resulted in the enrollment of many women who were really too old to do the work properly and excluded many who, unable to qualify for the Nursing Corps, found other avenues of service unrelated to the Dix regime. Therefore it helped to defeat one of Dorothea's main objectives for efficiency, to keep all the nursing services under her personal control. Among the women who managed to work outside her jurisdiction were some of the best known nurses of the war, like Clara Barton, Mary Safford, and the famous "Mother" Bickerdyke, that "cyclone in calico."

Curiously enough, the Dix requirements did not include nursing experience or stress the need for training, although at the time her release was published such a stipulation would have been almost useless. Except for the few young women trained in the New York Infirmary there were no trained nurses in the country. In fact, the very idea of nursing as a career for a woman, except as she plied her natural skills in the home, was as foreign to the popular concept of woman's role as that of doctor or lawyer. It was the crisis of war which, as in England during the Crimean struggle, suddenly thrust women into the public performance of a role they had played in private from time immemorial. They had nursed husbands and sons for every ailment from indigestion and measles to diphtheria and pneumonia, and it was natural that they should feel called to follow them into the miasmic hazards of military camps and even to the gory fields of battle.

The more surprising development was the tacit acceptance by military authorities and the general public that women should bear the brunt of nursing in time of war. Only a few masculine die-hards objected, among them Samuel Gridley Howe, who refused to let his wife, Julia Ward Howe, participate in war work beyond scraping lint and rolling bandages, but who, strangely enough, had once urged Florence Nightingale to study nursing! It was undoubtedly the work of Miss Nightingale, now a legend, which helped effect this startling development in the liberation of women. Her little book, *Hints on Nursing,* had appeared in Boston in 1860, and it found its way into many a woman's carpet bag along with her favorite herbs and liniments and emetics.

It was Dr. Elizabeth Blackwell who recognized the necessity of training for the new war nurses. In New York she became head of a screening committee for selecting candidates, who were then sent to her New York Infirmary for a month's training, then for a month's practical service at Bellevue or New York Hospital, a little enough preparation, she thought, compared with the thirteen months course which the infirmary had been conducting. In a series of nine lectures she tried to condense the necessary training into a capsule: ventilation, cleanliness, food, care of helpless patients, observation of symptoms, surgical dressings, bandaging, personal habits and precautions for nurses, and their moral and religious influence.

Elizabeth Blackwell was one of the few persons to whom Dorothea was willing to delegate responsibility, though the two never became friends. On the one occasion when they met, much later in the war, Dr. Blackwell was not impressed with the somberly dressed woman whose beautiful but harassed face revealed frustrating burdens which her sensitive spirit and insistence on perfection were finding almost impossible to bear. She had never approved of her superior's methods, which she considered dictatorial. But by that time Dorothea Dix herself would have become almost as severe in judgment of her work as her critics. Already the words she would later voice were shaping in her mind, a cry almost of desperation.

This is not the work I would have my life judged by!

2

Dorothea had spent summers in Washington before, and she had always regarded it as one of the dirtiest and unhealthiest cities she had been in. But viewed through the windows of the Congressional Library or from the carriage transporting her to her boardinghouse, its defects had been at least remote. Now, with new soldiers pouring in by the tens of thousands and herself responsible to a large degree for their health, she found the situation appalling. Refuse from the government slaughter house spewed into a canal; few houses had drainage, and slops were emptied into the streets; unsanitary privies mingled their stench with that of manure piles; flies swarmed over food in the shops and on the tables; only a few beds in the new

Dorothea Dix in later life.

makeshift hospitals were equipped with mosquito net curtains.

Conditions in the surrounding camps were even more horrifying. After choosing a dozen or more sites for hospitals on high ground with a maximum amount of pure air, Dorothea could have told the military authorities that the swamps around Washington were no fit places for camps — and she did, but too late. In wet weather the mud was ankle deep; in dry the dust was over the tops of boots. Garbage was left to rot. Some camps did not even have latrines. Water supplies were inadequate and contaminated. Hardtack, coffee, sugar, and beans were the main rations. As heat mounted, sickness was inevitable. Typhoid, malaria, measles, dysentery, even smallpox, were rampant. By the middle of May thirty percent of the volunteers were listed as sick. The number of temporary hospitals increased steadily, every sort of public building being pressed into use — the Capitol, the Patent Office, the Insane Asylum, colleges, hotels, warehouses, lodge halls, churches. And Dorothea was responsible for the nurses in every one of them.

The all-inclusive language of her official commission, she felt, extended her authority into the camps as well as the hospitals, and she was soon investigating their conditions and making stern recommendations. They were not heeded, nor were the reports of a committee sent down by the Women's Central Relief Association of New York to persuade the President and the Medical Bureau to establish a Sanitary Commission. This committee, composed of Dr. Elisha Harris, Reverend Henry Bellows, and others, declared conditions in the camps a "reflection on modern civilization." The surgeons of the Medical Bureau were not pleased, resenting the "unnecessary intrusion of petticoats and preachers," also the visits of Miss Dix who, they griped, came "prying and poking about" and "exceeded her authority." It was a conflict which was to continue through the war. In time, however, the United States Sanitary Commission was created by Acting Surgeon-General Wood to serve as a body of inquiry and advice. Headed by Dr. Bellows and including such eminent leaders as Samuel Gridley Howe, Dr. R. C. Wood, Dr. Wolcott Gibbs, it established regional headquarters and served as an information and coordinating center for all the independent aid societies throughout the North. Eventually it was to relieve Dorothea of a portion of the responsibility which was rapidly becoming intolerable.

"My life is so filled with crowding cares that I do not recollect what time passes between letters received or sent to my friends," she wrote Anne on May 27. "I never had so few moments for myself. I went three or four days ago to the Relief House to see and arrange for some sick soldiers of the Massachusetts Sixth and Eighth, and while I was in Colonel Jones' tent your brother, Fred, came in looking much better than I ever saw him. . . . There is soon to be active service, I fear, and our brave men must be provided for if wounded. . . . These are strange times, and this war truly seems now not unreal."

Its reality soon became stunningly apparent. After long weeks of delay General McDowell on July 9 gave the order to attack. On July 16 the army began to move, and the city, which had sunk into a sluggishness of inactivity, sprang into life. Crowds gathered along Pennsylvania Avenue to see the hosts march forth to battle. Flags waved. Voices cheered. Eyes turned with anticipation toward the rolling hills across the Potomac where the Confederate forces had long been waiting. It was generally accepted that victory would be won with the first skirmish or two. The exuberance of the soldiers, the colorful uniforms, the rousing music — all belied the report of the Sanitary Commission ascribing fatal weakness to the military forces as well as the medical corps. Dorothea did not join in the hilarious excitement. She was too busy preparing for the wounded who were sure to come, whether from victory or defeat.

News kept coming. On Wednesday the 17 the regiment was moving toward Fairfax Court House, slowly, for they were not trained to march, painfully, for the day was intensely hot, and dust clung to skin and clothes, parched their throats. Thursday they moved toward Centerville, in such scorching heat that many fell out from sunstroke and prostration. By Friday there had been mild skirmishes with the enemy and fighting at Blackburn's Ford. On Saturday it was predicted that the battle would be fought the next day. Still Dorothea was almost alone in her concern for preparation. Everywhere was the anticipation of victory. Sightseers were crossing the Potomac to get thrilling glimpses of a camp on the eve of battle, and, hopefully, of the enemy at Manassas among the distant hills.

Then it was the twenty-first. At 2:30 a.m. the men started marching. The sun rose with the same intense heat. More sightseers began riding out in carriages to witness the victory, taking picnic baskets, and forming a spectators' gallery on the ridge above Bull Run. The battle was on. Drums rolled, shells screamed, the hot sun gleamed on bayonets. "How splendid!" enthused one female onlooker. "We should be in Richmond this time tomorrow!" Until afternoon the picnickers continued to rejoice. Then suddenly the Union lines began to break. The battle became a rout, the Union soldiers fleeing for their lives. As the news reached Washington, Dorothea accelerated her preparations. There was no dearth now of grimly concerned women to lend assistance. In addition to her corps of nurses and members of the Sanitary Commission, there were hundreds of local citizens anxious to fulfill her orders. None of them slept that night. More churches, warehouses, private homes were outfitted as receiving stations, all flying the yellow flag which marked an army hospital.

At the first news of battle Dorothea had despatched nurses to Alexandria, and in a church near Bull Run a

makeshift hospital had been set up where the army surgeons could extract bullets and make amputations. But all
through the night wounded soldiers, draggled, exhausted,
bleeding, came trickling into Washington. The heat had
broken, and rain was pouring, adding chills and hazards of
pneumonia to the injuries of battle. By morning the trickle
had become a swelling stream. As Commissioner Olm-
stead of the Sanitary Commission described them, "a most
woebegone rabble. No two were dressed completely alike;
some were without caps, others without coats, others
without shoes. All were alike excessively dirty, unshaved,
unkompt, and dank with dew. The groups were formed
around fires made in the streets, of boards wrenched from
citizens's fences . . . others begging for food at house
doors . . ."

Wounded men poured into the hospitals, the Superintendent of Nurses and her corps working around the
clock. Some nurses went into the streets to attend
wounded men lying in the gutters. Dorothea was shocked,
disgusted, agonized by the woeful inefficiency of the War
Department. No one had given thought to preparations for
caring for the wounded. It had been assumed that each
regiment would do this with its own surgeons and equipment. Of course this did not work. Already the regiments
were hopelessly intermingled. Regimental hospital tents
were far in the rear. There was no ambulance corps and
few ambulances. Discovering the shortage, Dorothea purchased one with her own money and sent it to the
battlefield, where, it was reported, wounded men were
still lying. There was a shortage also of tents, cooking
equipment, uniforms. The army diet was causing out-
breaks of epidemics — fevers, scurvy, dysentery. In en-
suing days she went to the Sanitary Commission and
begged for an increase in healthful foods to supplement
the soldiers' diets — vegetables, jellies, jams, preserves,
dried fruits — to prevent the spread of scurvy. The response from the aid societies was heartening. Along with

the bandages, lint, shirts came boxes and baskets of vegetables and fresh fruits from nearby cities, jellies, jams, dried fruits from cities and towns farther away.

Of course this increased influx of supplies multiplied Dorothea's labors. Boxes and baskets and crates arrived at her door in huge vans. The house on H Street and the one on the corner of Fourteenth and New York were used as warehouses, with a staff hired at her own expense to aid in the sorting and distribution of supplies.

More temporary hospitals were necessary, in Alexandria as well as Washington. Private homes were commandeered: the Hallowell House on Washington Street, the Tibbs House, the Fowle and Johnson homes on Prince Street, the Grosvenor house on Washington, churches, and a theological school. Dorothea made it her personal responsibility to visit all of them. Not only had the debacle at Bull Run aroused the shocked sensibilities of northern women to a new concept of their task, but the performance of the nursing corps immeasurably enhanced the status of women nurses.

"What a blessed comfort a Nurses Department would be, following the Army," wrote one correspondent, after witnessing the work of volunteers. "For some kind gentlewoman to come in there to bind up wounds . . . would be invaluable. Then, if she had authority to draw for tea and little niceties on the Quartermaster and could carry them in her own wagon — say an ambulance — making her bed in this at night, and having all her little stores ready, so that in the confusion after a battle, she could at once bring forth tea and comforts for the sick, the field hospital would have a very different aspect and comfort to the poor fellows."

Tea and niceties were pleasant subsidiaries, but Dorothea's nurses were plunged into far grimmer activities than wheeling tea wagons: washing gaping wounds, handling bloody bandages, snatching a few hours sleep in some corner, writing letters to a wife or sweetheart at the dictation of dying lips. She was constantly appearing among them, issuing orders, relieving a wearied volunteer, sweet rich voice murmuring encouragement, fine proud features deep-lined with exhaustion but eyes burning with an almost fanatical dedication. So great were the needs during the emergency that she was soon disregarding her fine standards of age and dress and asking of applicants only one question: "Are you ready to go to work?"

On June 10 her official position had been further affirmed by her appointment as "Superintendent of Women Nurses, to select and assign women nurses to general or permanent military hospitals, they not to be employed in such hospitals without her sanction and approval, except in cases of urgent need." It was a broad and inclusive assignment, implying powers approaching those of a general. Women nurses were to be employed at the rate of one to every two males. For their services they would receive forty cents a day, rations, quarters, and transportation, while males received $20.50 a month besides rations, clothing, and medical attention. Later the wages of both were reduced. Army regulations allowed one woman nurse for every ten beds, a number later raised to thirty. At first the women nurses were restricted to service in base hospitals, but later when emergencies arose they were commandeered for temporary hospitals back of the lines.

Dorothea was not at all satisfied with the accommodations provided for the nurses in Washington, but it was the best she could secure. They were housed in a large parlor on the second floor of Ebbitt House, a rambling old hotel on F Street, near Willard's. Cots were set up for them, crowded into the space left over from stacked bundles of hospital supplies.

In the weeks and months following Bull Run base hospitals increased all over the country, and soon Dorothea was not only assessing applications and assigning nurses but venturing far from Washington on tours of inspection.

"Will you come here and organize these hospitals?" General John Charles Frémont telegraphed from St. Louis in August. "Full details have been written you. You can do vast good by coming, and you will be very welcome. I will repeat until answered."

Here once more she met Jessie Benton Frémont, acting as a nurse with her husband's regiment, such a whirlwind of energy and determination that she was dubbed "General Jessie." In St. Louis also was Dorothea's old friend, Reverend William Greenleaf Eliot, whom she had often visited, and who with other concerned citizens had organized a western branch of the Sanitary Commission to provide supplies for troops in the vicinity of St. Louis. Dr. Eliot had appealed to her for nurses. As she set about the organization of the hospital with her usual thoroughness, Dorothea encountered not only the strong opposition of the surgeons in charge and the commanding officers but a state of apathy among the citizens.

"Nine-tenths of the people," Dr. Eliot told her, "look on the work of the Sanitary Commission with contempt, and our Ladies' Union Aid Society has to work in secret."

Immediately Dorothea sent appeals to eastern friends for financial support, and it was soon forthcoming. New Englanders violently opposed to the extension of slavery were soon sending contributions, Boston alone donating $200,000 and all of New England more than $500,000. Dr. Eliot's Unitarian affiliations in his native Boston and other eastern cities were also helpful factors.

The surgeons in St. Louis were not the only ones who resented Dorothea's singlehanded activity in performing her duties. In September Commissioner George Templeton Strong of the United States Sanitary Commission wrote in his diary, "General Frémont seems to have set up a local Sanitary Commission of his own to act under the direction of Miss Dix! . . . This has doubtless been got up by that indefatigable woman. She is disgusted with us because we do not leave everything else and rush off the instant she tells us of something that needs attention."

Although the Medical Bureau at first planned to employ women nurses only in base hospitals, soon it was demanding them in the temporary hospitals set up behind the lines. Though she continued her relentless battle against nursing activities by women not under her control, Dorothea found the rule impossible to enforce. Local women, wives of Sanitary Commission agents and of military officers, even the inevitable "matrons" and "daughters" of the regiments, continued to enter the hospital tents after a battle and minister to the wounded and sick. Whether her violent antipathy to such unofficial activities was the result of her innate insistence on perfection or merely of that stubborn determination which had kept her doggedly pursuing any path she had chosen, she could not have told. She knew only that she had been given a responsibility, and she must fulfill it if it killed her. It nearly did.

Indefatigable. The commissioner had chosen the perfect word. During all the four years of the war she worked every single day. Even when ill and confined to bed that first August, she continued to direct all activities. In visiting hospitals all over the country she was as thorough in her investigations as in the asylums and almshouses, inspecting the wards, kitchens, sanitary arrangements, ventilation, water supply, consulting with the patients as to their needs and complaints, carrying in her ample carpet bag a supply of magazines, jellies, fruits. Patients greeted her coming with pathetic eagerness, surgeons and other officers with dismay and often high dudgeon. For she did not hesitate to express her displeasure with caustic energy, and she found much to displease — inefficiency, carelessness, drunkenness on the part of doctors on duty, which she considered unforgivable and worthy of dismissal. Frustration sharpened the tongue which for years she had schooled herself to curb into gentleness. The impossible burden she had unwittingly assumed and which increased beyond human capacity during the four years turned a genius for leadership based on firm but gentle persuasion into the domineering bluntness of a dictator.

Usually it was the careless attendants, the inept and indifferent surgeons, the inefficient nurses, who complained of her interference. Patients, often neglected, ill fed, unattended, knew her as an angel of light. Efficient nurses were her loyal devotees. Conscientious surgeons, at their wits' end for assistance and supplies, found her remarkable ability to cut red tape a godsend. And in the high echelons of government her right to authority remained long unquestioned. Edwin M. Stanton, who succeeded Cameron as secretary of war, gave her his unqualified approval and listened to her every complaint. Her visits to army hospitals, often unannounced and incognito, might arouse discomfiture, choler, muttered curses, but never disregard or indifference.

Once she heard that in a hospital not far from Washington the delicacies provided for sick soldiers were reaching the officers' tables instead of the patients' trays. She went at once and, without announcing her name, received permission from the surgeon in charge, through the sheer authority of voice and manner, to make an inspection of the wards. "You must change this immediately." . . . "This practice is highly unsanitary. Of course it must stop." . . . "The misuse of condiments intended for patients will end from this moment." As one firm directive succeeded another, the officer became, first amazed, then highly indignant. Finally he could contain his outrage no longer. "Madam," he thundered, "who are you, that you thus presume to invade my domain, and thus to dictate to me, the officer in charge?"

Drawing herself up to her full height, she replied quietly but in the compelling voice which had often restored a raving maniac to calmness, "I am Dorothea L. Dix, Superintendent of Nurses, in the employ of the United States Government." The officer also was reduced to startled meekness. When she had gone he approached an associate. "Who in thunder is that Miss Dix, and how could she speak with such authority?"

The other regarded him with pitying surprise. "Good heavens, man, don't you know her? Why, she has the rank, pay, honors, and emoluments of a major-general of volunteers, and if you have got her down on you, you might as well have all hell after you!"

On another occasion, while visiting the hospital at Hampton and engaged in the activities which her critics dubbed "spying about," she came on three convalescent soldiers who were enduring a most cruel punishment for some serious offense. (Legend would have it that she found them strung up by their thumbs.)

"Who ordered this?" she demanded in her most imperious tones.

"The surgeon in charge," she was told. She went at once to the officer in question and ordered that the proceeding be stopped. He turned on her in a rage. He would tolerate no interference, especially by a woman. Punishment of his soldiers was his business, and she had better respect his authority.

Dorothea waited to hear no more. She went directly to the department commander, who at the time was General Butler. "In this branch of the service," she inquired, "which one of us outranks the other, the surgeon in charge or myself?"

"Miss Dix, of course," he replied promptly. The matter was settled. The men were released from torture, and the officer was disgraced.

She cared not a whit for this vindication of her status, except as it made possible a more efficient and just administration. She relished such hostile encounters no more than her repeated skirmishes with touchy caretakers and legislators in more than a score of states and a dozen foreign countries. But, as for the last twenty years, she did not shirk them.

"I am no enthusiast," she said once to a friend during

this most frustrating period of her life. "What I have done is only from a determined will, and because I think it is my duty."

3

Three months? Soon it was for three years that volunteers were being demanded by the grim, gaunt Commander in Chief, who seemed to grow in stature with every agonizing month. For the third time Dorothea's life was intimately entwined with that of a President — Polk . . . Fillmore . . . now Lincoln, whose life she may well have saved.

"The President's respects to Miss Dix. Mrs. Edwards, Mrs. Lincoln's sister, was suddenly called home today by sickness in her family. Mrs. Pomeroy is now at the White House, and Miss Dix's permission for her to remain two weeks, or any shorter time, if so long is not possible, will greatly oblige Mrs. Lincoln and the President."

"Medical Director of Military Hospital at Winchester, Virginia. This introduces Miss Dix. Please receive her kindly and avail yourself of her services among the sick and wounded soldiers. A. Lincoln."

Before the war was over a hundred such passes were forthcoming, to hospitals, railroad transports, ferries, bridges, forts, steamers, all with the President's signature. But, though she was a welcome visitor at the White House and felt free to approach the President with any major problem, the relationship included no social function. She would not have gone if invited. There was no time. And, indeed, the mood for festivity had passed. Since Bull Run the city had turned dismally austere, a stage stripped clean of nonessentials. Picnickers in billowing skirts and lace cravats no longer fared forth to applaud the victors. They waited tense behind closed shutters for news of victory or defeat from Fort Hatteras, North Carolina, Ball's Bluff, Virginia, Belmont, Missouri, Forts Henry and Donelson, Nashville, Tennessee, Pea Ridge, Arkansas, Yorktown. Parades became wearying maneuvers. Drums and marching feet acquired an ominous beat. War had become a grim and bloody business.

And for almost the first time in its history women were in the midst of heroic action. Kady Brownell, color bearer in her husband's First Rhode Island Regiment and leader of her own company of sharpshooters, had been under fire at Centerville, fought and was wounded at Newburn. "Mother" Bickerdyke, after descending like a cyclone on the camps and hospitals at Cairo and resolving their shocking filth and disorder into decency, was continuing her whirlwind assault on dirt and suffering and death in the new hospital ships introduced by the Sanitary Commission on the Mississippi. Mary Safford, as refined and rich as Bickerdyke was uncouth and poor, was often her faithful ally. Anna Ella Carroll, credited with saving Maryland to the Union, had gone west as Lincoln's emissary in late 1861 and devised the military strategy which General Grant was to follow successfully. Mary Livermore was efficiently directing the work of the Sanitary Commission in the West. In Washington Clara Barton had turned her own house into a nursing home. And Julia Ward Howe, forbidden by her husband to soil her gentle hands in nursing, found a far more effective use for them with her pen. Riding through the streets of Washington in November, 1861, and caught in a traffic jam, she began singing the popular "John Brown's Body," and soldiers along the way took up the song.

"You could write better words to that fine tune," suggested a companion.

She did, and her "Battle Hymn of the Republic" with its stirring climax, "Let us die to make men free" helped infuse into a merely sectional struggle the idealism which would soon take form in the President's Emancipetion Proclamation.

The intrusion of females like Bickerdyke and Safford into the realm of military authority was often as much resented by surgeons as the "snooping interference" of the Superintendent of Nurses. Though Dorothea cared nothing for the antagonism of military personnel to herself, she suffered agonies over the opposition, sometimes approaching persecution, to the nurses in her corps. She fought for them like a lion protecting her cubs, yet she did not pamper them. She expected of them the same Spartan fealty to duty that she did of herself. At least one nurse could give vehement testimony to both facts.

Mary Phinney Olnhausen, a New England widow, though with no nurse's training, fulfilled all of Dorothea's requirements. She was over thirty, plain, practical, eager to serve. As usual, Dorothea kept her in her home for several days, then took her to the Mansion House Hospital, formerly a hotel, in Alexandria. "A stern woman of few words," Mary decided, looking sidelong at the straight, somberly dressed figure beside her in the jolting carriage.

"You may encounter difficulties," Dorothea told her. "The surgeon in charge is determined to give me no foothold in his hospital. But I expect you to take no notice of any opposition they may give you."

As they arrived at the old brick building ambulances were unloading victims from Cedar Mountain, and they edged their way in through a double line of stretchers, one with the wounded going in, the other with the dead being carried out. A grim introduction, thought Dorothea, to the horrors of war! But she had judged the new nurse accurately. Along with the whiteness of face, there was a straightening of shoulders, a tightening of lips. This woman would win in spite of opposition. They were two of a kind.

"If you need me," she said kindly, parting from the new

nurse with more reluctance than usual, "I am nearby. And God will be with you."

Opposition? It was obvious from the start. "Follow us," ordered the chief surgeon curtly. Obediently she accompanied him and his assistant through the dirty wards, so filled with cots that there was barely room to move, the smell of blood and pus overpowering in the August heat. Many of the men had been lying for days almost without clothing, their wounds not yet dressed. Mary was given the most repulsive task of changing dressings. There were no instructions, but if she failed to do what was expected, she was harshly reprimanded. She was given no place to sleep. Occasionally a nurse would let her use her room, and she would drag in a straw bed and place it on the floor. "We will make it so hot for her that she will not stay long," the chief surgeon was heard to say.

When after some weeks Dorothea went to inspect the hospital, she was tempted to give up the fight and remove her nurse at once, exactly what the surgeon wanted. But she recognized in the woman a toughness and stubbornness akin to her own. "You must bear it a while, my child." Mary repressed a smile, for she was almost as old as Miss Dix. "I have placed you here, and you must stay." Mary Olnhausen stayed, enduring not only the persecution but the confusion of inadequate equipment and an untrained staff. "I speak to nobody," she wrote home, "get what food I can and buy the rest." It was torturing but excellent preparation for her future career as superintendent of a training school for nurses. And her stubbornness and loyalty to Dorothea Dix won the day. Dorothea was finally able to replace the inefficient nurses in the hospital with those of her own selection.

Not that a majority of the military personnel rejected the superintendent's nurses or failed to take advantage of her services, especially in the provision of supplies. Her duties in this department were stupendous. Early in 1862 there was an epidemic of scurvy in the western armies, and all through that year and the next huge supplies of vegetables and fruits were commissioned and shipped to the armies operating under Generals Grant and Rosecrans — potatoes, onions, dried fruits, lemons, barrels of sauerkraut. Though the task of collecting and distributing was shared with the Sanitary Commission, Dorothea felt herself officially responsible for the handling of such supplies, and her refusal to cooperate completely with this organization led to misunderstanding, even conflict, with some of its executives.

In fact, if there was one major fault in her administration, it was her reluctance to delegate responsibility. She was like a housewife who, with an army of servants, must pry into each corner for dust and keep track of every grain of sugar. Even the most minor request and distribution of supplies came under her supervision. A hundred years later there would still be extant dozens of little memos, often mere scraps of waste paper, containing urgent demands for minutiae.

"Miss Dix, Will you be so kind as to let me have by the bearer an India Rubber cloth and a pillow to the head, also some of those pillows you spoke of to put under a patient with bed sores. Yrs. respectfully."

"Please send 2 oranges and a little tea, good bread for Ward 7."

"Please let the bearer have a few potatoes or a little fruit for a convalescent."

"Send egg nog for two men. They require strong stimulation."

"Please send 1 pint arrowroot gruel with a liberal quantity of brandy in it."

"Will Miss Dix please let the bearer have 1 dozen bed quilts."

From Yorktown: "1 yd lint, 1 yd muslin, 6 rolls bandages, 1 bottle good brandy, 1 yd oil silk."

From Wheaton Hospital: "Please deliver the bearer some gruel if you have it and a few oranges, or any other articles which will suit your convenience and will be wholesome for the sick."

"Miss Dix, please send me a pair of socks if you please. William Barry of Boston."

"Cocoa and a few loaves of soft bread if possible." . . . "Arrow root with port wine and much obliged." . . . "a few towels and oblige" . . . "Dr. Nichols needs shirts (worsted) and underclothing" . . . "a few pounds of dried apples for Ward B."

"A stern woman of few words," Mary Olnhausen said of Dorothea Dix. Yet her admiration and loyalty persisted through almost intolerable testing. Many of Dorothea's nurses were equally devoted to their chief.

"I saw a great deal of her during my hospital service," one of them, A. T. Perry, was to write years later. "A little old lady past sixty-five, but singularly youthful in her movements, looks, and especially in her voice, which was always so daintily modulated to fix its exact weight upon her every word, and yet, as far as I knew her, so invariably potent in holding her listener at arm's length, it especially impressed me as her feature of very marked individuality. In dress she was the perfection of neatness. . . . She was perpetually on duty, and so thoroughly did she give herself, heart and soul, to her work, she seemed to know no weariness."

It was in November, 1862, that Dorothea's eyes, lifted to greet a new applicant, brightened with unusual warmth. "My dear, I met your father many years ago. I admire his work so much. Like him, I used to be a teacher in Boston."

"I know." The young woman gave her a beaming smile. The blue eyes beneath the brim of the cavernous black bonnet sparkled. "Wasn't I raised on your *Conversations on Common Things?* And I simply adored your *Garland of Flora.* You know, I've always wanted to write myself."

Dorothea smiled back, a rare act nowadays. Refreshing to find an applicant who did not look at her with timidity and awe! "Since you're the daughter of Bronson Alcott, you should be able to write very well."

"Oh, I hope so. But just think! Your *Conversations* has gone into another printing after almost forty years! It's still selling in Boston bookstores."

"Is it?" asked Dorothea. Her teaching and writing career seemed to belong to another world. "I didn't know."

"Wonderful!" enthused the future author of *Little Women*. "If I could only write a book that would live that long!"

Louisa May Alcott had just turned thirty. Her clothes were sober enough, black bonnet, fuzzy brown coat, no hoop skirt. So far she fulfilled Dorothea's original requirements. But she was neither plain nor self-effacing. The blue eyes which had won her the nickname "Periwinkle" were brightly, almost boldly curious. They held a glint of humor, even mischief. The youthful figure was alive with pent-up energy. But Dorothea had long since ceased to apply her rigid rules in their entirety. She knew instantly that here was a far better nurse than many of the colorless, sober applicants she had so thankfully accepted.

She took the new nurse to the Union Hotel in Georgetown, now a hospital, which Louisa May immediately dubbed "Hurly Burly House." The budding author plunged into the work with a vitality unfazed by every experience, including a death on her first rounds and the illness of another nurse which thrust her suddenly into the superintendency of a ward with forty beds. In three days after her arrival the ambulances began bringing victims from the terrible blood-letting at Fredericksburg, hordes of gaunt, pale men, mud to their knees, bloody gangrenous battle wounds, bandages untouched for days, and she rushed from cases of pneumonia, typhoid, diphtheria, to those of amputations and festering sores, taking all in cheerful stride and managing all the while to keep a journal which, published the following year under the title

Hospital Sketches, would form one of the most lively and pertinent chronicles of the war.

I spent my shining hours washing faces, serving rations, giving medicines, and sitting in a very hard chair, with pneumonia on one side, diphtheria on the other, two typhoids opposite, and a dozen dilapidated patriots hopping, lying, and lounging about. . . .

Up at six, dress by gaslight, run through my ward and throw up the windows though the men grumble and shiver; but the air is bad enough to breed a pestilence; and as no notice is taken of our frequent appeals for better ventilation I must do what I can. Poke up the fire, add blankets, joke, coax, and command but continue to open doors and windows as if my life depended upon it. Mine does, and doubtless many another, for a more perfect pestilence box than this house I never saw — cold, damp, dirty, full of vile odors from windows, kitchens, washrooms, and stables. No competent head, male or female, to right matters, and a jumble of good, bad, and indifferent nurses, surgeons, and attendants to complicate the chaos still more.

After this unwelcome progress through my stifling ward, I go to breakfast with what appetite I may — find the inevitable fried beef, salt butter, husky bread, and washy coffee.

In her *Sketches* the description of food was even more graphic:"beef put down for the men of '76, pork just in from the street, army bread, composed of sawdust and saleratus, butter, salt, as if churned by Lot's wife, stewed blackberries, like preserved cockroaches, coffee mild and muddy, tea, three dried huckleberry leaves to a quart of water." She bought some supplements, cheese and crackers, but rats ate up the cheese, and bugs got into the crackers. Occasionally she was able to walk for a little in the streets, gulping the January air, mild as spring.

Her ministry lasted just six weeks. When she fell ill — pneumonia? diphtheria? — Mrs. Ropes, the matron, wired for her father, but long before he could arrive Dorothea was at her bedside with a basket filled with bottles of wine, tea, medicine, and cologne, besides a little blanket and pillow, a fan, and a Testament. The room was cheerless — two windows draped with sheets, five of their panes broken ("compound fractures," wrote Louisa May), a bare floor supporting two narrow iron beds ("mattresses like plasters"), pillows ("in last stages of consumption"). In the fireplace, with no shovel, tongs, andirons, or grate, burned a sluggish log. A mirror ("big as a muffin") hung over a tin basin, blue pitcher, brace of yellow mugs.

"There may be rats in the closet," said Louisa May with a wan but impish smile. "Better not open the door."

"This war," Dorothea had written Mrs. Rathbone a few months before, "is breaking my heart." The enormity of its suffering overwhelmed her now. She wanted to take the slender young figure with the brave fevered eyes into her arms and rock her, like a mother, against her breast, but, being Dorothea Dix, she of course did nothing of the kind. "You can't stay here," she said firmly. "You must be removed to Willard's."

But only when Mrs. Ropes died of the same disease did Louisa May consent to leave her post of duty and go home. Each day she remained in Washington Dorothea went, as she had gone to hundreds of other bedsides of nurses and patients, to bring what cheer and healing she could to the desperately ill young woman.

"She is a kind old soul," the latter wrote in her *Journal*, "but very queer and arbitrary."

Queer, perhaps. Arbitrary, certainly. Yet it was not these traits which Louisa May Alcott remembered best when she wrote her *Hospital Sketches*.

> Daily our Florence Nightingale climbed the steep stairs, stealing a moment from her busy life, to watch over the stranger, of whom she was as thoughtfully tender as any mother. Long may she wave! Whatever others may

think or say, Nurse Periwinkle is forever grateful; and among her relics of that Washington defeat, none is more valued than the little book which appeared on her pillow one dreary day; for the D. D. written in it means to her far more than Doctor of Divinity.

4

"Time rolls on," Dorothea wrote Anne in March, 1863. "We still measure its age by the flow and ebb of conflicts and battles. . . . I am full of care day by day within a space of ten square miles. I have nearly 180 nurses to control, besides all at a distance, and in Pennsylvania and most of the states I have delegated my authority to parties I have thought to be responsible. . . . As yet I have not been off duty for a day since the rebellion. I trust I have both grace and strength to carry forward my work till the end." She could not have borne the crushing burden without a stubborn faith that somehow healing would come to the country from the fearful blood-letting.

Though she had never compromised her work for the insane in the South by alleging support for the abolitionist cause, it was a relief that now her hatred of slavery could be avowed without question. For, though the war had begun as a patriotic struggle to save the Union, the Emancipation Proclamation had elevated it to a righteous crusade for human freedom. The soldiers were imbued with idealism. The increase of psychiatric casualties which she and Dr. Nichols had expected at St. Elizabeth's had not taken place. In his report for 1862–1863 Dr. Nichols explained this reversal of anticipated increase in the rate of insanity by this very idealism, a moral sense of justness in the national cause and a faith in its triumph.

In July came Gettysburg, a victory for the North but won at the tremendous cost on both sides of over 43,000 killed and 170,000 wounded and missing. Many of the latter were left on the battlefield, and the single line of railroad to Baltimore became a bottleneck. Hundreds of women vied for a chance to go, to search for the dead, to take food, to nurse the wounded, to serve in any way possible. Dorothea sent all her available nurses, then cooperated with Secretary Stanton in an endeavor to keep all unauthorized volunteers out of the battle area. The presence of such crowds would create pandemonium in a situation already hopelessly confused. She went to the Baltimore station and, standing for hours in the broiling July heat, tried to intercept all unauthorized women and keep them from boarding the train to the front. Many had passes from the Sanitary or Christian Commissions. Even these she subjected to sharp scrutiny, still attempting to apply her rigid rules as to age and sober appearance. In one such group all were elderly and plain except one girl, Cornelia Hancock, who stood out like a rose in a bunch of dandelions.

"I'm sorry," she told her kindly but firmly, "but you're much too young. You must go back home at once."

As soon as her back was turned the girl climbed into the Gettysburg train and hid there. In the hospital tents her services were welcomed without question. Later, inspecting one of these tents, Dorothea saw her working, hard and efficiently, in boots and a torn calico dress. Wisely she said nothing.

The opposition of some officers to her position was steadily growing. With equal vigor they resented the work of the Sanitary Commission, those "meddlesome sentimentalists" whose supplies were welcome but whose interference in their military powers was highly annoying. Friction with the commission was somewhat allayed when Secretary Stanton reorganized the Medical Bureau, but the officers still resented the visits of inspection, especially by the superintendent of nurses. Though most were loyal, the more voluble antagonists demanded her removal from authority.

The blow came in October, 1863, with an order issued by the assistant surgeon-general. Though it reaffirmed her sole right of assignment of nurses to the hospitals on application of the surgeons in charge, its third and fourth provisions constituted a subtle but decisive blow to her position. No females were to be employed without her certificates of approval *unless specially appointed by the surgeon-general.* In other words, the surgeon-general could appoint any nurses he wished. Moreover, women nurses were to be under the exclusive control of the senior medical officer and could be discharged by him "when considered supernumerary, or for incompetency, insubordination, or violation of his orders. . . . Such discharge, with the reason therefor, being endorsed upon the certificate, will be at once returned to Miss Dix."

It was a devastating blow. Secretary Stanton had always been her loyal supporter, yet he bowed to the demands of a few petty officers and for all practical purposes abolished her office. Pitilessly she analyzed her reaction to the stunning defeat. Was it her pride that was hurt? Yes, of course. She had given up her career for this work, labored without rest or pay for more than two years, expended strength, income, all her resources, only to be slapped down, discharged, like one of her "supernumerary, incompetent, insubordinate" nurses! But it was not pride which had received the deepest wound. She had wanted with all her fierce patriotism and compassion to serve her country and succor the sick and wounded. Now she was a soldier suddenly shorn of all weapons, left with only a smart uniform and title. What to do? It would be so easy to run away like a sick dog and lick her wounds. No. Twice before she had run, each time to the peace and luxury of Greenbank. Not again. She continued to work as if nothing had happened.

There was no time to lick one's wounds. The needs were too great. After Gettysburg came Chattanooga, Lookout Mountain, Missionary Ridge, all with their terrible tolls, their urgent appeals. She endeavored to answer them all, impartially, as generous to the few who had worked for her downfall as to the many who had always been her friends. She continued, with Secretary Stanton, to press for the institution of an up-to-date program of military hospitals, far removed from the crude tents or filthy warehouses in use behind the lines. By 1864 such a program was begun, and many hospitals were being built. Here Dorothea was on familiar ground, and, as at Chester, Pennsylvania, it was to her that plans for building and equipment were often submitted.

It was while traveling in Pennsylvania that her train was stopped by a band of Confederate soldiers. As the men in gray came through the cars, stern faced, bayonets raised, the passengers were terrified, all wondering what their fate was to be. At worst they might be taken prisoners; at best the train would be halted indefinitely.

"Why, it's Miss Dix!" exclaimed one of the Confederate officers, stopping by her seat. She recognized him immediately, one of the surgeons who had helped her campaign for the hospital in North Carolina. After greeting her cordially, he introduced her to his fellow officers.

"Tell me about the hospital," she begged eagerly. "It's so long since I've heard news." She inquired after some of their mutual acquaintances, and they talked for some time in friendly fashion. The surgeon whispered a word to his superior officer, who nodded and bowed in courtly fashion. Inasmuch as Miss Dix was on the train, he said, it would be released.

"Thank you," said Dorothea. "Some day when this war is over I hope to return to North Carolina and carry on our work together."

She could not think of the Confederate soldiers as enemies.

"To the Secretary of War, Sir," she once wrote an appeal, "I respectfully ask authority while I am inspecting the Hospital occupied by our Federal soldiers at Elmira to visit that of the Rebel prisoners in detention there. D. L. Dix."

On the back of her letter a surgeon wrote, "Everybody knows that whatever Miss Dix undertakes would be grounded upon the purest and most philanthropic purposes, and so far as she is concerned could not fail to be otherwise than right. But the policy of allowing communication with the prisoners by persons not connected with those responsible for their security is seriously doubted and is not recommended."

A few days later, however, the same surgeon reversed his decision. "I desire to say that while I do not recommend the practice, as stated, I not only have no objection to a visit, as proposed by Miss Dix, but approve it!

The new hospitals were not in use until late summer of 1864. Meanwhile Dorothea did her best to improve conditions in the makeshift facilities, traveling far and wide to make investigations. Often she met doctors, public officials, businessmen with whom she had worked intimately in approaching legislatures and establishing new hospitals, and these encounters invariably won her a courteous reception in situations where she might have expected noncooperation. On one trip she was introduced to a Dr. Buker, a surgeon, she was told, from Hampden, Maine.

"Hampden!" Her eyes lighted with warmth as she took his hand. "Why, I was born there, but I haven't been in the town since I was ten years old."

Yet they managed to discover mutual acquaintances, and the doctor knew her cousins in Dixmont. Hampden! She could think of it now with equanimity, even nostalgia. She knew that there had been beauty as well as pain in those harsh, repressive years when she "had never had a childhood." In the mud and blood and agony of a hospital tent it was good to remember the long elm-shaded road, the square substantial houses, the friendly meeting house, the path to the smooth-flowing Penobscot where she had run with Joseph to watch the ships with their proud white sails.

On one of her trips to City Point, Virginia, she was accompanied by Mrs. Annie Wittenmyer, an agent of the

Iowa Aid Societies, whom she met on the steamer going south down the river. It was Mrs. Wittenmyer's first meeting with the superintendent, whom she thought "the stateliest woman she had ever seen, very dignified in manner and conversation." As always, Dorothea wore a plain dark dress with neat linen collar and cuffs and no jewelry, not even a breast pin.

It was night when they arrived at City Point, unexpected, and they found both town and hospital crowded. "Don't worry about me," Dorothea told her much younger companion. "I'll find a cot somewhere in one of the nurses' tents." But Mrs. Wittenmyer, having found a place to sleep on a bundle of straw and shavings in a storeroom of the Christian Commission, with her carpet bag for a pillow, was getting ready to sleep when a knock came at the door. There stood "that stately woman with all her dignity about her."

"May I share your storeroom for the night?" asked Dorothea with a smile.

"As she was old enough to be my mother," Mrs. Wittenmyer was to write later, "of course there was but one thing to do, and that was to give up my bed of shavings and straw to her, and with the stub of an old broom, try to clear a place on another part of the floor for myself."

Her wonder and admiration grew as Dorothea arose early the next morning, apparently refreshed as if the straw bed had been of down, took a hurried breakfast, careful not to eat anything that a sick soldier might find palatable, and hurried off to inspect the patients, kitchens, and supply rooms.

Dorothea wanted neither praise nor admiration. In that same year of 1864 a writer, Josephine Dayton, preparing a number of sketches of representative American women, wanted to do one on Miss Dix the "Benefactor." She desired details about her present office, when it was conferred, its duties, its result. Would Miss Dix give her an interview in Philadelphia? Miss Dix would not.

The war dragged on. Victories for the North mounted. General Sherman started his campaign for the Carolinas. Columbia and Charleston surrendered. The battle of Five Forks . . . the fall of Petersburg . . . Richmond. And on April 9, 1865, Lee surrendered to Grant at Appomattox. Four years almost to a day from its beginning, the war was over. Washington went wild with rejoicing, then a week later was plunged into mourning with the assassination of the President. Must victory, wondered Dorothea, always contain the seeds of its own defeat?

She worked on. There were still hundreds of sick and wounded soldiers. Someone must be responsible for the nurses caring for them. All that hot summer she remained in Washington, visiting hospitals, conducting a voluminous correspondence in an effort to locate missing soldiers for their families, helping to care for the last remnants of the wounded. While many of the surgeons went away on vacations, she stayed on. One by one the hospitals were closed, the last stores of supplies distributed.

"No," in September she wrote Anne, who begged her to take a rest and come for a visit, "I cannot come at present, certainly not until the volunteers are mustered out. I never felt more need of labor in their behalf than now. I resigned in August the place of Superintendent of Nurses to take effect the 10th of September but did not thereby relieve myself of labor. I have turned over the house I rented to other parties and become while I am here, a boarder. I am resuming care for the insane as well and find life has its own returning obligation for the helpless and suffering."

5

It was eighteen months after the war ended that Dorothea considered her work finished. Perfectionist to the end, she was unsatisfied until she had located every missing soldier possible, written every letter promised for a dying soldier, secured pensions for many of the wounded men and her own nurses who had been invalided in their work. She pored over lists of soldiers in the War Department and in the files of the Sanitary Commission trying to correct their records. And soon she became committed heart and soul to another project.

There was a new national cemetery at Hampton, Virginia, near Fortress Monroe. It was a spot sacred to many memories, where soldiers she had comforted had given her dying messages, where many of them were buried. When someone suggested that they should have a memorial she gladly assumed this extra burden. She promised the memorial committee a thousand dollars, even if she had to pay it herself. But as a result of her urgent appeals the response was generous. She wrote for contributions to almost every state in the Union. Hannibal Hamlin, statesman of her native Maine, promised $300. Stewart, of the merchant press, gave her $200, Jay Cooke, the celebrated banker, $500. Before the year was over the necessary amount was almost raised, and she was able to write of her new task to Mrs. Rathbone:

"Lately I have collected in a quiet way among my friends $8,000 with which to erect a granite monument in a cemetery at Fortress Monroe where are interred more than 6,000 of our brave, loyal soldiers. . . . I had special direction over most of those martyred to a sacred cause, and never forget the countless messages of hundreds of dying men to fathers, mothers, wives, and children; never forget the calm, manly fortitude which sustained them through the anguish of mortal wounds and the agonies of dissolution. . . . Thank heaven the war is over. I would that its memories also could pass away."

A chance to build again! She loved the very touch of the raw materials — stone, iron, lime, cement. Hard and stubborn though they were, so much more malleable than politicians! She spent many days traveling and visiting quarries in Vermont and along the coast of Maine, trying to find stone which would do justice to the shining quality of the men it would memorialize. She made all arrangements for the quarry stones, vessels to carry them, workmen.

By December 11, 1867, she could write to Mrs. Torrey: "Reaching Washington, I proceeded at once to the Ordnance Bureau to see Major General Dyer, asking for 1,000 muskets and bayonets, 15 rifled guns, and a quantity of 24 pound shot, with which to construct my fence. I am rather gratified that every bill has been paid."

A good use for the outmoded instruments of war! If not beaten into plowshares, at least they should remain forever harmless, symbols and warnings of the destruction and death they had wrought. She watched the rise of the monument with the joy of a Michelangelo creating a Pietà. By mid-1868 it was finished — a noble obelisk of syenite seventy-five feet high, resting on a huge base twenty-seven feet square, inclosed in a circular fence of musket barrels, bayonets, and cannon set in great blocks of stone. It bore the simple inscription: "In Memory of Union Soldiers who Died to Maintain the Laws." Like those of the hospital buildings she had helped to create, its site was impressive. It was the first object sailors would see coming from the sea to the Roads, a slender finger like a church spire, a symbol of hope rising out of death. "It will stand for centuries," she declared with satisfaction, "unless an earthquake shakes it down." On May 12 Secretary Stanton, always her friend and supporter, wrote a letter of acceptance, expressing the nation's gratitude.

Dr. Isaac Ray wrote her in lighter vein: "I congratulate you on the completion of your Monument. With so much stone and iron on your shoulders, I do not wonder you got sick. Pray, do take a lighter load the next time you shoulder other people's burdens."

With her dead beneath the monument Dorothea buried also the bitterness and frustration of this most bitter and frustrating period of her life. For no one knew better than she that much of the opposition she had encountered had been merited. *This is not the work I would have my life judged by!* Yet she knew also that she could not escape that judgment. Many would forget the astounding successes of the forty years in her chosen ministry and remember only the weaknesses of the four, when, a sick and tired woman of sixty and more, driven by an overpowering zeal and purpose, she had attempted an impossible task, arousing the enmity of many who fell short of her high standards of perfection.

Not that the judgment would be uniformly critical. Said the historian Lossing in his *History of the Civil War:* "Like an angel of mercy she labored day and night for the relief of suffering soldiers. She went from battlefield to battlefield when the carnage was over, and from camp to camp, giving with her own hand comforts to the wounded and soothing the troubled spirits of the dying. The amount of happiness that resulted from the services of this woman can never be estimated."

Even more intimately revealing was the testimony of her friend Dr. Caroline A. Burchardt, who was closely associated with Dorothea through the war.

"She was a very retiring, sensitive woman, yet brave and bold as a lion to do battle for the right and for justice. She was very unpopular in the war with surgeons, nurses, and any others, who failed to do their whole duty, and they disliked to see her appear, as she was sure to do if needed. . . . She was one who found no time to make herself famous with pen and paper, but a hard, earnest worker, living in the most severely simple manner, often having to be reminded that she needed food. . . . Every day recalls some of her noble acts of kindness and self-sacrifice to mind. She seemed to me to lead a dual life, one for the outside world, the other for her trusted, tried friends."

And Secretary Stanton, more closely associated with her officially than any other person during this period, had always been her keenest admirer and supporter. What could her country do, he inquired of her at the close of the war, to show its gratitude to this tireless servant who had been first on the ground and last to leave? Could there be a great public meeting presided over by high government officials? Could Congress vote her a gift of money?

"No." Dorothea's reply was swift and vehement. "Most certainly not."

Then what?

"Nothing, unless — the Flags of my Country," she suggested on impulse, not really seriously. It was a mere figure of speech, expressing her loyalty.

But he took her at her word. A stand of beautiful flags was specially made for her by the government and shipped to her in Boston in January, 1867. The presentation was made by General Sherman. When the great case was opened and she saw them, she wept.

"Sir," she wrote Secretary Stanton, "I beg to express my sense of the honorable distinction conferred on me by the Secretary of War in the presentation of a Stand of United States Colors. . . . No more precious gift could have been bestowed, and no possession will be so prized while life remains to love and serve my country."

All her life, yes. Then they would be hung at her request in the Memorial Hall at Harvard University dedicated to the sons of Harvard who had died in the war to preserve the Union.

❁ *Eight* ❃

Restless Pilgrim

*No one will consider the day ended
until the duties it brings are
discharged.*

1

THE WAR WAS OVER . . . and just beginning. Concern for the mentally ill, for four years submerged by national madness, now sprang into life. The country discovered that insanity had greatly increased, that out of a total number of mentally ill estimated at over 54,000, over 7,000 were totally unprovided for, that existing institutions were inadequate, understaffed, and out of repair, that legislatures, swamped by the financial exigencies of war, were in no mood for what were termed charitable appropriations. Where turn for help? Where, indeed, but to that worker of miracles, the "angel of mercy," the "patron saint of the helpless?"

Appeals began coming. Could Miss Dix help choose a site for a third hospital in Pennsylvania? Could she advise about separate facilities for the Negro insane in Tennessee? Could she suggest a new superintendent for a hospital in Ohio? She had been promising for years to come to California. Why not now?

There were other appeals. William Rathbone wrote, rejoicing that the shedding of blood was over. He regretted the rift between their two countries over the trend of British sympathies toward the South and mourned the appalling tragedy of Lincoln. "I trust the universal expression of horror and consternation on this side of the water will convince your people what our feelings really are." Surely this was the time for her to come to England for a rest! "Are we never to see you again in your English home?" wrote his wife.

"Come . . . rest . . ." Again and again the words were repeated, by Anne Heath, brother Joseph, the Emersons and Mrs. Torrey in Boston, the Eliots in St. Louis, the Burnaps in Baltimore, the Hares in Philadelphia, the Doremus family in New York. At the end of the war Dorothea did manage a few days in New England, visiting Joseph and his wife in Dorchester and Anne in Brookline. But Boston was no longer home. Even its contours had changed. The old house and garden in Orange Court, once close to the bay and almost in the country, was now surrounded by a populous network of streets. The Round Marsh at the bottom of the Common had been turned into a Public Garden, with a lake formed from the waters of the old Frog Pond. The congregation of Dr. Channing's church on Federal Street had moved to a new building on Arlington. Though the old familiar houses on Mt. Vernon Street remained unchanged, with Mrs. Channing and Miss Gibbs long since gone, they might have been always the homes of strangers.

The people had changed most of all. Anne and her sisters looked surprisingly old, especially Anne, who had long been afflicted with eye trouble and lameness. Abby had lost her husband, Mr. Barnett, and was overcome with grief. Susan, who had helped Anne make most of Dorothea's dresses for many years — always dark and severe in style with just a hint of white at the neck — was gray and wrinkled. Yet they were near her own age, Anne not much older than Dorothea.

Have I also grown old? she asked herself, taking time for a rare self-appraisal in the mirror. True, she was painfully thin, less than a hundred pounds. There were hollows beneath the high cheekbones, and little networks of wrinkles furrowed the high brow. But the thick reddish-brown hair drawn in smooth loops over the ears and coiled high at the back was scarcely touched with gray. The long narrow head was as straightly poised as ever on the slender neck, and the eyes, deep-set under heavy brows, shone with the same eager zest as when she had started on her crusade a quarter of a century ago. For the first time she noticed, with surprise and delight, that it was almost as if Grandfather looked back at her, the same strongly shaped nose, square chin, bright eyes under heavy, beetling brows.

She plunged into the new crusade with as much relish and determination as if she were again in her forties instead of midsixties. She must visit all the institutions she had helped establish. There were now fifty-four hospitals for mental disease in operation and six in the process of being built. But the needs were tremendous. Huge funds must be raised, legislatures approached, old institutions approved, new ones built. Often the results of her investigations were discouraging, if not heartbreaking.

"It would seem," she wrote Mrs. Torrey, "that all my work is to be done over so far as the insane are concerned. Language is poor to describe the miserable state of these poor wretches in dungeons and cells. I did not think I was to find here in this year of 1868 such abuses."

But the prospect was not all discouraging. There were signs of outstanding progress. In May, 1868, Professor Silliman, her old friend to whom she had sent so many botanical specimens, wrote her from New Haven:

"It is just two years this month since you came here to move this matter, and now the first patients are in the new hospital building. How much we all owe you for your timely aid, courage, and energy, without which this noble work would not have been undertaken, certainly for many years! And it was all done so quietly! The springs of influence were touched in a way which shows how possible it is to do great and noble things in public assemblies without a lobby or the use of money!"

In Washington at the army and navy hospital, its burdens increased a hundredfold by the casualties of the war, there was similar success. Her appeal to Congress for funds for additions was honored without question. And in Pennsylvania she helped meet the increased demands in a remarkable way.

"Tomorrow," she wrote a friend, "I go to the Northeastern district of the state to find a farm of 300 acres for the third hospital, for which I have got an appropriation of $200,000."

Progress in this state was one of her greatest joys. The hospital at Harrisburg, one of her first "offspring," second only to her "first born" at Trenton, had clocked a quarter century of efficient service. Dixmont, namesake of her beloved grandfather, was even closer to her heart.

"I trust," wrote Mr. John Harper, its treasurer, "when the warm weather comes, you will visit Dixmont and see for yourself what a monument for humanity has been erected and put into prosperous operation through your foresight and exertions. Do you remember the day in my room at the bank, when you urged the establishment of a new rural hospital, and a certain Judge opposed you so bitterly? The judge was a man of great eloquence and influence, but you beat him, to his astonishment."

She traveled constantly. In the summer of 1867 she was in Nova Scotia, visiting the hospital which after long delays and much litigation had been built in Halifax. Its superintendent, James DeWolf, had kept her informed of all details of both construction and administration. Now, he feared, he was to be replaced by some member of Parliament. Such personal problems of workers, often confided to her, were always treated with the deepest sympathy and interest, though she made it a principle to exert influence only in the rarest of cases.

Her travels were not all a retracing of steps. There were new frontiers to be explored. So far her contacts with institutions in the far west had been largely by correspondence. Now their demands for her presence became imperative. "I am leaving for California," she wrote Anne in April, 1869, "to execute a long delayed work at Stockton. I cannot, of course, say how long I may be absent or how I shall return. Providence permitting the execution of my plans, I may be back before September."

The trip made possible brief visits with friends, Dr. William G. Eliot and his wife in St. Louis, and Jessie Benton Frémont, with whom she had been so closely associated in the war. Then, while inspecting hospitals and prisons in Portland, Oregon, she stayed in the home of the Eliots' son, Thomas Lamb Eliot, who was pastor of the city's large Unitarian church. The frail health of Tom, burdened with his many duties and an increasing family, worried her, and she begged him and his young wife Henrietta to take life more easily.

"Strange words coming from you!" he returned wryly.

These old friendships were increasingly precious to Dorothea, as the ranks of the best beloved were becoming steadily depleted. The death of William Rathbone just a year ago had left a wound which would never heal. Over and over she had read the tribute sent her by the family, a full page in the Liverpool *Mercury*, extolling the life of the city's fearless leader in liberal government and selfless humanitarian. She knew now that she would never again go to England. Greenbank without William Rathbone would be like Eden bereft of its creative Spirit. Only twice before had she felt such bereavement at the death of a loved one — William Channing, and Grandfather.

For three years she had concentrated on institutions in the North and West. Now — dared she turn South? Of course there were friends who would welcome her, in spite of her active participation in the war — Francis and Matilda Lieber in Columbia, South Carolina, the Dobbinses in North Carolina, the Clays in Alabama. And she was constantly receiving appeals from the heads of hospitals struggling with far greater problems than most of the northern institutions. But — how would the *people* receive her? Surely the glad welcome once received in all the southern states was gone forever! Would their bitterness jeopardize any work she might be able to do? And what of her own reaction? For she too had felt bitterness, especially at the sight of prisoners brought back from southern prisons in a state of half starvation and misery. Could she conquer or even hide the old antagonisms? Might not her coming hurt more than help?

The fine dream in which she and others had seen a purified and more godly nation emerging from the holocaust had turned into a nightmare. The Union had been saved, yes, but at a price of frightful disunity. Graft, corruption, exploitation were rampant. The war had drained the financial resources of the North so that there was no mood nor money for philanthropic enterprises, but in the South it had consumed them to the dregs. In the wake of the despoiling armies had come the "carpet baggers," like a plague of grasshoppers. The mental hospitals were on the verge not only of bankruptcy but of disintegration. Cries of despair had long been coming to her, especially from the Carolinas. She must come and help.

Of course she went. And to her surprise and delight not only did she herself feel no remnant of bitterness, but she was welcomed by the people with open arms. The war might never have been. Arriving in South Carolina, she was confronted with a situation of desperate need. Here the "carpet baggers," arriving with little more than an extra shirt and a pair of socks, plus the rapacity of scavengers, had not only fleeced the people but acquired political power in the legislature, packing it with newly freed Negroes, who became their ignorant but willing tools. The policy of such a legislature wreaked havoc with state institutions. No sooner had Dorothea arrived than she was besieged by pleas for help.

"My dear Madam," wrote Alfred Huger from Charleston in January, 1870, "I have just heard of your arrival at Columbia! The Past, the Present, and the Future are by this announcement grouped before me. It is the instinct of the afflicted to be aroused and encouraged when your name is mentioned. Our poor little state is sinking under a weight of calamity and woe, our temples are draped in mourning, and our hearts are in the dust. Still, we flock to the altar when the High Priestess is there.

"I was one of the founders of the lunatic asylum. Everywhere and at all times I have watched its progress. During the war I was in daily, almost hourly interchange with our valued friend, Dr. Parker. We have heard, like a summons to meet death, of his possible removal and we have heard also of your providential advent. If the authorities that rule over us selected this man as a victim or if Dr. Parker can endure his suffering no longer, then there is an agony upon us, and may we not appeal to you for succor and for help?"

The statement, though effusive, was not exaggerated. Conditions were indeed desperate. Two-thirds of the hospital's board of regents were uneducated Negroes controlled by the rapacious northerners. They had combined three offices in the asylum into one and bestowed it on a totally unfit person. When Dr. Parker had reported the man's delinquency to the board, the man had written, "Everything will go on well, if you can have your own way, but not if the Superintendent is to have his." Fortunately there was one Negro regent more qualified for his responsibility. "The Superintendent is the man to have his way," he admonished, "and we will not have two bosses."

But Superintendent Parker was in imminent danger of removal. "If any one can save our cherished institution from ruin," he wrote Dorothea, "you are the person."

He was not removed.

Her travels through the South continued. In North Carolina she was the guest of Governor Holden. She was invited to take a seat on the floor of the senate, a chair being put in a proper and convenient place in the chamber, and as she entered, the senators all rose to their feet. She was welcomed by the president, who made a courtly speech to the "Honored Lady." Later Representative Moore introduced her to members of the house.

"Mr. Speaker and Gentlemen of the House of Representatives. I have the honor of introducing Miss Dix, the eminent philanthropist. I need not inform you who she is. Her name is a household word wherever civilization and Christian charity are known and respected."

Later, when she returned to Raleigh in January, 1871, to help with additions to the woefully inadequate hospital, she would write Anne, "The citizens and public functionaries have met me with such unmistakable cordiality that I needs must put out of my mind the terrible past during the rebellion and take up the line of work where I left it in 1860. Strange to say, none are heartier in welcoming me home to North Carolina than the Democrats and Confederates, so that my plans are accepted and acted upon with an alacrity that hourly surprises me."

But friendly welcomes could not compensate for the agonizing disappointments of seeing so much of her previous work in retrogression if not in ruins — buildings out of repair, hospitals overcrowded and understaffed, and, worst of all, a return to some of the old horrors of chains, purges, straitjackets, dungeons. Of course she labored day and night trying to correct such evils, and, as usual, the extra exertion took its physical toll. In Louisville she was forced to take to her bed with a troublesome cough. Later at Columbus, in April, 1870, she was again taken ill.

"Have been in North Carolina, South Carolina, Georgia, Kentucky, Tennessee, and Ohio," she wrote Anne. She was leaving the next week for Cleveland, then on to Dixmont. But the cough was still continuous, and on the eve of leaving she was seized with severe chills. Not Ohio, after all, nor Dixmont, but Trenton, the place which seemed most of all like home. She arrived in a state of total collapse.

"Malaria," pronounced the doctor. "Your system has been saturated with it for years."

Not for years had she been so ill. For days it was a struggle between life and death. But by mid-June she was writing Anne, "Gaining strength slowly but surely. Was partially dressed yesterday and wearing a lilac and white house dress which you gave me almost twenty years ago, as 'gude as new.' "

2

"A divine spinner for the House of God," Fredrika Bremer had called Dorothea, watching her in the recess at the Capitol, where, "amid the fiery feuds, she silently spins her web for the unfortunate."

All through the decade of the seventies the web continued to strengthen and expand, its tendrils crossing and criss-crossing as the spinner continued her ceaseless casting of threads from Canada to the Gulf, from the Atlantic to the Pacific and beyond.

"Angel," too, she had often been called, and, though still a fighting one, like Michael with his sword, her role became more and more that of guardian angel, jealously protective of her numerous "children" and hastening to their aid in answer to every urgent appeal. They were many and constant, coming from eminent psychiatrists, prison wardens, state legislators, obscure hospital attendants, mothers of missing soldiers, destitute nurses, the mentally ill and their relatives, personal friends, and hundreds of others. She endeavored to answer them all.

From C. S. May in Middletown, Connecticut. "I am proud of this hospital for which you have done so much, and I want to point out to you the need of still further provision for the insane in the state and obtain advice as to the best course to pursue. *Come.*"

From A. Armstrong in Harrisburg, calling her attention to the state of things at the School for Feebleminded Children at Medea.

From M. E. Baker, matron of the Children's Home in Providence. She is having trouble and needs help. Could Miss Dix send a bill of fare which was proved useful in other institutions?'

From Dr. Bemis at the Worcester Lunatic Hospital. "I have succeeded in obtaining bonds with right to purchase 200 acres of land midway between the city and the lake. Well wooded, southern exposure and pleasant view. Pure water, 600 apple trees, 300 pear. Good drainage." He is thinking of South Framingham also. Will she give suggestions? He gladly accepts her gift of a carriage. It will give the patients much pleasure.

From William Lockhart at the Indiana Hospital for the Insane. Funds are needed to complete the hospital. They must have help. . . . He wishes to make a change. Is tired of staying and contending with a man unscrupulous. Will she write him a recommendation to Jacksonville, Illinois?

From William Peck at the Ohio Central Lunatic Asylum at Columbus. "Your anxiety about our Ohio hospitals for the insane is not without foundation. . . . New building still dragging. Dayton without a competent superintendent. Politicians are at the bottom of our troubles." Is in dilemma. Which one should he take as matron?

From Dr. J. A. Reed at Dixmont. "I am following your advice strictly. . . . I have never gone wrong when I followed where you led."

From Dr. John Woodbury Sawyer, superintendent of Butler Hospital. "Sorry to say the Board contemplates the erection of 'cells'! Their ideas of management are crude."

In February, 1871, she was back in Washington after her severe illness, trying to obey the doctor's order to "take it easy."

"What do you find to do?" inquired Anne, confounded by the idea of an idle Thea. The reply was scarcely a recital of leisure activities designed to kill time.

"Mail brings requests from ex-soldiers to look after their back pay and pensions, requests from seven persons who have lost money registered and not transmitted by mail through various post offices, to present their cases to the Depredation Bureau of the post office. One case of an effort to sell counterfeit money makes a communication to the assistant secretary of state necessary; a request to get three children, one an infant three months old, into the Foster Home; a request for a contribution to the Young Men's Christian Association; another for clothing for two families; another to aid a foreign mission, the last being declined having no cash on hand; a request to examine and present a petition for a Revolutionary claim to be paid; opinions on the Women's Rights and their fitness for the learned professions, etc., and the best method for organizing and sustaining reform homes for fallen women, etc.

"Now if you think I am idle any part of the working time for the twenty-four hours, you are mistaken. I have all the time and have always as much as I can do."

She was constantly involved in problems of Civil War participants. For months she endeavored to locate Mary Ann Bickerdyke, whose whereabouts were unknown from 1870 to 1874. Was she deranged, her son James worried, destitute? Dorothea set to work. No matter that "Mother" had been one of the nonofficial nurses, resistant to her authority. After much travel and reams of correspondence she located the "cyclone in calico" alive and well and in her right mind in Bethany Institute in New York doing missionary work. Deranged? Not a bit of it. She had merely been in straitened circumstances for five years and had not wanted to be a burden to her family.

"All due to you," James wrote Dorothea. "A thousand times grateful!"

It might almost have been thirty years before. Back and forth, up and down, the length and breadth of the country she traveled, investigating, advising, carpetbag filled with books, pictures, stereopticon views, scripture tracts for patients, toys and other gifts for the children of superintendents. Travel was a bit easier now, more railroad branches into small towns, more bridges spanning rivers, and she yielded to increasing age and the pleas of friends by avoiding the more rigorous and hazardous adventures — although on her trip to California she had spent ten or twelve days in the saddle and ridden twenty-five miles in one day. The slight, straight figure in its dark dress and bonnet and shawl, the barest frosting of white at the throat, was a familiar and respected traveler almost everywhere she went. She carried a pass on most major railroads, was greeted with deference on steamboats and stages, given the best room in both well-known and obscure hotels.

"It's Miss Dix!" Usually the relayed announcement was "Open Sesame" to respectful treatment, willing cooperation, delighted greetings.

Not always. For wardens, superintendents, matrons, attendants deficient in duty she was Nemesis. Board members, legislators engaged in raising funds, official inspectors, usually announced their arrivals well ahead of time, and machinery could be oiled, special foods prepared, the stage set for their cursory conducted tour. Not Miss Dix. She merely arrived with that quiet but irresistible display of authority and proceeded to penetrate every function of an institution — wards, kitchen, laundry, cellars, bathrooms, her sharp if aging eyes ferreting out every slight evidence of careless or inefficient management. The older doctors in the major institutions welcomed her visits, solicited her comments, which were invariably pertinent. Not so all the younger men, unfamiliar with her previous activities and self-confident in their freshly acquired knowledge. Some resented the intrusion of this unofficial lay-man with her assumption of authority, her uncanny ability to see all, hear all, and then to speak all. Others made sport of what they dubbed the "Dix cult" and the "self-consti-tuted lunacy commission," and indulged in much mer-riment over her unexpected visits.

On one occasion, arriving at an asylum at an un-seasonable hour, she requested the attendants to give a trial of the fire-extinguishing apparatus. It was woefully out of order and completely useless. She summoned the young superintendent and administered a stern rebuke. The incident became the butt of numerous jokes shared with his associates.

"Imagine! My frightful consternation! Seven o'clock in the morning, and the hoses not working! I'm amazed she didn't come at midnight, get the cook out of bed, and de-mand a demonstration of his breakfast preparations!"

Possibly the brash young doctor would have more sober second thoughts less than a decade later, hearing of the total destruction by fire of an immense insane asylum in Montreal, Canada, where a hundred victims were roasted alive, an asylum provided with a complete fire-extinguish-ing system, yet with its hose disconnected from the pumps and the wrench mislaid. Or, in December, 1880, when in a fire at the Minnesota Hospital for the Insane at St. Peter thirty-one patients lost their lives, or, a few years later, of a destructive fire at the asylum in Augusta, Maine, where, fortunately, all patients were evacuated in safety and no lives lost.

But far more typical was the reaction of Mrs. Harriet C. Kerlin, wife of the superintendent of an institution for feebleminded children in Elwyn, Pennsylvania.

"Among our many visitors, there has never been one so ready to praise the good found, and so agreeable to reprove mistakes or failures. . . . If she were found at 5 o'clock a.m. in an unusual place, watching the early movements of our large family, her kindly manner of telling what she had seen, right or wrong, made us feel that sympathy with the superintendents prompted her desire for as perfect management as possible, and that no spirit of pleasure in spying out wrong had caused her unexpected early walk. She never gossiped about the weaknesses or faults of others. Her judgment was given with consideration of accompanying circumstances. Her language, voice, and manner were thoroughly gentle and lady-like, yet so strong was she in intelligence and womanhood that at times I ranked her alone, and above all other women."

Such was the tribute not only of her intimate associates but also of well-known authorities in the area of mental disease. In 1877, when she was seventy-five, Dr. Charles F. Folsom of Boston wrote of her in his book *Diseases of the Mind*, "Her frequent visits to our institutions of the insane now, and her searching criticisms, constitute of themselves a better lunacy commission than would be likely to be appointed in many of our states."

In the homes of many superintendents her welcome was more that of a beloved relative than of a visiting dignitary, or even of a friend. Especially did she endear herself to children. There were always gifts for each one in her treasure bag. She knew more about science and nature than many of their teachers and delighted to share her knowledge. All her life she had loved puzzles, riddles, enigmas, and was ready to propound them by the dozen.

"Why are brokers like Pharaoh's daughter? Because they get a small profit from the rushes on the bank."

"What kind of sweetmeat did they have in the ark? Preserved pears."

"What is the champion conundrum? Life. We all have to give it up."

Her concern for children was no here-today-and-gone-tomorrow affair.

"Thank you for the paper that you sent me. I like it," wrote young Alvah Godding from the hospital in Washington. "I had a velocipede Christmas and I ride on it in the hall and sometimes out of doors. We have three red squirrels and one gray one in our schoolroom. Did you know that I go to school every day and am learning to read and write? My canary is very tame and will eat from my fingers. Papa gave me a postage stamp album one day, and I am filling it with stamps. I have already more than fifty. When are you coming here?"

"I have received four envelopes of pictures since I wrote you," it was Dr. Bemis's small son Johnny writing from Worcester, "for which please accept a *great many thanks*. My papa and mama and grandma are well, and all send their regards to you."

Another letter acknowledged the receipt by young George Sawyer of a gyroscope and thanks. He has shown the fireworks and egg to his father.

At least one of these young admirers was inspired to follow her example. Sitting in his study in a dormitory room at Andover with her Christmas gift before him, pictures of some of the "bright-winged birds" which had been their common interest, he had written her back in the sixties, "I used to listen to your story as a boy. Hero worship stirred my heart toward one noble woman who, with 'scrip' in hand, went from city to city. . . ." Now, in the seventies, she was recommending Charles Parker Bancroft, a graduate doctor, for a position in one of the great hospitals.

In her wake sprang up budding inheritors of her name, if not of her vocation. From little Dora, daughter of the Eliots in Portland, Oregon, through Dorotheas, Dorothys, Eldoras, Theodoras, Theodosias, Dollys, all across the country she could count her namesakes, and these "gifts of God" were recipients both of countless little presents and of her lifelong affection for all children. Indeed, for all *persons*. She had been a reformer, creating social change. But the impulse for such creativity had sprung always from an acute sensitivity to the needs of persons, a young woman in a cage, an Abram Simmons in a frost-crusted dungeon, a fevered sailor on a steamboat, a prisoner with empty eyes and hands, a sick woman in a hotel room.

"I often think of your thoughtful care of that forlorn woman in the cars," her friend William Eliot had written when he was trying to raise the endowment for George Washington University in St. Louis. "It was a rebuke to me. I can spend or be spent for an institution or for humanity, but if I had seen the 'certain man between Jerusalem and Jericho,' I should have been the priest or Levite. Perhaps *they* were at work for something on a *large* scale, and could not see the *small;* or perhaps they had no relish for charity in detail."

Dorothea did. As her beloved Trenton hospital was her "first born," so all the others were her children," not institutions, but persons, hands to be occupied with meaningful tasks, eyes opened to beauty, minds enriched with knowledge, souls stirred to spiritual awareness. She could not do enough for them. Her letter files bulged with notes of gratitude.

Charles F. Stewart in the Nebraska hospital in Lincoln, for the generous donation of 114 pictures. "Will add much to the cheerfulness of the wards."

Clara L. Knapp from the Kansas State Insane Asylum. "Thanks for the gifts sent. Everything was admired, but the patterns of fancy work were just what we needed."

H. M. Harlow of Augusta, Maine. She has sent a package of music.

John Curwen at Harrisburg. "The lap robes for the carriage came."

C. J. Bennet at the Minnesota hospital. Miss Dix is to be responsible for half the cost of a piano. "A Chickering is most desirable."

John H. Heywood, Louisville. "Warmest thanks for the organ which came last week."

Richard Gundon, at Southern Ohio Asylum. She has sent music. "Our band has already incorporated some of the pieces."

Such expressions were legion. Boxes, packages, crates wove the same vast network as her travels. Her income, thanks to Grandmother, was adequate for her frugal needs, but it took scrimping to provide for all her many charities. She had always been a scavenger, never throwing anything away that might be made useful, enlisting her friends to sew the odds and ends she brought them into layettes and petticoats, collecting cast off clothing, books, pictures from everybody along the way, even children.

"You can help," she would inspire them to share their toys, puzzles, collections of flowers, butterflies, minerals with needy patients. Tears were sometimes shed, no doubt, in her wake, and in more than one case precious collections and toys were secreted when it was known she was coming.

Her charities also were legion — books, hundreds of them for prison and hospital libraries . . . pictures . . . lithographs . . . music . . . money . . . flower seeds, shrubs . . . clothing for almshouses and orphanages . . . $500 for the widows and orphans of lost fishermen . . . $100 to the Colonization Society to send Henry Russell, aged thirty-six, to Liberia . . . help through Wellesley College for a girl named Isabelle Cromwell . . . food and clothing for the Portuguese whom a severe fire had left homeless and destitute in Boston . . . a package to one of the superintendents who had lost much in a fire.

"It seemed to me so like my mother," wrote Mary Blatchford from Evanston, "and it's really remarkable how many things you sent replace to me and the children precisely what the fire took away, books for the children, pictures, comfortable shoes. You must have the gift of second sight."

3

The web she had spun through the years remained firm, even those tendrils stretching into distant lands. On her European trip, while interesting herself in conditions in hospitals and prisons in Prague, she had aroused the admiration of a group of Bohemian women. In 1868 they had sent her a picture of their group, and in return she had sent through the State Department of the American minister in Berlin a photo of herself executed in porcelain, enclosed for protection in a hermetically sealed tin case. Now, in 1873, there came to her a beautiful box of dark, highly polished wood inlaid with an inscription in metal: "To Miss D. L. Dix, From the American Club of Bohemian Ladies." It contained two large pictures of Prague, a volume of Bohemian poems, Dorothea's own story in Bohemian, two albums full of 250 photos of members of the club, a quarto volume of Bohemian songs, a map, and other treasures.

There were other indications that her work in Europe had survived and grown. In 1876 Dr. J. P. Bancroft of the Concord, New Hampshire, Asylum for the Insane visited Rome and saw the asylum erected by Pope Pius IX which her efforts had probably originated. In spite of many obstacles it had improved, then serving 650 patients. There were also good reports from Scotland and the Channel Islands.

It had long been her dream to cast tendrils, too, across the Pacific. Years before, in Washington, she had sought out a chargé d'affaires from Japan, Jugoi Arinori Mori, a man of intellectual ability and humanitarian interests, and tried to impress on him the need for enlightened institutions for the mentally ill in his country. Now, in 1875, she learned of his success.

"My dear Miss Dix," he wrote from Tokyo, "During the long silence, do not think I have been idle about the matter in which you take so deep an interest. I have given the subject much time and attention, and have successfully established an asylum for the insane in Kyoto, and another in this city is being built and will soon be ready for its work of good. Other asylums will follow, too, and I ardently hope they will be the means of alleviating much misery."

Good! Fortunately the map on which she was accustomed to mark each new hospital with a small cross was one of the world, not merely of her own country. Already, before these two, there were thirty-two crosses, each representing one mental hospital which she had helped either to found or to enlarge greatly.

Yet the work was barely begun. Buildings were overcrowded. Unnecessary restraints were still being employed. Obsolete methods of treatment were still in use. A few years before, Dr. E. T. Wilkins of California had made a survey of the country's institutions, visiting 149 of them. He had found practices to recommend, such as workshops, gymnasiums, games, courses of instruction, libraries, music. Yet space everywhere was inadequate. Purgatives and emetics, hot and cold baths, were being used indiscriminately.

In 1875 John Charles Bucknill, a prominent English psychiatrist visiting the United States, lamented the lack of exercise, the overdried and overheated air, the lack of health which pervaded the institutions of the country. He considered the Pennsylvania hospital equal to the best in England, and spoke well of Utica. He saw eight apparently quiet patients in straitjackets at St. Elizabeth's. He disliked the "lodge wards" at McLean and the pavilions for wealthy inmates. And in 1876 Dr. Daniel Hack Tuke, writing in the *Journal of Medical Science* on his survey of American institutions, while giving much commendation, compared the position of American psychiatrists on the question of restraints unfavorably with that of English psychiatrists on this subject.

"Their position, succinctly expressed, is simply this — Restraint, in some form or other must be employed, whether by bricks and mortar, manual tension, of fastenings on the person, or 'chemical restraint.' Whichever be adopted, *physical* and not moral restraints are resorted to."

He quoted from one of Dorothea's letters in his report. " 'I can at once state two facts,' writes Miss Dix to me, 'concerning the state of communities in the United States, an acknowledged obligation to *provide suitably* for *all* insane persons, whether chronic or recent cases. . . . Much is said on the supposed rapid increase of insanity in the United States. I do not think this is a sound proposition. Of course, the number of insane persons is vastly larger than ten years since, but the amazing increase of population by a continually inflowing immigration from Europe, with the natural increase of native inhabitants, will create imperative need for a multiplication of hospitals for care and treatment.' "

Need, yes. In her lifetime they had barely touched its edges. If only she were in her forties instead of her seventies!

To her dismay and extreme displeasure she was forced to yield to the insistent demands for her portrait to be hung in some of the hospitals she had helped to found. It was hard to refuse the importunities of Trenton, her "first born."

"Will you lend me the daguerreotype which represents myself?" she wrote Anne. "I suppose I will have to concede to have a portrait made life-size for Trenton. If you should go to that beautiful state institution, you may find me suspended in image though not in effigy."

Then, of course, she had to give the same privilege to Dixmont. It was presented to the hospital by an anonymous donor.

"You know, sir," Mr. Harper wrote this man, "in the olden time, each institution sacred to charity had its patron saint. The Dixmont Hospital, notwithstanding our Protestant and iconoclastic ideas, has a patroness whom we respect and love; indeed who is canonized in our affections quite as strongly as were saintly ladies in the medieval age. The mission of 'our Lady' is to create those noble institutions which aid in the restoration of the dethroned reason, and Dixmont Hospital is one of the jewels which will adorn her crown hereafter."

Soon there were many hospitals which had life-sized

portraits of her in oil. McLean had one in Somerville. Tennessee had two, Harrisburg and others had one. There was one in the Boston Athenaeum, as well. All were made from a daguerreotype she had given Anne many years before and borrowed again and again.

She was at St. Elizabeth's, the army and navy hospital outside of Washington, when one of these portraits arrived and was hung. Dr. and Mrs. Godding, the superintendent and wife who had succeeded Dr. Nichols, and several others gathered around to look at it. Some were enthusiastic, others had reservations. Mrs. Godding thought it flattered the subject, showed her looking too young and too beautiful.

"I think it is a good likeness," pronounced Dorothea. "Still, if it is not, I shall not accept it. I certainly don't wish to be flattered nor caricatured. I know!" A thought accurred to her. She turned to Mrs. Godding. "Let's let your little daughter come look at it and decide. I can depend on her to be honest."

Mrs. Godding was reluctant. She was afraid the three-year-old would not even recognize the picture. But she called her in. "Come, dear, and see what we have here."

The child came in, and before her mother had a chance to question her, she pointed to the picture. "Oh, thee! Ith Mith Dicth!"

Dorothea kissed her and announced with satisfaction. "See, it is a good likeness."

Only once did she ever allow herself to pose for a painting. Rose Lamb, sister of her attorney and good friend, Horace Lamb, in Boston, was a very fine artist. Somehow she persuaded the reluctant Dorothea to sit for her. The result was disappointing. It showed her not as a woman in her prime, like the daguerreotype, but as she was, a woman long past middle age. It was a good likeness, she had to admit. "But it is not the way I wish to be remembered," she said frankly. She gave it to her friend Horace, requesting that he show it to no one.

She was growing old, of course, yet so seldom did she study herself in the mirror that she scarcely noticed the physical changes. It was the sight of Anne, a mere shadow of her old self, that shocked her finally into awareness of the relentless passing of time. Then, one day in February, 1878, she was summoned from Trenton by a telegram telling of her brother Joseph's death following an intense illness of only fourteen hours. In his home on Center Street, where she had visited many times, she sat alone, thinking back more than seventy years to the endless folding and stitching of paper, the dust and clutter and shabbiness of the little house in Hampden — yes, and to wild runs along the river paths, the smell of apple blossoms, the thrill of climbing a birch and swinging down to the ground. It all seemed very long ago and far from reality. Yet equally unreal seemed the resolution of the Prudential Committee of the Harrison Square Unitarian Society praising the noble life and character of a man named Joseph Dix.

A few months later, in May, she was writing Abby about Anne's death. "When I saw her last, it did seem to me that the 'golden bowl was almost broken,' and the light flickering in the socket."

For three years more she kept on, traveling, inspecting, though at an ever slowing pace. She should have been satisfied with her achievements. There had been thirteen institutions for the mentally ill in 1843; by 1880 there were 123, seventy-five of them state-owned, one federal, the others private. She had helped to found thirty-two of the state institutions. She could take pride also in fifteen training schools which had been established for the feeble-minded. There were over 91,000 mentally ill persons in the United States, and over 50,000 of them enjoyed institutional care. But of course she could never be satisfied. Her concern for suffering had never been whetted to a finer edge. It extended even to dumb creatures.

Once, when driving through Custom House Square, a congested section of Boston, she had noticed the draft horses straining and sweating in the struggle to pull their heavy loads. What a blessing if someone could be constantly at hand to draw pails of water to refresh them! Better yet, how wonderful if there could be a fountain where the poor beasts themselves could take refreshment, one which would never run dry. Immediately she began making plans for such a fountain.

She had heard the poet Whittier repeat an inscription which he had seen in Arabic on just such a fountain in the East, and she remembered the thrill it had given her. She wrote to him asking if he would send her the translation.

"My dear friend," he wrote back from Oak Knoll in 1879, "I cannot recall the Arabic inscription I referred to for the fountain, and have written one myself, taking it for granted that the fountain was to be thy gift, though thee did not say so.

"Such a gift would not be inappropriate for one who all her life has been opening fountains in the desert of human suffering, who, to use Scripture phrase, has 'passed over the dry valley of Baca, making it a well.' With love and reverence thy friend, John G. Whittier."

The poem accompanied the letter.

> "Stranger and traveler!
> Drink freely and bestow
> A kindly thought on her
>   Who bade this fountain flow;
> Yet hath for it no claim
>   Save as the minister
> Of blessing in God's name."

4

Stranger and traveler! These she had always been. She had had many homes — and none. The little house in

Hampden and Dix Mansion had been only stopping places. The Hares in Philadelphia, the Heaths and Torreys and Emersons and brother Joseph in Boston, the Henrys in Washington, the Burnaps in Baltimore, the Liebers in Columbia, the Rathbones in Liverpool — all had welcomed her, begged her to call their homes her own, but she had come to them like a pilgrim, always swiftly moving on.

"I prefer to be a citizen of the United States," she said often, "not of any one place."

In these last years there were only two places where she felt she belonged, the rooms reserved for her in the institutions closest to her heart, the State Hospital at Trenton and St. Elizabeth's, the army and navy hospital, near Washington. Next to these in her affections came Dixmont, in western Pennsylvania, the only one except Dix Hill which bore her name.

The rooms in each were always ready for her coming. Except in cases of emergency no one else ever occupied them. She could put away a skirt, a shawl, a bonnet, a bit of ribbon, a packet of letters in drawer or closet and know she would find it in exactly the same place when she returned. Years ago Dr. Nichols had set aside for her a room in the army and navy hospital, near his own apartment, and when Dr. Godding succeeded him, his wife continued the arrangement. Dorothea's visits were sporadic. She might stay a night or a month, or even two, but she was always welcome.

The room at Trenton was even more personally her own. It was under the pediment of the beautiful Greek portico which formed the front of the main building, and she could look out over the expanse of lawns, gardens and fields to the shining curves of the Delaware River. As the years passed the periods of retirement to Trenton grew longer and more frequent. Yet long after her body should have yielded to increasing weakness, her indomitable will continued to fire it with energy, like a candle flame that

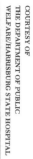

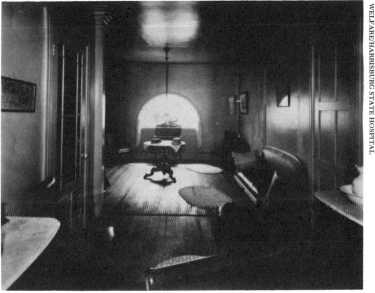

Living quarters at Trenton Hospital.

persists in burning even after the tallow has been consumed. She was seventy-eight in 1880 and still maintaining her grueling rounds of hospital visitation. Though
she tried to avoid the severe winters of New England by
traveling south as soon as snow came, the winter of 1880
found her still responding to the insistent demands of
northern institutions. Perhaps she sensed that the day of
activity was near its end and, like a mother with a great
brood of children, she must see that each one was well fed,
prayed over, tucked in before the coming of night.

"She arrived at my house in Boston," remembered Dr.
George F. Jelly, superintendent of McLean Hospital,
"after nightfall one bitter, snowy winter evening. She
seemed chilled to the marrow, said she would go straight
to bed. I offered her assistance in mounting the stairs, but
she declined. The furnace drafts were opened, a large fire

kept blazing in the grate in her bedroom. My wife and I piled five or six garments on her, and I administered a warm drink. In spite of it she kept shivering and would, I felt, succumb to pneumonia. But she was on one of her tours of inspection and had ordered a carriage for early in the morning. Nothing would make her change her plans, and when morning came she was ready to start. It was still a bitter snowstorm. I begged her at least to let me go with her to the station, for I feared she might die before reaching her destination. No. She would go alone. As soon as she got through with her work in New England, she would go farther south."

South she went, to Virginia and Carolina in March, Florida and Georgia in May, traveling fourteen hundred miles before the increasing heat drove her north again. In June she was again in Trenton, so exhausted she dared not make plans for summer. But as requests came, she could not refuse them.

No one will consider the day ended until the duties it brings are discharged. The favorite quotation was becoming a prodding spur. The day? Say, rather, the life! It was October before the weakening body conquered the imperious will. She arrived in Trenton in a state of complete collapse.

"She is very ill," young Dr. Ward reported to the board of managers. "I doubt if she ever recovers to continue her work."

Instantly the board took action, meeting and passing a unanimous resolution: "That the members of the Board hereby express their deep sympathy with Miss Dix in her affliction and indulge the hope that she may speedily be relieved and restored to her usual health.

"Resolved, that the Superintendent be authorized to make all necessary provision for the convenience and comfort of Miss Dix while she remains in the Asylum."

To the end of her life, the resolution implied if not expressed, for so serious was her condition that everyone understood, Dorothea most of all, that recovery was a vain hope.

"Let the silver cord be loosed swiftly," she was tempted to pray, "and the golden bowl of the lamp be soon broken — that is, if it be your will."

But the cord was steel-tough in spite of its slackness, the bowl fired with a white-hot heat that resisted many seams and cracks. The flame within flickered, almost died, then bravely returned to a feeble but persistent glow. Early in 1882, she had recovered sufficiently to write letters again and read the poems, hymns, scriptures she so much loved.

"My precious Rose," she wrote Rose Lamb, in February, one of the few times she had ever permitted herself to address a friend in such intimate language, "I am still in invalid dress or rather undress, mostly on the bed, with no prospect of being abroad when spring flowers spring, bloom and blossom. There has been little wintry weather, the fields are more green than brown. One heavy snowfall afforded two days sleighing for patients. I gain strength slowly and have a vivid sense of aloneness except when I read the cheering blessed promises and example of our Lord."

The weeks of waiting became months, the months years. She was in increasingly frequent pain. Ossification of the arterial membranes, doctors diagnosed, and they could give no relief. But far worse than the pain was the confinement of a restless spirit within four walls, often the narrow compass of a bed. Suffering . . . imprisonment . . . the two evils she had struggled so hard to combat in human life. The irony produced no sense of injustice or self-pity, only a keener, if possible, sensitivity to those whose helplessness she now shared.

> If I am cold, they also are cold;
> If I am weary, they are distressed;
> If I am alone, they are abandoned.

She was weary, yes, infinitely so, but not cold; lonely, but certainly not abandoned. Her rooms in the tower were warm and cozy. She was surrounded by her dearest possessions: books, the little chest from the Ladies of Bohemia, a leaf from a magnolia tree at Mt. Vernon planted by Washington, a lock of Reverend Mr. Gannett's light brown hair cut off back in 1845, a little piece of stone from Palestine taken from the ancient bridge connecting the temple with Mount Zion. Though unable to leave her rooms, she could look out over the parklike expanse of the grounds, watch the patients enjoying the fullest liberty possible — men and women whom her efforts may well have spared the misery of chains and dungeons.

She was well cared for, even though her little nurse-companion, Annie, was a great trial, impertinent, untidy, reluctant to follow her minute directions. But Dr. John Ward and his lovely young wife Horrie were far more attentive and devoted than her own relatives. When he had come bounding into her room announcing joyfully the news of his first-born child, she had burst out happily, "Yes, and born under the roof of *my* first-born child!"

Now that she could not go to the world, it came to her. Friends were constantly dropping in — George Emerson from Boston, Henry Bellows from New York, Thomas Eliot from Portland, Oregon, Dr. Daniel Hack Tuke, who was visiting the United States gathering material for his new book, *The Insane in the United States and Canada.* Letters poured in. Superintendents kept her informed of the growth and problems of her thirty-two "children," sent her their annual reports, asked her advice. Even her old pupils remembered her.

"I never think of you as grown old," wrote Mrs. John Kebler from Cincinnati. "You always come to me as I knew you first, crowned with rich brown hair, the like of which no one else ever had. . . . Always shall I connect with you, if I remain longer than you, that lovely hymn of Whittier, and my prayer shall be —

Still, let thy mild rebuking stand
Between me and the wrong,
And thy dear memory serve to make
My faith in goodness strong.

It was fitting that she should quote from Whittier, a life-long friend of Dorothea.

"How well I remember with comfort and cheer," she had once written him, "your calls when I was at Danville. You did not suspect the good you were doing me; your presence bringing to recollection so much you had written inviting to a deeper hope and trust in Divine Providence, a more profound reverence for the Great Creator and a deeper conviction of the truths of the gospel of our Lord and Savior, Jesus Christ. I do not think, Mr. Whittier, you have ever realized the wide reaching blessing of your public works."

Now, learning of her illness, he wrote her, "I am glad to know that thou art with kind friends. Thou hast done so much for others that it is right for thee now, in age and illness, to be kindly ministered to. He who has led thee in thy great work of benevolence will not forsake thee. With a feeling of almost painful unworthiness I read thy over-kind words as regards myself. I wish I could feel that I deserved them. But compared to such a life as thine my own seems poor indeed."

He sent her the manuscript of a poem he had written in 1882, "At Last."

There were many letters from the Eliots. To Thomas's children and to the Goddings in Washington Dorothea kept sending little remembrances — books, pictures, bean bags, needle cases.

"What can I send them?" she wrote Etta Eliot as late as October, 1886, "and how many have you? Will another five dollars get anything for Thanksgiving or Christmas?"

She lived now with but one purpose, to use what time and money she had left in the service of others. There were many individuals dependent on her for financial assistance. They must be provided for. But the bulk of her capital must be preserved for worthy charities. Her estate would amount to fifty or sixty thousand dollars. She was opposed to leaving money merely to institutions. She wanted it to aid individuals, especially to educate young men and women, not to come to cities and be clerks, but for men to be taught useful mechanical trades, for women to learn to be nurses or teachers or good mothers and wives. The provisions of her will, arranged after many consultations with Horace Lamb, were explicit. There were personal bequests to friends and relatives. A thousand dollars would go to General Armstrong for his Institute for Negroes and Indians at Hampton, five hundred to the Society for the Prevention of Cruelty to Animals for the drinking fountain in Boston, five hundred to Gloucester for the wives and children of lost fishermen. The remainder, all she had been able to save through her frugal life, would constitute a trust fund, its income to be used as loans to assist worthy young people through school.

With her usual meticulous attention to detail she made known her wishes about other effects. Her collection of autographs at Newton were to be sold. The battle flags had already gone to Harvard, the medals of honor to the Massachusetts Historical Society. Religious books would go to the Meadville Theological School. Dr. Godding should have her field glasses and other effects left at Washington. A silver cup given her in the South would go to Dr. Grissom at Dix Hill for his daughter, one of her many namesakes. Her collection of gold Syrian coins and silver pictures were to be sold and the proceeds given to charity.

Her biography! For years the prospect had been rearing its head like an unpleasant serpent. She wanted none of it. But pressures were persistent. Not for herself, she was urged, but for the cause.

"I never cease to regret that thee did not keep a journal of thy life and labors," Whittier had lamented.

Her close friend General John Dix had written to the Honorable Alexander Randall of Annapolis, who, with his wife Elizabeth, was one of Dorothea's old friends: "I wrote to Miss Dix urging her to make full notes of what she had done for the insane. There is no record like hers — I do not except Howard or Mrs. Fry; and it is due to our country to give a faithful account of the labors of her life. . . . I have pressed this duty on her for years, and trust your solicitations and those of other friends may decide her to perform it."

Randall had obediently bombarded her with letters. "How comes the memoir? You owe it to our country properly to attend to it yourself. I know you will not charge me with flattery when I say that if any other female in the country had accomplished half as much as you, she would have procured her life to be written or written it herself."

Even Anne had not understood her Thea's horror of publicity. Long before her death she had written, "Some quack will seize the pen and write your life, stating that you were born in the British provinces, placed in early life by your friends in Brattleborough, where at the water cure you attained great strength of constitution. It will sell well. The world will fall to and read it, remarking at the close, 'What kind relations to give her such a powerful help at starting!' . . . Since the voracious public will have a story, give them a true one. I will supply you with ink and give you a glass of milk and keep off intruders."

She finally yielded and turned her papers over to Horace Lamb, discussing with him what details should be omitted or emphasized.

"Not much about the Civil War," she insisted. Fortunate for her peace of mind that she could not know that her positive commands to her many friends to destroy her private letters had been happily disregarded, and eight or nine thousand of them were still extant. Had she had her way, the biography soon to be written by Reverend Francis Tiffany, a Unitarian minister, would have been dry as dust.

Three years . . . four . . . five . . . Pain was constant now and increasingly severe. But she was no stranger to pain. Had she not once written Anne, "the hour of bodily suffering to me is the hour of spiritual joy. It is then that most I feel my dependence on God, and his power to sustain." She was growing very deaf also, and her sight was impaired. "But I don't think it right," she commented, "to get such numbers of spectacles that nobody else can use, and which do me no good."

One of her friends brought her an ear trumpet, but its reverberations pounded like hammer blows against her head. "Try to put this tube in my ear so as not to pain," she would beg, "and yet allow me to hear what you have to say."

She could no longer read easily, but the hymns and poems so dear to her had long since been memorized, and she repeated them for hours on end. Propped on her pillows, she could still write letters, her unsteady hand composing them with painful slowness and almost always adding lines from a beloved poem or hymn. In spite of the shaky writing, she thought wryly, they were doubtless more legible than the hasty scrawls about which Anne and others had made such disparaging remarks!

"Would you recognize me?" she demanded curiously of Mrs. Miller, an old friend from Princeton, New Jersey, who had not seen her for some years. Then, sensing that she had embarrassed the visitor, she hastily changed the subject.

The golden bowl was indeed tarnished, its flame flickering low, but the silver cord clung by a tenacious thread. As long as she could make some contribution to the human life about her, she did not want to die.

On one of her visits Mrs. Miller saw that the patient wanted to say something confidential, and she tried to maneuver the nurse out of hearing, unsuccessfully.

"Never mind now," she comforted. "Tell me when I come again."

"Ah, yes," Dorothea said faintly, "if I am here, if I am here."

"Oh, I hope you will be here for many years to come!" It was a mere gallantry, for she assumed death would be welcomed by the sufferer. She was amazed when the patient started up from her pillows with agitated eagerness. "Oh, my dear friend, if you hope that, pray for it, pray that I may be here. I think even lying on my bed I can still do something." She was even more surprised when at her leaving Dorothea threw her arms about her and exclaimed with unaccustomed tenderness, "O, darling!"

It was a phrase which occurred over and over in the fragments of letters she wrote now to her friends. "O, darling!" At last the shield of impenetrable reserve which had so long separated her from the world, even from friends like the beloved Anne, melted away, letting the innate but long-concealed tenderness break forth.

Another spring . . . She saw it only in the tops of trees and an expanse of sky, as if already her vision was focused on objects far above the earth. A feathering of green, a burst of buds, soaring wings, and a flurry of racing clouds. Reality was mingling inextricably with the past. The treetops might have been shading the steep path to the rocks above the Penobscot, the clouds racing toward the bay with the white-winged gulls over Boston Common. She wrote a letter to Matilda Lieber, one of the last with her own hand, and in an absent moment wrote across the margin, 85 Mt. Vernon Street. Friends who came now felt secretly that each visit was goodby.

"They try to repair the one hoss shay," she said to one. Then, "I am as unstable as the sea."

Summer came swiftly, a sudden burgeoning of bright emerald and vistas of dazzling blue.

"Don't give me anything," she begged Dr. Ward. "None of those anodynes to dull senses or relieve pain. I want to — feel it all. And — please tell me when the time is near. I want to know."

"I will," he promised, "if it is possible."

But the end came as suddenly to him as to her, on July 17, 1887. He was sitting at the tea table when the nurse in attendance ran in to report that she was dying. He rushed up the stairs. Just as he arrived at her bedside she gave a last quiet sigh.

She was buried, as she had wanted, in Mt. Auburn Cemetery in Cambridge. The clergyman spoke briefly from the text, "I was an hungered, and you gave me meat . . . I was in prison . . ." He read Whittier's poem, "At Last," a well worn manuscript copy of which had been found under her pillow.

> When on my day of life the night is falling,
>> And, in the winds from unsunned spaces blown
> I hear far voices out of darkness calling
>> My feet to paths unknown,
> Thou who hast made my home of life so pleasant,
>> Leave not its tenant when its walls decay;
> O Love Divine, O Helper ever present,
>> Be Thou my strength and stay!

It was just as she would have wanted it, as simple as the bonnet and shawl, the unadorned dark dress with its fluff of white at the throat which she had worn entering cells and dungeons, palaces and halls of state, which had absorbed the dusts and muds and cinders of the length and breadth of two continents. The marble marker erected later would bear neither epitaph nor date, only the words: DOROTHEA L. DIX.

There followed innumerable tributes, resolutions of distinguished bodies and heads of state, glowing newspaper eulogies. But none could equal the simple words with which her old friend Dr. Nichols closed a letter to Dr. Daniel Hack Tuke:

"Thus had died and been laid to rest in the most quiet, unostentatious way the most useful and distinguished woman America has yet produced."

Bibliography

PRIMARY SOURCES

The major collection of Dorothea Dix Papers is in the Houghton Library, Harvard University, Cambridge, Massachusetts, catalogued under Ab MS Am #1838. It contains twenty-nine boxes of letters, manuscripts, clippings, pictures, mementos, and other personal effects. The letters, numbering thousands, are from a wide variety of correspondents: family and intimate friends, superintendents of hospitals and other doctors, ministers, nurses, teachers, writers, statesmen. These include many noted persons, such as Millard Fillmore, Abraham Lincoln, Horace Mann, Fredrika Bremer, William Ellery Channing, John C. Frémont, Sarah Grimké, Oliver Wendell Holmes, Henry Wadsworth Longfellow, Samuel Gridley Howe, Francis Lieber, Elizabeth Peabody, John Greenleaf Whittier. Included in this collection are the Heath-Dix Papers, hundreds of letters written by Dorothea Dix to her friend Anne Heath during many years.

Other collections which include pertinent materials are:

Boston, Massachusetts. Public Library. Chamberlain Autographs, containing letters from Dorothea Dix to George Barrel Emerson. Also in the library are fragmentary letters in the Dorothea Lynde Dix Collection.

Boston. Massachusetts Historical Society. A few letters from Dorothea Dix in various collections.

Buffalo, New York. Historical Society. The Millard Fillmore Papers contain many letters from Dorothea Dix.

Cambridge, Massachusetts. Arthur and Elizabeth Schlesinger Library, Radcliffe College. The Jane Gray Dodge Papers and the Loring Family Papers contain correspondence with Dorothea Dix.

Liverpool, England. Papers of William Rathbone V contain letters of Dorothea Dix to Mr. and Mrs. Rathbone, 1837–1875.

Maryland Historical Society Library. The Alexander Randall papers contain diaries relating to the campaign on behalf of the insane by Miss Dix.

Minnesota Historical Society. The Charles Edwin Mayo Papers contain data on Miss Dix.

Pennsylvania Historical Society. Papers of the Powel Collection contain letters to Dorothea Dix.

Pittsburgh, Pennsylvania. Western Pennsylvania Historical Association. The John L. Harper Papers.

Raleigh, North Carolina. Historical Commission. Papers of James E. Dobbin. Also letters of D. L. Swain regarding Miss Dix's work in North Carolina.

San Marino, California. Henry E. Huntington Memorial Library. Lieber Papers.

Washington, D. C. Library of Congress. Dorothea Dix Papers. Fragmentary.

Williamsburg, Colonial. Galt Family Papers.

OFFICIAL DOCUMENTS

Documents of the United States Christian Commission, 1861–1865. Adjutant's Archives, War Department. Washington, D. C.

Memorials of Dorothea Dix to state legislatures and Congress: "Memorial to the Legislature of Massachusetts." Boston: Directors of the Old South Work, Old South Meeting-house, 1843.

"Memorial to the Honorable Legislature of New York." Albany, 1844.

"Memorial Soliciting a State Hospital for the Insane, Submitted to the Legislature of New Jersey." Trenton, 1845.

"Memorial Soliciting a State Hospital for the Insane of Pennsylvania." Harrisburg, 1845.

"Memorial to the Illinois General Assembly." Springfield, January, 1847.

"Memorial to the General Assembly of North Carolina." Raleigh, November, 1848.

"Memorial to the United States Congress Praying a Grant of Land for the Relief and Support of the Indigent Curable and Incurable Insane of the United States." Washington, D. C. Senate Document No. 150, June 27, 1848.

"Memorial Soliciting a State Hospital for the Insane, Submitted to the Legislature of Alabama." Montgomery, November 15, 1849.

"Memorial Soliciting Adequate Appropriations for the Construction of a State Hospital for the Insane in the State of Mississippi." Jackson, February, 1850.

"Memorial to the General Assembly in the Behalf of the Insane of the State of Maryland." Annapolis, February 25, 1852.

"Memorial to the Senate and House of Representatives, to accompany Bill S.44." Washington, D. C., January, 1854.

"Memorial for an Insane Hospital in Nova Scotia." Contained in Hurd, Henry M., *Institutional Care of the Insane in the United States and Canada.* Vol. I. Baltimore, Maryland, 1916.

Report No, 487. House of Representatives on "Indigent Insane Persons," to accompany bill H. R. No. 383. Report from the Select Committee to whom was referred the memorial of Miss D. L. Dix for an appropriation of land for the relief of the insane. Washington, D. C., August 8, 1850.

Report No. 57. Senate of the United States, to accompany Bill S. 44. Report of Committee on Public Lands to whom was referred the bill making a grant of public lands for the benefit of the indigent insane in the several States. Washington, D. C., January 23, 1854.

Probate Office, Penobscot County, Bangor, Maine. Vol. X, pp. 283–285. The will of Dorothy Dix, Dorothea's grandmother.

BOOKS AND PAMPHLETS

Alcott, Louisa May. *Hospital Sketches.* American Century Series. New York: Sagamore Press, 1957.

American Psychiatric Association and American Association of the History of Medicine, Editorial Board. *American Psychiatry.* New York: Columbia University Press, 1944.

Applebee, Robert B. "Talks on Sailing Vessels of Maine." Mimeographed. Bangor, Maine: Public Library, 1961.

Bacon, Edwin M. *Rambles Around Old Boston.* Boston: Little, Brown, 1914.

Beach, Seth Curtis. *Daughters of the Puritans: Dorothea Lynde Dix.* Boston: American Unitarian Association, 1907.

Beath, Charlotte M. H. "Dorothea Lynde Dix" in *Just Maine Folks*: Maine Writers' Research Club: Lewiston, Maine: The Journal Printshop, 1924.

Beedy, Helen Coffin. *Dorothea Lynde Dix, A Brief Sketch of Her Life Work.* Bangor, Maine: Charles H. Glass, 1901.

Bremer, Fredrika. *Homes of the New World.* London: A. Hall, Virtue, 1853.

Brockett, Linus Pierpont, and Vaughn, Mary C. *Woman's Work in the Civil War.* Boston: R. H. Curran, 1867.

Brooks, Gladys. *Three Wise Virgins.* New York: E.P. Dutton, 1957.

Bibliography

Brown, Arthur W. *Always Young for Liberty: a Biography of William Ellery Channing.* Syracuse University Press, 1956.

Clark, James Freeman. "Dorothea L. Dix" from *Sermons of James Freeman Clarke.* Vol. 1. No. 9. Boston: George H. Ellis, 1887.

Dannett, Sylvia G. L. *Noble Women of the North.* New York: Thomas Yoseloff, 1959.

Dix, Dorothea Lynde. *American Moral Tales for Young Persons.* With ten engravings. Boston: Leonard C. Bowles and B. H. Greene, 1832.

———. *Conversations on Common Things: Guide to Knowledge with Questions.* 3rd edition. Boston: Munroe and Francis, 1828.

———. *Evening Hours.* Boston, 1825.

———. *A Garland of Flora.* Boston: S. C. Goodrich, and Carter and Hender, 1829.

———. *Hymns for Children.* Boston, 1825.

———. *Letter to Convicts in the Western State Penitentiary of Pennsylvania.* Washington, D. C., 1848.

———. *Meditations for Private Hours,* 5th edition. Boston: Munroe and Francis, 1841.

———. *Remarks on Prisons and Prison Discipline in the United States.* Boston: Munroe and Francis, 1845.

———. *On Behalf of the Insane Poor.* Selected Reports, in series *Poverty, U.S.A.: The Historical Record.* Edited by David J. Rothman. Contains ten of the Dix Memorials to state legislatures. New York: Arno Press and the New York Times. 1971.

———. *A Review of the Present Conditions of the State Penitentiary of Kentucky, with Brief Notices and Remarks upon Jails and Poorhouses in Some of the Most Populous Counties.* Frankfort, Kentucky, 1845.

Flexner, Eleanor. *Century of Struggle: The Woman's Rights Movement in the United States.* Cambridge, Massachusetts: The Belknap Press of Harvard University, 1966.

Foucault, Michael. *Madness and Civilization: A History of Insanity in the Age of Reason.* New York: Random House, 1965.

Grimké, Archibald H. *The Life of Charles Sumner.* New York: Funk and Wagnalls, 1892.

History of Penobscot County, Maine. Cleveland: Williams Chase, 1882.

Holbrook, Stewart H. *Dreamers of the American Dream.* New York: Doubleday, 1957.

———. *Lost Men of American History.* New York: Macmillian, 1946.

Holland, Mary A. *Our Army Nurses.* Boston: B. Wilkins, 1895.

Kane, Harnett, and Arthur, Ella Bently. *Dear Dorothea Dix, The Story of a Compassionate Woman.* New York: Doubleday, 1952.

Kennard, Caroline A. *Miss Dorothea Dix and Her Life Work.* Pamphlet. In Houghton Library, Cambridge, Massachusetts.

Kirker, Harold, and Kirker, James. *Bulfinch's Boston, 1787–1817.* New York: Oxford University Press, 1964.

Lamb, Rosamond. "A Great Woman of America, Dorothea Lynde Dix." A talk given in the Council Chamber of the Old State House at the Annual Meeting of the Society. Boston: Bostonian Society, January 19, 1937.

Lowe, Corinne. *The Gentle Warrior: A Story of Dorothea Lynde Dix.* New York: Harcourt, Brace, 1948.

Malone, Mary. *Dorothea L. Dix, Hospital Founder.* Champaign, Illinois: Gerrard, 1968.

Marshall, Helen E. *Dorothea Dix, Forgotten Samaritan.* Chapel Hill: The University of North Carolina Press, 1937.

Stranger and Traveler

McCord, David. *About Boston: Sight, Sound, Flavor, and Inflection*. Boston: Little, Brown, 1948, 1964.

Melin, Grace Hathaway. *Dorothea Dix, Girl Reformer*. New York: Bobbs Merrill, 1963.

Norman, Gertrude. *Dorothea Lynde Dix*. New York: G. P. Putnams' Sons, 1959.

Olnhausen, Mary Phinney. *Adventures of an Army Nurse*. Boston: Little Brown, 1903.

Pickard, Samuel. *Life and Letters of John Greenleaf Whittier*. Vol. 2. Boston: Houghton, Mifflin, 1894.

Rice, Madeleine Hooke. *Federal Street Pastor, The Life of William Ellery Channing*. New York: Bookman Associates, 1961.

Rittenhouse, Jack D. *American Horse-Drawn Vehicles*. Los Angeles: Dillon Lithograph Company, 1948.

Rossiter, William. *Days and Ways in Old Boston*. Boston: R. H. Stearns, 1915.

Rowe, Alfred S. *Dorothea Lynde Dix*. Paper read before the Worcester Society of Antiquity, November 20, 1888. Worcester, Massachusetts: private press, 1889.

Sinclair, Andrew. *The Emancipation of the American Woman*. New York: Harper and Row, 1965.

Sprague, John Francis. "Maine's Joan of Arc." Kennebec Historical Society's Brochures, Series 1, Number 2. January, 1924.

———. "Dorothea Lynde Dix." In Sprague's *Journal of Maine History* 5:199.

Tharp, Louise Hall. *The Appletons of Beacon Hill*. Boston: Little, Brown, 1973.

———. *The Peabody Sisters of Salem*. Boston: Little, Brown, 1953.

———. *Until Victory: Horace Mann and Mary Peabody*. Boston: Little, Brown, 1953.

Tiffany, Francis. *Life of Dorothea Lynde Dix*. Boston: Houghton, Mifflin, 1891.

Tuke, Daniel Hack. *Chapters in the History of the Insane in the British Isles*. London, 1882.

———. *The Insane in the United States and Canada*. London, 1885.

Wasson, George S. "Sailing Days on the Penobscot." Salem, Massachusetts: Marine Research Society, 1932.

Waterston, Robert C. "Memoirs of George Barrel Emerson." *Massachusetts Historical Society* 20:232–259.

Weston, George F., Jr. *Boston Ways: High, By, and Folk*. Boston: Beacon Press, 1957.

Whitehill, Walter Muir. *Boston, a Topographical History*. Cambridge, Massachusetts: The Belknap Press of Harvard University, 1859.

Wilson, Dorothy Clarke. *Lone Woman: The Story of Elizabeth Blackwell, the First Woman Doctor*. Boston: Little, Brown, 1970.

Winsor, Justin, ed. *Memorial History of Boston*. Boston: James R. Osgood, 1881.

Wittenmyer, Mrs. Annie. *Under the Guns: A Woman's Reminiscences of the Civil War*. Boston, 1863.

Woolsey, Jane Stuart. *Hospital Days*. New York, 1870.

Young, Agatha. *The Women and the Crisis: Women of the North in the Civil War*. New York: McDowell, Obolensky, 1959.

PERIODICALS

Alter, Bette. "The Life and Work of Dorothea Dix and Her Influence on the Present Day Care of the Mentally Ill." Other papers on the same subject by Bernice Albertson and Julda Martens. *Ohio Nurses' Review*, July, 1928.

Bibliography

Bangor Daily News. Account of dedication of Dorothea Dix Memorial Park in Hampden. Bangor, Maine, July 5, 1899.

————. "Life Magazine Tribute to Dorothea Dix." January 15, 1947.

————. "Hampden Park to Honor Memory of Benefactress Dorothea Dix." May 19, 1953.

————. "Century Old Hospital Honors Memory of Dorothea Lynde Dix." March 3, 1955.

————. "Dorothea Dix, Hampden Native, Nominee for Hall of Fame." May 12, 1955.

Bangor Daily Whig and Courier. "Dorothea Dix, Fitting Honor to Memory of a Noble Woman, A Big Day in Hampden." July 6, 1932.

Bangor Semi-Weekly News. "Dorothea Dix Park is a Reality at Last — A Brief Description of Its Many Beauties." October 14, 1903.

Barth, Ramona Sawyer. "The Stormy Petrel of Compassion." *Journal of Liberal Religion.* Spring-Summer, 1949.

Boston Sunday Herald. "Noble Woman's Life, Dorothea Dix, to Whom a Monument is to Be Erected." October 20, 1901.

Browne, William J., M.S.M.D. "A Psychiatric Study of the Life and Work of Dorothea Dix." *American Journal of Psychiatry.* Read at the 124th annual meeting of the American Psychiatric Association. Boston: May 13–17, 1968.

Chadbourne, Ava H. "Maine's Dorothea Dix Was Militant Crusader." *Lewiston Journal Magazine.* Lewiston, Maine, September 9, 1952.

Christian Life. "Dorothea L. Dix." London, England. Taken from "Eminent Christian Women." Read before the St. Louis branch of the Women's Western Conference, 1885.

Liverpool Mercury. "The Late William Rathbone." Liverpool, England, February 6, 1868.

Maine Sunday Telegram. "Dorothea Dix Love Letters Found." Portland, Maine, March 23, 1969.

National Intelligencer. "Miss Dix" with poem in her honor. March, 1852.

Sturges, Florence M. "Maine-born Reformer Dorothea Lynde Dix." *Lewiston Journal Magazine,* Lewiston, Maine, August 29, 1970.

Thompson, Mary Lou. "Dorothea Dix Put Religion into action." *Unitarian-Universalist World,* November 1, 1974.

Tuke, Daniel Hack. "On the Past and Present Provision for the Insane in the United States." *Journal of Mental Science.* London: J. and A. Churchill, April, 1876.

Other newspapers for general research on Dorothea Dix and her activities:

Baltimore American, 1861
Baltimore Clipper, 1861
Baltimore Sun, 1852, 1861–1865
Boston Beacon, 1887
Boston Courier, 1841–1843
Boston Daily Advertiser, 1841–1843, 1860–1865, 1887
Greensboro Patriot, North Carolina, 1848, 1852
The Liberator, edited by William Lloyd Garrison, 1843, 1861
New York Times, 1861–1865; 1887
New York Tribune, 1855, 1861–1865, 1887
Providence Journal, 1844
Raleigh Weekly Register, 1854

Index

351

Index

Index

359